WITTGENSTEIN'S INTENTIONS

D0208234

GARLAND REFERENCE LIBRARY
OF THE HUMANITIES
(VOL. 1443)

WITTGENSTEIN'S INTENTIONS

edited by

John V. Canfield
Stuart G. Shanker

GARLAND PUBLISHING, INC. • NEW YORK & LONDON
1993

Library of Congress Cataloging-in-Publication Data

Wittgenstein's intentions / edited by John V. Canfield, Stuart G.
Shanker.
    p.   cm. — (Garland reference library of the humanities ; vol.
1443)
  ISBN 0-8153-0067-0 (alk. paper)
  1. Wittgenstein, Ludwig, 1889–1951. I. Canfield, John V.
II. Shanker, Stuart. III. Series.
B3376.W564W59   1993
192—dc20   92-28556
                                         CIP

Printed on acid-free, 250-year-life paper
Manufactured in the United States of America

It will be obvious that my heart is not so much in the interpretive task as in the insights that may emerge in the course of struggling with it, and even if I am unable to decide what were Wittgenstein's intentions, I am content if something I have come upon that might have been his intention is itself philosophically interesting. I read philosophy with no other end in view then that of gaining philosophical enlightenment, and hence if I come away from my attempts to understand Wittgenstein with a new thought I am delighted, and the only point of view from which I care whether this was the thought Wittgenstein intended is that if it is not, perhaps there is some other, even more interesting thought still to be uncovered, or perhaps there is a mistake in the thought I now have, the understanding of which would be instructive.

J.F.M. Hunter, Understanding Wittgenstein

CONTENTS

PREFACE

It seems only fitting that, in a book dedicated to John Hunter, we should begin with a Hunteresque preface. Anyone familiar with the genre will immediately expect us to challenge the sharp demarcation between scholarship and philosophy: particularly as this applies to the study of Wittgenstein's later writings. The effort to understand Wittgenstein's thought yields interesting and possibly important philosophical insights. His arguments raise all sorts of difficult problems: both philosophical and exegetical. Sometimes it is beneficial to apply Wittgenstein's techniques to questions which he did not address, or on which there is further to be said. And sometimes the best way to come to terms with Wittgenstein's intentions is to work through the same problem on one's own, where one hopes to arrive independently at the same conclusion that Wittgenstein reached for validation that one has appreciated the spirit and point of his thinking.

No Hunter preface is complete without some reference to the cautionary note on which Wittgenstein ends his Preface to *Philosophical Investigations*: "I should not like my writing to spare other people the trouble of thinking. But, if possible, to stimulate someone to thoughts of his own." Hunter's work exemplifies the point: both in terms of his own response to Wittgenstein and the demands which he in turn imposes on us. No one can go away from Hunter's writings without having had thoughts of his own stimulated; and no one would ever dream that Hunter's writings had spared other people the trouble of thinking.

The same can be said for each of the following papers. If there is a single principle which each of these authors shares, it is that Wittgenstein's intentions defy a simple linear explanation. To turn Wittgenstein into a theorist — the figurehead of some distinctive school of thought — is to undermine the essence of his message about the nature of philosophy.

There are many examples of such 'reductionist' interpretations. For example, there is the idea that Wittgenstein developed a theory of names: one that Searle improved upon and Kripke and Donnellan subsequently refuted. On the notion that Wittgenstein had a hand in such a theory, he is granted, among other such things, a minor role in the history of that branch of the philosophy of reference that runs through Russell, Wittgenstein, Searle, and Putnam, up to Kripke and Donnellan and beyond. But what is wrong with that picture is that Wittgenstein is no theorist at all, in the way that holds true of Searle and the others.

Again, a popular 'refutation' of Wittgenstein holds that, as an ordinary language philosopher he is hopelessly conservative. For why should philosophers be restricted to the common, natural-language use of words? To so hem them in would be as ridiculous as holding a scientist to the ordinary use of, say, 'force'. The refutation presupposes that Wittgenstein is a kind of Miss Manners of philosophy, admonishing people not to break the rules of use of common words. Except she operated at least in the cause of civility, rather than that of an unmotivated conservatism. So here the reduction of Wittgenstein's intentions goes via the idea of Wittgenstein as one of those now happily-defunct ordinary language philosophers. As so often happens, Wittgenstein was quite aware of the possibility of the sort of criticism in question, and answered it; but the critics do not see enough of his view of language and philosophy to understand their mistake.

The sort of uncomprehending misreading we have been speaking of has perhaps its worse consequence for what is arguably Wittgenstein's greatest work, the two-volume *Remarks on Philosophical Psychology*. This collection speaks to numerous current issues in philosophy as well as in allied areas in psychology and the social sciences — not to mention such fields as AI, cognitive science, and primatology. But by and large its treasures go unremarked; there is little attempt made to bring Wittgenstein's insights to bear. We have even met the remark that his executors, in publishing the posthumous works other than the *Investigations* are scraping the bottom of the barrel — the important Wittgenstein, to the extent that he is important, having already made his appearance.

The present book, a collection of essays on or directly related to the later Wittgenstein, aims to improve our understanding of him, and to show something of the philosophical wealth remaining untapped in his writings. It also aims to pay tribute to the work of John F.M. Hunter. In celebration of his long and on-going career, and for his brilliance, dedication, style, for his ability to pin-point intriguing problems in the reading of the *Investigations*, and proffer equally intriguing solutions to them, for his illuminating, Wittgenstein-inspired studies in philosophical psychology in general and the problem of intention in particular, and finally for his being who he is, moral and kind to a fault, honest, sarcastic, warm, loyal and lovable, we dedicate this volume to John Hunter.

J.V. Canfield
University of Toronto

S.G. Shanker
York University

THE CONTRIBUTORS

Alice Ambrose is Emeritus Professor of Philosophy at Smith College. She is the author of *Essays in Analysis* (1966) and co-author with Morris Lazerowitz of *Essays in the Unkown Wittgenstein* (1984) and *Necessity and Language* (1985) *inter alia*. She is the editor of *Wittgenstein's Lectures: Cambridge 1932–1935* (1979). President of Eastern Division, American Philosophical Association, 1975.

Robert L. Arrington is Professor of Philosophy at Georgia State University in Atlanta. He is the author of *Rationalism, Realism, and Relativism: Contemporary Perspectives in Moral Epistemology* and the co-editor of *Wittgenstein's "Philosophical Investigations": Text and Context*.

John V. Canfield is Professor of Philosophy at Erindale College, University of Toronto. He is the author of *Wittgenstein: Language and World*, *Looking-Glass Self*, and the Editor of the fifteen-volume collection *Philosophy of Wittgenstein*.

Roderick M. Chisholm is Professor of Philosophy at Brown University. He is the author of *Perceiving: A Philosophical Study* (1955), *Person and Object* (1976), *Metaphysics* (1989), and *Theory of Knowledge* (1991).

John W. Cook taught at the University of Oregon and is author of "Magic, Witchcraft and Science," "Kirkegaard and Wittgenstein," and "Wittgenstein and Religious Belief."

Jeff Coulter is Professor of Sociology and Associate Faculty member of Philosophy at Boston Univesity. He is the author of *Approaches to Insanity, The Social Construction of Mind, Rethinking Cognitive Theory*, and *Mind in Action*. His specialised areas are the philosophy of the social sciences and the sociology of knowledge. He has been working on the reconstruction of topics in cognitive science along sociological lines for some years.

Bernd Frohmann received his doctorate in philosophy from the University of Toronto, where he is now an Assistant Professor in the Faculty of Library Information Science. He has co-edited several volumes of *The Collected Papers of Bertrand Russell*.

P.M.S. Hacker is a Fellow of St. John's College, Oxford. He has written extensively on the philosophy of Wittgenstein, on Frege, and on subjects in the philosophy of language and philosophical psychology. His most recent books are *Appearance and Reality* (1987) and *Wittgenstein: Meaning and Mind* (1990).

J.F.M. Hunter has taught at Edinburgh University and the University of Toronto. He is the author of *Essays after Wittgenstein, Intending, Understanding Wittgenstein, Wittgenstein on Words as Instruments*. He has published many articles, mostly on ethics and philosophical psychology, and Wittgenstein.

Eike von Savigny teaches philosophy at the University of Bielefeld, Germany. Besides numerous articles he has published eleven books, among them a study of ordinary language philosophy (1969), *The Social Foundations of Meaning* (1988), and a two-volume commentary on the *Philosophical Investigations* (1988–9).

Stuart G. Shanker is Professor of Philosophy at York University. He is the author of *Wittgenstein and the Turning-Point in the Philosophy of Mathematics* and the Editor of *Ludwig Wittgenstein: Critical Assessments* and *Gödel's Theorem in Focus*.

The late Alan Richard White was Ferens Professor of Philosophy at the University of Hull. Among his major books were *G.E. Moore: A Critical Exposition* (1958), *Attention* (1964), *The Philosophy of Mind* (1967), *Truth* (1970), *Modal Thinking* (1975), *The Nature of Knowledge* (1982), *Rights* (1984), *Grounds of Liability* (1985), *Methods of Metaphysics* (1987), *The Language of Imagination* (1990), and *Misleading Cases* (1991).

LIST OF ABBREVIATIONS

The following abbreviations are used for Wittgenstein's primary sources in this book:

NB *Notebooks 1914–1916*, G.E.M. Anscombe and G.H. von Wright (eds.), G.E.M. Anscombe (trans.). Oxford: Basil Blackwell, 1961.

TLP *Tractatus Logico-Philosophicus* (1921), D.F. Pears & B.F. McGuinness (trans.). London: Routledge & Kegan Paul, 1961.

RLF 'Some Remarks on Logical Form', *Proceedings of the Aristotelian Society*, vol.9 (1929).

LFW 'A Lecture on Freedom of the Will' (1946), *Philosophical Investigations*, vol.12 (1989).

PI *Philosophical Investigations*, G.E.M. Anscombe (trans.). Oxford: Basil Blackwell, 1953.

RFM *Remarks on the Foundations of Mathematics*, G.H. von Wright, R. Rhees, and G.E.M. Anscombe (eds.), G.E.M. Anscombe (trans.). Oxford: Basil Blackwell, 1956.

BLB *The Blue and Brown Books*. Oxford: Basil Blackwell, 1960.

LA *Lectures & Conversations on Aesthetics, Psychology and Religious Belief*, Cyril Barrett (ed.). Oxford: Basil Blackwell, 1966.

Z *Zettel*, G.E.M. Anscombe and G.H. von Wright (eds.), G.E.M. Anscombe (trans.). Oxford: Basil Blackwell, 1967.

PG *Philosophical Grammar*, Rush Rhees (ed.), Anthony Kenny (trans.). Oxford: Basil Blackwell, 1974.

PR *Philosophical Remarks*, Rush Rhees (ed.), R. Hargreaves and R. White (trans.). Oxford: Basil Blackwell, 1975.

AWL *Wittgenstein's Lectures, Cambridge 1932–1935, From the Notes of Alice Ambrose and Margaret Macdonald*, Ambrose, A. (ed.). Oxford: Basil Blackwell, 1979.

WWK *Ludwig Wittgenstein and the Vienna Circle*, B.F. McGuinness (ed.), J. Schulte and B.F. McGuinness (trans.). Oxford: Basil Blackwell, 1979.

CV *Culture and Value*, G.H. von Wright (ed.), Peter Winch (trans.). Oxford: Basil Blackwell, 1980.

RPP1 *Remarks on the Philosophy of Psychology* vol. I, G.E.M. Anscombe and G.H. von Wright (eds.), G.E.M. Anscombe (trans.). Oxford: Basil Blackwell, 1980.

RPP2 *Remarks on the Philosophy of Psychology* vol. II, G.H. von Wright and Heikki Nyman (eds.), C.G. Luckhardt and M.A.E. Aue (trans.). Oxford: Basil Blackwell, 1980.

LW *Last Writings*, G.H. von Wright and Heikki Nyman (eds.), C.G. Luckhardt and Maximilian A.E. Aue (trans.). Oxford: Basil Blackwell, 1982.

GWL *Wittgenstein's Lectures on Philosophical Psychology 1946-47*, P.T. Geach (ed.). Chicago: University of Chicago, 1989.

Wittgenstein's Intentions

CHAPTER I

Wittgenstein's Intentions

John V. Canfield

What a strange phenomenon that a child can actually learn human language! That a child who knows nothing can start out and learn by a sure path this enormously complicated technique.
— Wittgenstein

The child's magical-seeming passage into language interested Wittgenstein profoundly. Studying his view of that transition leads to a new understanding of it. Conversely, examining speech acquisition from his perspective increases our understanding of the perspective itself. This paper seeks to establish that positive feedback loop. I focus here on children's mastery of intention-utterances, but with the overall aim of opening a route to a wider series of examples that will illuminate language acquisition and Wittgenstein's philosophy, and that as a result will facilitate coming to an overview or reflective understanding of a number of our key concepts.

Wittgenstein's goals and manner of achieving them differ radically from those of contemporary theorists of language acquisition, even in the case of those to whom he may seem close, such as Jerome Bruner. So it is appropriate to begin by discussing Wittgenstein's method.

On Method. The idea of observing language use is obviously *echt* Wittgenstein. The famous line from *Philosophical Investigations*, "Don't think, look!" finds many echoes in his work. For example in his statement that his aim is to provide a "clear view of the use of our words" (§122), or in *On Certainty*, §501, where he speaks of *looking* at the practice of language.

At the end of his life, Wittgenstein wondered whether it was after all possible to describe the "logic" (or depth grammar) of language; nevertheless his writings are chock full of such descriptions.[1] Numerous of his philosophical remarks report on language use. Although he believes such descriptions embody logically necessary truths, at the same time he thinks they characterize language; we should therefore be able to test them for accuracy.[2] We can do so by observing the uses they attempt to delineate, and indeed it is only through such observation that we can fully understand the descriptions. For example Wittgenstein claims that in stating an intention one does not depict something inner but rather produces an "Äusserung" — often termed an "avowal" in the secondary literature (RPP I §§215, 593). His claim can be comprehended fully and adjudicated only after one has seen into the workings of the corresponding pieces of language.

Of course the figure of looking or observing is not the only one operative here. Wittgenstein also speaks, for instance, of "studying" use, and of making "conceptual investigations" (philosophical investigations!).[3] He assumes, one might say, some way of confronting use.

The assumption is manifest also in the plot line of his philosophical commentaries. The trajectory in those familiar paragraph-long remarks is commonly from illusion to illumination. They often begin by evoking in the reader (or in Wittgenstein's alter-ego) a philosophical delusion, concerning, for example, the nature of *intention* or *self*. Illusions about such things naturally arise in an inquirer's mind; one becomes captivated by philosophical pictures originating in misunderstandings of our own concepts: by the picture, for instance, of an intention as some inner state or mental object. Or the picture of "I" as a referring expression. Wittgenstein calls such a picture the convincing statement of a conviction (PI p.223). (The exact nature of the alleged picture will become clear only when the contrast term *use* is properly understood.) The pictures, he would have it, operate at a naive and deep level, the level one might say of proto-philosophy. Deeply ingrained illusions are the root source of metaphysics, and thus Wittgenstein's efforts to, "bring words back from their metaphysical to their everyday use" (PI §116).[4] The illumination I spoke of comes when a picture or "metaphysical use" is matched against everyday use, whereupon the misleading character of the former becomes plain. But of course to make the comparison we must be able to observe "use."

It is one thing to speak of "confronting," "observing," and the like, if there exists a known way of doing so, or if one is able to provide a new way, as with Galileo's telescope. In Wittgenstein's case, the idea of "use" he employs and, correspondingly, the type of "observation" he presupposes are uniquely his; he did not simply apply some known method of observation. Thus a necessary condition for understanding Wittgenstein is to master the art of perceiving language in the way he advocates; to do that is to "confront" use. What, then, is Wittgenstein's "telescope" — what method does he provide for viewing language at work?

There is not one such method but several: "There is not a philosophical method, though there are indeed methods, like different therapies" (PI §133). Many of these are familiar, in name at least, either from the secondary literature, or from Wittgenstein's writings, including the following sometimes overlapping ones: Noting some of the bounds of sense, and drawing conclusions therefrom. Testing grammatical remarks against ordinary uses, and dealing with alleged counterexamples to the remarks. Constructing simple, imaginary language-games. Inventing more complex uses, where differences between invented and actual language-game highlight features of the latter. Drawing "auxiliary lines," for example by considering a would-be soulless tribe.[5] Pondering how changes in nature might influence our concepts (for instance if given shapes never varied in colour). Imagining such alterations in our way of life as might be exhibited by the "meaning blind" or again, the "intention blind."

In addition to these methods, there are two further ones that, used together, yield a clear perception of language employment. They reveal something of the *depth* of Wittgenstein's view of language, of what he finds hidden beneath "surface grammar." Of course Wittgenstein says that in a way nothing is hidden: "For what is hidden... is of no interest to us" (PI §126). He almost immediately goes on to say, however, that "The aspects of things that are most important for us are hidden because of their simplicity and familiarity.... One is unable to notice something — because it is always before one's eyes..." (PI §129). This is not a case of "our forgetful authors"; rather Wittgenstein speaks of two ways of being hidden. The depth of language is not concealed, but is right before our eyes, were we to look in the right places; it is "hidden" only in that, perhaps through familiarity, we do not see it.

Norman Malcolm explored the first of the two methods I am interested in, in his essay "Language as Expressive Behaviour."[6] The second one, though well known by name, has not been the subject of much scrutiny.

Both ways of proceeding have to do with the idea that to use a word is to utter it as a move in a language-game. Many language-games, including some of special philosophical interest, have roots in primitive or instinctive behaviour. One method for observing "use" is to explore those roots.

Wittgenstein frequently speaks of the notion of primitive behaviour. For example:

> 475. I want to regard man here as an animal; as a primitive being to which one grants instinct but not ratiocination. As a

creature in a primitive state. Any logic good enough for a primitive means of communication needs no apology from us. Language did not emerge from some kind of ratiocination.

The essay "Cause and Effect: Intuitive Awareness" is central for understanding Wittgenstein on the "primitive." He writes there, for instance:

The origin and the primitive form of the language-game is a reaction: only from this can more complicated forms develop.
Language — I want to say — is a refinement, 'im Anfang war die Tat' (p.420).[7]

Instead of "primitive form" he later speaks of the "proto-type" of the language-game (p.421). He speaks of "instinctive" behaviour, as when a person "instinctively" (or perhaps better, *naturally*) looks from the effect to the cause, for example looking to see what has just stung him. He also refers to the "biological function" of these "primitive forms" of behaviour, as in this quotation:

The game doesn't begin with doubting whether someone has a toothache, because that doesn't — as it were — fit the game's biological function in our life. In its most primitive form it is a reaction to somebody's cries and gestures, a reaction of sympathy or something of the sort (p.414).

Wittgenstein says our language grows out of primitive, instinctive, or natural forms of behaviour, in particular those constituting our interactions, and that we can come to significant insights into our concepts by examining those roots.

The following quotation shows how the two methods I am interested in are linked:

Believing that someone else is in pain, doubting whether he is, are so many natural kinds of behaviour towards other human beings; and our language is but an auxiliary to and extension of this behaviour. I mean: our language is an extension of the more primitive behaviour. (For our *language-game* is a piece of behaviour.) (RPP I §151).

The second method of looking at language comes into play at the point just after the one that examines primitive behaviour. I shall call the proto-typical behaviour Wittgenstein mentions the "proto language-game". What arises from it — by "extension" as he says — is the simple or primitive language-game. At this stage words occur as functional elements within human interaction patterns.

Wittgenstein sometimes refers to such primitive language-games. For example, in a statement noted by Peter Geach we read:

> There is an advantage in considering simplified techniques. E.g. we consider the use of a signal to mean "I am depressed" (GWL 46).

These "simplified techniques" come to the same thing as the following "primitive language-games," mentioned in Geach's notes:

> Primitive language-games are specific and cannot be taught by explanation because they correspond each to a special use of language e.g. "apple" for a wish, "throw" when you are going to throw. If a child lacks such a reaction, you certainly cannot give it to him by *explanation* (GWL 25).

In §163 of RPP I Wittgenstein speaks of "a more primitive form of expression" which the child may first learn in mastering the language-game; and in §351 of the same work, he says: "But instead of the expression "It tastes exactly [like sugar]" I might more primitively use the exclamation "Sugar!". In RPP II §177 he mentions a "primitive utterance" of fear; the term translated as "utterance" is "*Äusserung*," and this indicates he is referring not to a cry of fear but to a word in a simple language-game where fear is expressed. The idea of a simple or primitive language-game is also implicit in the following well known passage in the *Investigations*, concerning a human's learning to speak of pain: "A child has hurt himself and he cries; and then adults talk to him and teach him exclamations and, later, sentences. They teach the child new pain behaviour" (§244). Those exclamations, like the "Sugar!" mentioned above, occur within a primitive language-game.

There are in turn two ways of approaching primitive uses of language. One, already mentioned, is by studying imaginary models of language use, such as that of the builders of PI §2. This familiar method is especially prominent in the *Brown Book*. I am interested here in a second way. Wittgenstein often recommends this method, but for whatever reasons, philosophers have by and large not followed up upon it in detail. It is to study how children might learn to speak of such things as their intentions, desires, pains, emotions, and so on. And, my suggestion is, we can drop the "might" by observing children as they actually take up the use of the words we are interested in. For children at some point in acquiring language do suddenly pick up a mastery of simplified or primitive language-games, for instance of requesting or intending. They do so in the context of the natural behaviours or interaction patterns I have called "proto language-games." Studying language learning can bring to light salient details of both aspects of the primitive that I have emphasized.

Of course it is well known that Wittgenstein wants his readers to examine how children come to learn to use language. In the late fifties that knowledge supported a folk-philosophical "refutation" of Wittgenstein, who was said to have committed a genetic fallacy, confusing how one learned something with what one learned. Wittgenstein had anticipated such a criticism when he wrote:

> Am I doing child psychology? — I am making a connection between the concept of teaching and the concept of meaning (RPP II §337; Z §412).

The connection in question involves the idea of a "centre of variation" shared by primitive language-games and their subsequent more complex forms. In travelling from the complex interchanges of everyday life toward primitive versions of them, and in particular toward the simple language-games that appear when children first master language, one presupposes some important common element in the various groups of uses thus surveyed. I shall discuss this key idea later.

To sum up: The way of observing use that I am interested in here combines two of Wittgenstein's practices: focusing on proto language-games, and on related primitive-language-games. To examine these things we must be able to produce examples of them. Exactly such examples arise when children learn to speak. Thus I propose to examine first language acquisition in a Wittgensteinian manner.[8]

It may perhaps be objected to this enterprise that its vocabulary is arcane. Isn't it bad enough coping with such terms as "language-game," "use," or "picture," without adding new ones — "primitive language-game," "proto-typical behaviour," "centre of variation" and so on? But how in general are such terms, whether familiar or less usual, to be explained? Not by means of other general words. Defining those terms of art by means of one another does not help, and they cannot be defined successfully from outside Wittgenstein's system, since they too "correspond to ... a special use of language." Rather the terms must be explained through examples. (That they admit of such explication gives them the advantage over many another special term in the in fact overlapping areas of language acquisition and metaphysics. Contrast, say, the term "mind," or the term "intention" when it is assumed to stand for some mental object.) For Wittgenstein an understanding of such ground-level concepts as that of *intention* must also be based paramountly on a consideration of examples.

To exemplify and explain my present approach to Wittgenstein, I shall adopt the following expository strategy. I shall take as a target one of Wittgenstein's more mysterious high level "grammatical" or "logical" discussions of intention, and as part of spelling out what he is up to there, I shall introduce material about children's coming to a mastery of the language-game of intention-stating.

Text and preliminary exegesis.

RPPI §788. Why do I have doubts about his intention, but not about mine? To what extent am I indubitably acquainted with my intention? What, so to speak, is the usefulness of my *knowing* my intention? That is, what is the usefulness, the function, of the expression of intention? That is, when is something an expression of intention? Well, when the act follows it, when it is a prediction. I make the prediction, the same one as someone else makes from observation of my behaviour, *without* this observation.[9]

This passage is strikingly obscure, both in its over-all message and in detail. The first of its initial string of questions makes sense (seemingly), but the second is enigmatic, and the subsequent ones seem to be, or reflect, nothing so much as *non sequiturs*. The passage's last two remarks make difficult reading, and it is particularly hard to understand how they answer, or are even relevant to, the problem initially posed. Let us see.

"Why do I have doubts about his intention but not about mine?" The natural answer is that, while I can only hypothesize his I have some special, direct, and inward relationship to my own. My intention is present to me somehow; I am immediately aware of it, in so far as it *is* my intention. I know that I intend to get the book. That intention is nothing I can see or sense outwardly. Rather my getting-the-book intention is present to my mind. It is an object of direct acquaintance. I confront it much as I might one of my pains or thoughts — or so I am inclined to say. Whereas I have only an external contact with another person's intention.

The basic picture at work here assumes a comparison with this sort of case: When playing poker, why do I have doubts about what his hole card is, but not about mine? Obviously because I can look at mine but can only try to figure out or guess what his is. Similarly, it is in some super-strong way impossible for another to see my intention, but I confront it directly.

What is that direct relationship? The basic picture of confronting one's intention inwardly may be elaborated in a number of ways. Hobbes might have said the intention is a mental image of the intended object or act. Some contemporary thinkers readily forego any actual image. For some the intention is propositional, and having an intention is one of the propositional attitudes. Such theorists may hold that there is no phenomenological counterpart to the having of such an attitude. Perhaps instead there is an unconscious scanning of the intention *qua* propositional object. Such scanning outside of consciousness might nevertheless be counted as a direct and inward relationship. Whether one is conscious of the intention-as-inner-object or not, still one has a direct relationship to it, some form of confrontation with it, whereby one knows it.[10]

One might embellish the basic picture further by assuming an innate language of thought, within which the intention *qua* propositional object is expressed or understood. Perhaps this inherited language comes equipped with a concept of intention, an intention "marker" as it were, so that a proposition radical like "Go to the store, me" might get marked either with an *I* for intention, a *P* for prediction, or a *D* for desire, depending on which it is I think. To think the proposition radical together with the intention marker (perhaps also along with something that functions like Frege's assertion sign) is to have that intention, and there is no room for doubt. I have no such direct relationship to anyone else's intention; hence in the first-person case, certainty, while in the third-person case, doubt.[11]

788b. "To what extent am I indubitably acquainted with my intention?" ("*Inwiefern kenne ich unzweifelhaft meine Absicht?*")

In response to Wittgenstein's first question, the reader forms a picture of the intention as an inner object known immediately or directly, an object, it might be said, that one is indubitably acquainted with. Hence the target of 788b.

The idea of an indubitable acquaintanceship highlights two elements in the picture of an intention. The first is that of some sort of bare "of-ness" relation, some direct mental confrontation with or immediate perception of the intention — this in keeping with the fact that 788b uses the verb "kennen" and not "wissen." The contrast is with knowing *that*. But that side of the contrast is present too, at least implicitly, as we see when we consider the indubitability of our acquaintanceship. Mere knowledge by acquaintance will not establish certainty (lack of doubt) unless it is at the same time discursive.[12] Doubts imply a propositional or discursive attitude toward something; they require something which is, in a term Fodor has used, "cognizable." The intention itself, then, must be propositional. I do not doubt *that* I am going to get the book, say. If my relation to my intention is some form of awareness or attention, then, this relationship must also allow me to read the intention's propositional content, to the extent that I "see" or "know" that I intend to do a certain thing. Acquaintanceship *with* must involve also knowledge *that*.

It is easy to be misled by the question Wittgenstein asks about that indubitable acquaintanceship. For one thing, the word translated "to what extent" may if taken literally send one searching for the limit of the extent. But *inwiefern* can also be translated "in what way?" or "how so?" I believe it is best to take the word in that more relaxed way, and to read Wittgenstein as asking simply, "What *is* this idea of being indubitably acquainted with my intention? What does it come to?" The question leads naturally on to the next one.

788c. "What, so to speak, is the usefulness of my knowing my intention?" ("*Was ist, sozusagen, der Nutzen davon, dass ich meine Absicht weiss?*") The reference to "knowing" in 788c shows I was correct in reading the indubitable acquaintanceship mentioned in 788b as implying knowledge; that is, the picture of being indubitably aware is a picture of knowing one's intention.

But what of the puzzling reference to what I have rendered as "usefulness"? The key here is to realize that Wittgenstein is taking a certain path toward answering his previous question. 788c can be read as saying, in effect: "To find out what this indubitable acquaintanceship (which gives a knowledge of my intention) amounts to, investigate what it accomplishes, or what good it is; what, so to speak, its usefulness is." One might think initially that this interpretation supports the idea of Wittgenstein as some kind of pragmatist, but the "usefulness" he has in mind is of a particular sort, and because it is, his view is not really foreshadowed by the American pragmatists, at least not in any interesting detail.

I suggest we are asked to consider that "usefulness" exactly in order to get us to focus on the phenomenon of *stating* one's intentions. For whatever usefulness an inner confrontation with my intention — or my knowing it — may have, it must at least include this: that it allows me to and justifies me in stating the intention, telling others about it. This is a minimal usefulness it must have. (Wittgenstein's "pragmatism" here comes down to an insistence on examining how words are used — how they function in language-games; but the pragmatists did not possess Wittgenstein's idea of what such functioning comes to.)[13]

What exactly have I won to, when I have gone from inner intention to outer statement of intention? If inner knowledge must yield outer statement, but if one suspects, as Wittgenstein does, that the outer statement is *not* to be understood simply as saying out the content of what one knows inwardly, then one will do well to study the phenomenon of voicing one's intention. Hence his next question:

788d. "What, that is, is the usefulness, the function, of the expression of intention?" ("*Was namlich ist der Nutzen, die Funktion, der Absichtsausserung?*") The transition between 788c and 788d is mediated by the assumed answer to 788c, which is something like, "Its usefulness includes its allowing one (in principle) to express in speech what one knows inwardly." 788d then focuses on the issue of what it is one is thereby justified in saying. What is the content of the intention-as-expressed? What do I say when I say what I know in knowing my intention?

The question 788d marks a switch in Wittgenstein's point of view. In 788a—788c his attention is directed at the philosophical picture of the inner intention. In 788d he turns to an examination of how we actually use the words by means of which we "express our intentions." The term "Nutzen" is pivotal here. In 788c "usefulness" is used only to get us to think not just about the inner intention, but about what we say when we tell our intention. But in 788d usefulness stands now for proper Wittgensteinian *use*, as is suggested by the fact that he paraphrases "usefulness" with another of his standard terms of art, namely "function". (In his later philosophy Wittgenstein uses "function" in an extended way, applying it to a new field.)[14]

Wittgenstein's second and third questions lead toward an examination of the concept of an intention, for only if we have a reflective understanding of that concept can we test our original picture of an intention. In 788d he asks after the concept from inside his own view of language. We are to inquire into the use of intention-expressions. That is allegedly the way to discover the content of first-person intention utterances, and hence the way to find out whether when we know our intention-qua-inner object we also know our intention-as-stated.

Wittgenstein's next question, however, seems baffling once again. After motivating a query about the function of the intention-statement he suddenly seems to switch gears and asks about *when* something is an intention-statement, and this new question is linked to the old by another "namlich": 788e "That is to say, when is something an intention-utterance?" (*"Wann, namlich, ist es eine Absichtausserung?"*)

Despite appearances to the contrary, the transition to this final question is justified. To study the "function" of intention-stating words we must be able to pick out uses that do indeed state one's intentions from those that do not. Thus we can ask ourselves when, or under what conditions, we will count something as an intention-utterance. It will be when the utterance is made as a "move" in a certain sort of language-game. So now we must be able to pick out instances of that language-game. Once we have isolated the language-game, we can discover the use or function of the utterance in question, since its function depends upon its being imbedded in that language-game. Thus I suggest that Wittgenstein's question in 788e amounts to this: "What is a distinguishing mark of the language-game in which intention-utterances occur?" Why then didn't he ask *that* question, instead of the one about when something counts as an intention-utterance? Because the two come to the same thing. The answer to the question about the language-game will be something like "When the utterance serves as a 'prediction' of a certain kind, as in this that and the other case, and not when it serves, for example, as a request, as in such and such other instances." So in turn we shall pick out the language-game by noting the interactions taking place there. The "when" in 788e will be answered by detailing what those interactions in that context are.

Wittgenstein has moved us a considerable way by his series of questions. We start, prompted by his first question, by picturing an intention as something mental that we are acquainted with (the intention as inner object). Given that picture, it is clear why we can have no doubts about *our* intentions. A series of further questions brings us to the boundary of Wittgenstein's view of language and meaning. If we are to say what the usefulness of "knowing" the inner object is, we must observe the use of intention-expressions closely. The underlying assumption is that such observation will reveal the epistemological question in 788a to be incoherent. Its appearance of coherence derives from a misleading picture.

I now want to recall my initial methodological remarks. If we are really to adjudicate the last two sentences in 788, or even understand them, and consequently comprehend Wittgenstein's response to the question about doubt, we must *ourselves* scrutinize the language-game of intention stating. It is here, then, that students of use must get about their job. One way they may do so, I have suggested, is by looking at language mastery, and I turn now to that phenomenon.

An Interpolation. One of the child's initial language-games, that of making requests, provides a useful contrast case for the study of intention-statements. I start with a cross-species comparison.

For Wittgenstein to speak a language is to engage in a form of life. A form of life significantly like ours, and one where there is a rudimentary grasp of concepts, or a simple form of symbol use, is that of chimpanzees in the wild, as made known through the work of primatologists. The contrast between the two life ways deserves close study; here I shall only indicate some features common to the two. The point of special interest is the close, long-term relationship between mothers and their offspring. This takes place within a fixed social group. The newborn chimpanzees, who would not survive on their own, are protected, fed, and raised. As they grow they learn to forage and to take a role in the group's cooperative and social activities.

The chimpanzees have simple forms of communication, simple "gesture language-games," one might call them (including hooting and other vocalizations as gestures). The gestures are produced in certain contexts and responded to in certain ways. The begging gesture is perhaps the most striking of these. If a stronger animal, a dominant male, say, has food — for instance meat from a recent kill — a weaker band member may "know full well" (as *we* might say) that it would be impossible successfully to commandeer some of it. But sometimes chimpanzees will share their food with weaker group members. Such behaviour marks their "form of life"; frogs, say, do not behave that way at all, and on the other hand humans are much more given than are chimps to sharing food with family or band members. The begging gesture functions inside the context of their form of life. The behaviour constituting the gesture language-game can be conceived of as a variation on still more primitive behaviour, where the smaller chimp tries to take food from the stronger, is perhaps violently rebuffed, but continues to make muted attempts to grab off some of the booty, or else perhaps stands plaintively looking on, but then maybe is finally allowed a small share in the kill. Instead of that possible mode of interaction, begging comprises a variation in which a new movement appears. (That is, for our purposes we can imagine things developing this way, whether or not they did in historical or biological fact.) As a supplement to, or perhaps a substitute for, its attempts to grab food, the smaller chimp makes a begging gesture and the stronger one sometimes responds by giving.

Now consider the human child. That the child pursues various things, wants various things, is obvious. It soon develops a repertoire of gestures which serve to tell its attendant adults what it wants. For example here are some observations on an eleven month old child:

> Moves my hand holding bottle toward her mouth — a gesture; me as servo-mechanism.
> "Arrar..." and arches back — to be let down from S's lap to floor.
> Cries and holds up hand — wants balloon.
> Hands bottle to parent, saying, in effect, feed me!

And at thirteen months:

> The wiggle signal — when she wants out of her high chair, wiggles downwards and makes unhappy noises (of course she "knows" you are there and paying attention, and may well give her what she wants).

There is a series of such cases, some elaborations of and some alternatives to earlier ones, as in this list of gesture requests and proto gesture requests:

> Cries; reaches; reaches with "eh"; reaches with hand opening and closing; reaches with pronounced wanting noise; points to where desired object is.

The baby's earliest crying will hardly count as a gesture, and it is perhaps impossible to mark a sharp boundary between those "instinctive" reactions and movements that are clearly gestures. But we soon do reach members of the series that plainly count as gestures indicating what, as we say, the baby wants.[15] It soon learns to make some of its wants unmistakeably clear, for example when it looks at the parent and reaches for its bottle, opening and closing its hand and making the noise it commonly makes when it wants something; and when given it, puts it to its mouth and drinks hungrily.

In these examples the child's gesture-requests and the begging gesture of the chimpanzees serve the same function — that of informing the other party in the interaction what the first party "wants."

In the human case the developmental series indicated above has a natural extension: in an appropriate context, the gesture of reaching or pointing is accompanied not merely by a generalized "wanting noise" but by a word from the language spoken by the parents. And this word is, in that language, the name of the thing the child wants (or wants to have put on it, for instance).

A further extension of the series would be the use of the word by itself, in the proper context, unaccompanied by a reaching or pointing gesture. A further extension would be to supplement the single word with others, for instance for the child to say, "I want juice." Or "Juice, please."

For the sake of concreteness I will give the first word of the child on whom the above observations were made; it fits the case exactly.

> First word "shoe" said of her new black shoes so we would put them on her. The shoes were lying on top of her dresser and she saw them as S was carrying her out of the room. It is clear she wanted them put on. [She had for a considerable time shown a marked interest in such things as trying to dress herself and trying to put on her own shoes, and it was clear that shoes had a special fascination for her.]

Already at the age of fifteen months or thereabouts the child has left the wild chimpanzee behind forever. Spontaneously it issues *words* which, as we say, refer to various objects, or various situations or actions that the child wants. I say "spontaneously" because there was no specific "training" in the use of "shoe", and no "conditioning" or "reinforcement." On the other hand the adults frequently spoke in the presence of or to the child, saying such things as "I'm putting on your *shoe*." The child's spontaneous issuing of the word is thus hardly magical, although it manifests a marvellous human ability.[16]

At some point the child just does step into language, and begins to participate in, or "play," a language-game with the adult. It is a two or more person game. The child says something, for instance "Down" and the parent reacts, in the default case (though there are of course countless exceptions) by an appropriate action, such as getting the child out of its highchair. At this point already there is a full blown and complete communication between adult and child. The child is speaking, and doing as good a job as it will ever do, as regards communicating, say, its desire to get down from the chair. (Again, we must be careful here not to say, "something ordinary, — with the wrong gesture" (RPP I §791). It is perfectly natural to speak of "communicating a desire"; that does not mean that the child is telling about something inner. No more is it when it stretches its arm out trying to get its bottle.) The child will learn over time to phrase its requests more fully, add polite forms, modulate its tone of voice in a certain way, so that it is asking and not demanding, and so on. But the core of the language-game will remain unchanged over the years. It is a simple language-game. Player A asks for something; player B responds in some appropriate manner, by getting it, or refusing to get it, or pointedly ignoring the request, and so on. When the child grows to adulthood, and asks a friend if she might have some tea, the language-game in play between the two is just that ancient one the child learned at fifteen months or so; it is essentially the same.

One must not think that the previous remarks bear out St. Augustine's view of language and not Wittgenstein's. The language-game of requests is one only. There are others ("categorially different" ones) that we can recognize in observing the child's gradual mastery of language. For instance, the child learns something like negation early on — a way of rejecting things proffered to it that it does not want, or of objecting to certain actions. Or there is the language-game of greeting, learned very early. There is the language-game of make believe, which is an important part of the child's earliest speech. And there is our concern, the statement of intention.

As the above discussion illustrates, the request language-game is an extension of the natural behaviours, on the part of child and adult, of the child's seeking various things and the adult either helping it get them, or substituting something more fitting, or warning the child of danger or bad consequences, and the like. The pattern of interaction between child and parent becomes complicated along what might be called social lines, since we might say that if an interaction essentially involves the use of language it is social (a matter, first of all, of acculturation, and second of all of the learning of or adopting certain custom-ruled patterns of behaviour). The word is the thing that allows the speaker and hearer to collaborate; for instance the word "down" allows the adult to move the child to where the child wants to be. Such language-games involve an inevitable social element, a co-operation or collusion between people.

First language: intention.

I return now to the issue of intention-claims. If the approach I am following is correct, then in seeking, through an examination of first language, some primitive language-game of intention-stating, our initial aim should be to inquire into the background behaviour, the proto-typical actions and reactions out of which those simple language-games grow.

As an examination of examples shows, there are several ingredients to that proto-typical behaviour. The child has certain *projects*, as I shall say (apologies to Sartre). It *interacts*, in a certain distinctive manner, with the adults who are raising it. And there is an element of *complicity* between child and adult. In many of their engagements the adult is aware of the child — watches it — and the child is aware that the adult is aware of it. But I do not mean by these general remarks to explain that proto-typical behaviour; rather the sorts of examples I give below explain those general terms, as I am using them here.

We can often see that the child is trying to do something or is actually doing something. We see, that is, that it acts with an aim or purpose. This of course is something we share with other animals. Goodall relates how a young chimp often wanted to walk in a direction opposite to that being taken by the band, which included its mother, and would make its desire clear by walking off that way. Similarly, a child may cry if one does not walk in the direction the child favours — toward the corner park, say; the child digs in its heels, cries, turns in the direction it wants and tries to go that way, until carried bodily off on the other heading. Again, what the child wants becomes obvious for example when, on its walks, it strikes out perpendicularly to the adult's line of march, wishing to explore each branching sidewalk and lane-way encountered. Or a simpler case: a preverbal child busy putting small stones inside a bottle, one after the other. In such cases I speak of the child's projects. As opposed to what? As opposed to the infant's moments of quiescence, of just existing in the world, or the child's accidentally falling, and the like.

The child's projects will often involve the second element I mentioned, a direct interaction of a certain kind with an adult, as when the pre-verbal child holds out its foot so that the adult can put its shoe on, or holds out its hands so that the adult can hold it while it climbs some stairs encountered on a walk. Or the pre-verbal child will play certain made-up games with the adult, initiating a simple "game" of being tickled, for example, or indicating by an unmistakable gesture that it wants to be turned and held upside down. We might name these patterns "co-operative interactions," recognizing however that the behaviours thus collected are extremely varied, and loosely linked by "family resemblance."

That the adult, in the necessary role of parent or surrogate parent, is often keenly aware of the child is obvious: reciprocally, the child often wants to be watched or observed. After it learns to speak the child may explicitly tell the adult things like, "Don't read. Watch me." "Or: watch me jump." And of course the child can tell if its request is carried out or not. What the speaking child can say the pre-verbal child can indicate or show, for instance by pulling the adult's hand in order to gain his attention. The mutual awareness that often shows itself, and especially during interactions, I call the element of complicity.

The proto language-game that lies at the root of intention-stating is a form of interaction between adult and child. It consists in the adult's awareness of the child's projects, and its reaction to those projects, such as praising or prohibiting or helping, where the child is aware of this reaction, and will often modify its behaviour as a result of it. For instance it will stop doing something the adult prohibits. The pre-verbal child approaches the wall socket; the parent calls out, "Don't touch that," and the child pauses, looks at the parent as if to ascertain the seriousness of the prohibition, and then desists.

The following reports of a child's behaviour further illustrate the points in question, and constitute observations on a proto language-game out of which develops the primitive language-game of intention-stating.

16th month. Makes astonishment noise — indrawn breath and open mouth — ohhahh — quite deliberately when looking — with me — at her picture book — at life-like drawings of cats and dogs, and so on. [I say "quite deliberately" in contrast to earlier instances, where the same "ohh" reaction was spontaneous, triggered immediately by what she saw. Now it is clear that she is making that sound, doing it deliberately. (It is in exactly this kind of case, among many others of course, that we speak of deliberate action.)

17th month. Interaction. Step game — climbs up step, then signals for both her hands to be held so she can step down. She signals by holding up her hands in position to be helped, sometimes also making a sound indicative of wanting.

Plays 'peek a boo' — in effect: Looks through crack in woven chair back, then sticks her head out into view and waves. We say, 'Where's Z.? There she is!'

Shakes empty pop can to see if any is left in bottom. She wants to pour out what is left — but knows I won't let her, so she goes into the next room and pours it out.

Drops her milk bottle on side and looks up at me and makes fake "oh" sound (with rounded lips) as if she regretted it happening (whereas she loves the chance to paint with milk and will try in various ways to get around our prohibition of it.)

Has become very social. Approaches with clear idea of playing, interacting. For example, brings books for you to look at with her. Or a ball for catch.

Likes when S and I both play with her — e.g. 3-cornered 'catch', with her having beach ball handed to her and then carrying it to S so S can throw it to me.

Tries to feed flies some of her cereal!

18th month. Opens drawer of her dresser and takes out all the clothes, "trying" them on then discarding in big pile, till drawer is empty. Now she is at the roll of toilet paper from her changing table, but seemingly knows she is not to take it and so pulls out pieces and uses them in mock blowing of nose, thus "justifying" her action.

19th month. Yesterday — playing with keys — started throwing them down on S (on whom she was sitting, as S lay in bed). Heavy keys. S said "No" (as it hurt). Z seemed aware of the prohibition — then waited awhile — and then threw them.

These examples support my earlier claims: There is a proto language-game of intention that consists in the child undertaking projects in the presence of the adult, the adult's reactions to those projects, the child's further reactions, and so on, where the child may be said to be aware of the parent's awareness of it. There is a wide range of these reactions. (Note that I do not want to make something called "awareness" lie at the bottom of intention-stating; for one thing, some Cartesian might then want to argue that such awareness presupposes cognitive capacities, and indeed an innate language. Rather what counts as such awareness is again given by a range of examples, including the child's keeping a look out for the adult's response, as when in warily approaching an electric socket it casts glances at someone who had previously warned it off such adventures. In the same way, the "psychological" word "wants" used so much previously is to be understood in terms of examples — of engaging in "projects," say, and not as a primitive theoretical term presupposed by my account.)

In the subsequent primitive language-game the proto-behaviour of the sort in question is supplemented by the child's voicing its intention (aim, projected act) and by the adult's reacting to that voiced intention as it might have reacted had it independently discovered — by observation or by inference from prior knowledge — what the child is up to.

The Primitive language-game of intention-stating. In the transition from the proto-behaviour to the simple or primitive language-game, the child steps spontaneously into language. It voices its intention inside the above indicated context of interaction. The use or function its intention-stating words have, as well as Wittgenstein's notion of the interactive nature of language use, can be seen very clearly when we realize how the simple language-game grows out of the proto language-game that precedes it. To make all this clear, I shall again discuss the relevant points in the light of examples, and in particular will now give some instances of a child's initial engagements with a simple language-game of intention-stating.

20th month. Simple one word use indicating where she is going or what she is up to — "up" going up stairs.

21st month. Statement of intention: while doing stacking toy with me says "off" as she starts to take a whole stack off.

22nd month. Sitting in chair by herself — leaning back — says "down" and repeats twice as she slides forward and gets down.

Turn to next book — but she wants to read the bird pop-up book and says — rejecting the other book — "Birdie" meaning — I want to read the bird pop-up book. "Z. get it," I say. "Z., Z., — birdy birdy" — she says as she sets out to the book shelf to look for the book in question (a known one of her favourites)

23rd month. "Show me Daddy watch" This meant in effect "I'm going to show Daddy the watch;" it was not a request. She had the watch, and after making the statement she proceeded to show it to me.

"Climbing chair" — statement of intention before trying to climb chair.

Make believe game of going to store — leaving room with toy shopping cart — saying what she is going to get: "Cottage cheese..., rice..., noodles."

24th month. "Duck, frog downstairs" — stating her intention of taking duck and frog downstairs.

"Out Teddy Bear" (throws it out of her toy shopping cart so she can play at fixing the wheels of the cart, as she has seen S do).

"Jump first, then shirt." She was going to put on her shirt (which she enjoys doing) but wanted to jump first when she saw the hammock.

26th month. "Walk downstairs," meaning in effect "I am going to walk downstairs."

"My do self that" — then proceeds to peel paper off crayon as I had been doing for her.

"One hand." Statement of intention — intends to go upstairs with one hand held.

"I'm going to put it in garbage. I put it in garbage." First she did as she said she was going to, then she said what she had just done.

27th month. "Give big hug." And then she does. (She parcels out her hugs.)

30th month. "First I eat my popcorn, then I poo, then I go outside."

42nd month. "When I get to Daniel's I'll have a drink of juice."

Function. The intentional statement, in the primitive forms I have noted, is taken by the hearer as saying what the child is going to do — get a book, go up the stairs, and so on. Since the reference of the primitive claim is to the future, it is taken as a prediction (of sorts). The "of sorts" is important, of course.

Wittgenstein's observes that agreement in judgment can be essential to a language-game; and it is essential in our case.[17] To illustrate the general point, it would not be our language-game with "red" or "three" or "Mother" unless there was in fact near universal agreement among the speakers of the language about this being red, this being three, this being the person the child calls "Mother" and so on. So too, concerning the primitive language-game of intention-utterances, agreement about what counts as the birdy book, what as getting down or going up the stairs, and so on, is presupposed in the smaller linguistic community of the child and its attendant adults.

There is also presupposed a certain relationship between the child's "prediction" (in stating its intention) and its act — namely that it can be counted upon to do what it has said. With exceptions, of course; that is, barring accidents, and certain interventions or intrusions, such as a third party rushing in with an attention-grabbing present. The loose class of exceptions aside, in what we can call the default case, the child does what it has said it is going to do.

As several of the above examples show, we recognize something as an intention statement precisely because — in an appropriate context — the child goes on to do the thing it mentioned: proceeds to go down stairs after having said "Down stairs" proceeds to bring its toy duck and frog down stairs after saying "Duck, frog, downstairs" and so on. If the child said the latter words and then waited for the adult to transport the things downstairs, then we would take it rather as a request.

I have been emphasizing the reliability of the "prediction" in the default case. That such reliability is an essential property of primitive intention-utterances becomes clear when we examine the function the latter fulfil.

To speak of a word's function (in Wittgenstein's sense) presupposes that it occurs as a move or significant gesture in a language-game, in some patterned human interaction. Words can no more have functions outside language-games than bits of machinery can have functions outside some whole within which they operate.

We are speaking here in particular of words in a primitive language-game with a behaviourial prototype. That the words have the function they do presupposes the continuation of the sort of aware, interactive behaviour found in the proto language-game. The words are an addition to that game. The case of intention illustrates clearly Wittgenstein's claim that "Our language is but an auxiliary to and a wider (further) development of ... more primitive behaviour" (RPP I §151).

In the primitive case, parent and child are aware of one another and tune their actions accordingly, in a certain way. For example the parent moves to block the child when he sees that what it is going to do has bad consequences. The statement of intention — "Throw!" "Up stairs" and so on — is an added element inside the same pattern. Hearing "Throw!" the adult may respond by saying "No! Don't do that!" just as it might have if it had seen the child preparing to throw an object it shouldn't. The words take on the function they do because they are added into *that* pre-existing, proto language-game. The words take over and a function previously fulfilled (in the simplest case) by the observable behaviour of the child.

The following schematic characterization indicates what the proto language-game has in common with the primitive one, as well as the point where the two differ. The child A and an adult B are at least potentially aware of and responsive to one another; B anticipates A's future activity (either through observation or prior knowledge, or through A saying what he will be up to); B then takes the opportunity to respond, by acting, acquiescing, prohibiting, warning, arguing, encouraging, and so on.[18] In the proto-language-game, B's response is based solely on observation or past knowledge; in the primitive language-game, A utters a word indicative of what he will be up to, such as the word "Down" or "Birdy book." Hearing the word takes the place of reading the future action from the child's present behaviour. The word has the same function in the enlarged language-game that A's future-action-revealing behaviour filled in the earlier one.

The words of the child's intention-utterance, then, occur as terms in a certain familiar interaction pattern. In that context, and only there, they function to tell the parent what to expect, what the child is up to. The words we might say name the future activity of the child, but again they do so only in the presupposed context. ("Birdy book" might on another occasion name what the child wants; here too the language-game context must be taken into account if we are to understand the child's words. It is not enough to suppose that what the child means is determined by the fact that it has learned to *refer* to that particular book.) In context, the child's words give the adult the opportunity of preparing in advance for the action that has been "named."

It order to form a judgment about what is essential to intention-utterances we can imagine certain of the features I have mentioned changed. It may be possible to suppose that some parts of the language-game or proto language-game change, while we are yet willing to attribute intention-utterances to the people in question. But if all the elements of the language-game that I have emphasized were to change we could not sensibly speak of there then being intention-utterances. For example, in a world in which adults were not aware of or paid no attention to what their children were doing, someone might still be tempted to say that the children make intention-utterances, provided they go on to act in accordance with what they said. Having said "throw" they then throw, though no one else pays any attention to what they say. The case is suspicious, however; it might be that the children are merely predicting their own actions. Another feature common to the proto and simple language-games is that the adults often adjust their behaviour, in a certain distinctive manner, to the anticipated behaviour of the children. A world is possible in which parents never react in this way, but go about their own business, quite indifferent to their children's future actions, even if these are known. Here again it would be dubious that the children make intention-utterances. Again, if children's behaviour (in a context) were not often a reliable indicator of what they are up to, what project is under way, then there could not be the proto language-game that in fact precedes our simple language-game of intention-utterance. Linked to this, if children could not be relied upon to act in accordance with their simple intention-utterances, moving to get the bird pop-up book when they say "Birdy book", and so on, then the simple language-game would not exist, and the words in question would not have the function they have for us. If we consider now all of those features, it becomes clear that there could be no intention-utterances in a world in which all were lacking. There could not be intention-utterances in a species where each animal is totally indifferent to what the others are doing, and where neither their acts nor words are reliable indicators of their future actions.

But someone might object: suppose there *is* an innate language of thought, and suppose a given animal in that imagined species thinks to itself, in that language, that it intends to throw a certain rock, and says, in a would-be simple language-game, "Throw!"; and suppose this sort of thing went on quite often. Should we not say that these animals are expressing their intentions? Wouldn't we certainly say that if we could ourselves have access to their intentions-as-thought? Well, we shouldn't say that. To take the first question, we would have no right to say these animals are expressing their intentions. We hear them say things that *sound* like "Throw!" "Down!" "Out!" "Show Daddy watch!" and so on; but in that context we cannot make the usual sense we make of such sounds. We can't make head or tail of these animals and their sounds. Can we suppose those noises are correlated with something inner, something private to those who utter them? What are they correlated with? Some image, a brain state, a thought-token, a certain inner-voiced "proposition" — or what? Those inner things no more bear their meaning on their sleeve than do the noises themselves. Let the inner something or other be written out, in some symbolism. Then the question is, how do we read the symbols? Nothing in their lives gives us a handle on how to read them. Why, for instance, are they not expressions of desire rather than intention? (We can suppose, similarly to the above, that these animal's alleged words of request are broken free of the salient features of the proto and simple language-game of request-making.) And the same considerations that hold for "thought-tokens" hold also for allegedly shared "thoughts"; nothing should make us say that in the imagined context these creatures are thinking to themselves, "I intend to do such and such."

To return to the issue of the reliability of the primitive intention-utterance. It may be too strong to say that this feature per se is essential; perhaps in a world where the other features discussed were present, and where there was only a partial such reliability (in the default case) we might still see enough similarity to our language-game to wish to speak of an intention-utterance. But to get that result we must speak of a partial and not a total lack of reliability. In any case the disjunction of features is essential.

Extending the simple language-game. Often the parent will respond *verbally* to the child's simple intention-utterances. Those responses help bring the child to a mastery of various ensuing complications of the language-game, and additions to it.

Among those complications are: (1) An enlargement of the intention-utterance to include the first person pronoun and to include other appropriate syntactical additions. "Throw" becomes "I am going to throw this," for example, and subsequently the latter may be rendered "I intend to throw this." (2) The ability to speak of various details of the intended act, such as for example *where* the child is going to throw the thing, or *what* — by name — the child is going to throw (items that are in the initial cases given by the context of utterance). (3) Tying in *reasons* to intention statements. The parent prohibits the child from fulfilling its stated intention — and says why: It's too dangerous, or noisy, or there's not enough time, and so on. Later the child will be able itself to ask for reasons why it can't do what it wants or intends and it will also learn to defend its intended actions by positive, countervailing reasons. (4) The inclusion of temporal reference makes up another twist in the language-game: "After my nap I'll ...." Time words, including, in the future, use of terms from clock and calendar systems of reference, are amalgamated to the expression of intention. This is a melding of the language-game of telling time with that of stating intention. But note that a language-game like that of stating clock time will naturally be amalgamated to such additional language-games as requests, intention-statements, narrative descriptions, and even make believe. We do not merely tell time, which isn't to deny that we might wonder purely out of curiosity what time it is. (5) Along a quite different axis of variation, the child subsequently learns the use of second and third person singular and plural present tense intention-statements. The child learns to say, for instance, "Molly is going to throw the doll." The logic of such statements differs markedly from those in the first person.

To enlarge a bit on the last point, what the child masters initially is the first person use. In saying this I assume a continuity between such early utterances as "Throw" — said as an intention-utterance — and later ones such as "I am going to throw" where the "I" is explicit. The continuity in question concerns the function of the utterances. The function of "Throw!" *qua* intention-statement is the same as the function of "I am going to throw!" If we examine the earlier or more primitive instances especially, and contrast them with the quite different second or third person uses, we can get a clear sense of what lies behind Wittgenstein's famous "logical" distinction between first and third person use. For example, in learning to say "Throw!" (qua intention claim) the child does not have to master any means for picking itself out, or for, as it were, attaching a label to itself; nor does it when it subsequently learns to replace "Throw!" by "I am going to throw!" Whereas in learning "She is going to throw" (or even to learn a primitive but functionally equivalent version of that) the child will have learned to pick out one thrower from another. These sorts of examples are also relevant to assessing Wittgenstein's rather notorious claim that "I" in present tense psychological uses does not refer. Note too that Wittgenstein treats the first person expression of intention as a different language-game from that of second and third person intention-expression. Examining details of simple language-games shows that the differences lying behind that distinction are striking indeed.

Centres of variation. I want now to address the idea of a "centre of variation" for it is through this notion that one can justify Wittgenstein's concern with primitive language-games. Consider the adult's intention-statement, uttered as he starts for the stairs: "I'm going to get the pop-up bird book." How does this compare with the child's "Birdy book" uttered as *she* starts for the stairs? "Birdy book" is the child's name for that particular pop-up book; the adults know the name and themselves use it in talking to the child. So adult and child are talking about the same book. They are both saying that they are going to fetch that book. If left to their own ends, they would each have returned with that particular book. What does a hearer get from the two statements? In each case a knowledge of the speaker's future action. It is as if the hearer now possessed a reliable prediction of the action. (Of course I am discounting character flaws in the speaker, or other such complicating factors; the class of features that take an intention-utterance out of the default case grows as the language-game becomes takes on complications.)

The two statements it is clear have something important in common, viz, their *point*. Having heard the intention statement, of either child or adult, the hearer is in like position: the hearer has been enabled to act appropriately. If he has information relevant to the intended act, he can state it; if he has a reason for prohibiting the act he can do so. And so on. The two utterances, in their contexts, have the same function, of alerting the hearer to the speaker's future action. That function is the centre of variation of the language-game. The centre remains the same when complications, such as references to time, and so on, are added. But for the functions to remain the same through variations in the language-games, it is (logically) necessary that the language-games themselves retain some central core. The centre of variation is really the basic pattern of interaction that is already visible in the proto language-game. The primitive and gradually more complex language-games growing out of the proto-behaviour share something. In the case of intention it is the behaviour pattern of people who co-operate (and so on) in a certain way through anticipating the other's actions.

Given the phenomenon of a "centre of variation" we can say that the child's "Birdy book" is in one sense (meaning as use) already a full-fledged, fully effective act of communication. The words serve the same central function they fill in certain more complex forms that the adult language-game of intention-statement takes on. The adult understands the child perfectly, and the child has performed what is in itself, surface grammar aside, a complete act of communication.

To say however that there is a central element of the language-game — a central pattern of interaction — that remains the same is not to deny that the language-game changes and develops in numerous ways. Differences may be as important as similarities, obviously; but what one should be wary of is reading back into some earlier form of the language-game features that only obtain in some later forms.

Prediction. As Wittgenstein noted, the speaker does not make the "prediction" contained in the intention-utterance on the basis of observation. The adult observes that the child is about to throw a book. The child does not similarly anticipate its own actions through observation. It does not watch its taking hold of the book, or its lifting it back to throwing position; does not "predict," on the basis of what it has perceived: "[I am going to] throw!"

We might speak here of two connected talents the child has. The first is the ability of undertaking various projects, achieving, as we say, various goals or ends. For example, it climbs up on the hassock and then, straining its developmental capacity to the utmost, jumps off of it. Then does this again and again. It wants to jump. The second talent manifests itself when one day, out of the blue, the child *says* what it is about to undertake. It is as if it had the ability to point into the future, to indicate or pick out some future act. It does this pointing or indicating with a word that it has heard adults using. But again it does not rely on self-observation to instruct it on what it is about to do, and hence what word it should pronounce.

Naturally not, someone may object: it relies on its inner awareness of its intention! It outwardly voices what it inwardly perceives, namely that it intends, say, to jump.

As opposed to that picture-generated assumption, I would counterpoise a different idea, one made concrete by my earlier remarks. This is that the child *just does* make the "prediction" that, in the proper context, constitutes its stating its intention. And what the child can do the adult can as well, since the core of the language-game of intention-stating, or its first-person branch, is already present in the child's usage.

The final remarks in 788. The first person intention-utterances we have been looking at are the target of Wittgenstein's depth grammatical remarks in the final sentences of RPP §788. We are now in a position to judge how close he has come to hitting the target.

In 788d he asks about the *function* of the expression of intention, and then moves, somewhat mysteriously, to the question of when something is an expression of intention (788e).

His answer is: 788f "Well, when the act follows it, when it is a prediction." Here it might be objected that the mere making of a correct prediction does not constitute an intention statement. It could instead be something quite different, namely a mere empirical prediction, made on whatever grounds. But to understand Wittgenstein correctly here we must take into consideration 788g as well: "I make the prediction, the same one as someone else makes from observation of my behaviour, *without* this observation." So the "prediction" in 788f is one of those special ones, where the speaker does not rely on observation. When we understand 788f—g together in this way, it can be seen from my earlier observations that Wittgenstein is right.

We take the child's issuing of certain words to be an expression of intention precisely when we are justified in taking them to be a prediction (of that special sort) and when the act indicated by the child's words is then performed by the child.

We can now see also why answering the "when" of 788e also provides an answer to 788d: the when-question gets the response, "When it serves as a 'prediction'" (in the special sense); and that response also characterizes the function of the intention-utterance, which is to serve, in the appropriate circumstance, as a 'prediction'.

The element of "predication," when we take into account the role it plays in the language-game, distinguishes the child's intention-utterances from its requests, even though the two might be expressed in exactly the same words. The words may be the same, but the context, what comes before, what things are like now, and what happens subsequently, will be different, as we have seen in several examples. In the historically first case, there may be doubts about whether a word states an intention. But when the child in later episodes naturally and consistently proceeds to act in accordance with its seeming intention-expression, then we have no hesitation in saying that it has expressed its intentions. In these subsequent cases too, however, the business about prediction still marks off the class of intention-utterances. Of course we allow special cases — the child falls and injures itself, or is interrupted, and so on. But putting those recognizable exceptions aside, we can say that "prediction" is the mark of intention.

The language-game of intention-stating presupposes the existence of a certain pattern of interaction among its speakers. Their form of life must be characterized by a certain generality. It is a generality holding not of one person, still less of one person's mind, but of a people — a culturally coherent group of speakers. The presupposed pattern is that the person who says a phrase like "Birdy book" then acts as he or she had "predicted," by going after the book, and the hearer in turn reacts to the prediction in one of the ways characteristic of the language-game. Without that regularity, in that context of interaction, the expression of intention, as we know it, could not exist.

The particular claim made about observation in the last sentence of 788 can also be seen to be accurate. We can often predict what the child will do by observing it. The child *says* what it is going to do, but not as a result of observing itself. It just does say what it is going to do.

The original question. "Why do I have doubts about his intention, but not about mine?" Wittgenstein's implicit answer is that the question contains a mistake. The conundrum is a fantastic growth rooted in one's picture of the intention as inner object. I speak confidently of my intentions. They must be *something*, and what else but something inner? I can have doubts about such a thing when it is inner to another, and hence another's intention, so the idea of doubting the thing makes sense. On the picture of the intention as inner object, the issue of doubt can be raised for the first person case, even though the answer is plain, namely that I cannot doubt what I directly confront.

Wittgenstein believes that a careful and full observation of the language-game of intention-stating will drive one from that picture. I have certainly not attempted a full description of the language-game here. Nevertheless enough has been said to lend credence to the idea that our common picture is misleading. I shall review some of the reasons for thinking it misleading, but first let me enter the following quotation, which makes Wittgenstein's attitude to the picture unmistakable:

> Does something happen when I ... intend this or that? — Does nothing happen? — That is not the point; but rather: why should what happens within you interest me? (His soul may boil or freeze, turn red or blue: what do I care?) (RPP I §215)

Examples of the sort I have examined carry the burden of indicating why Wittgenstein takes the picture of the intention as inner as misleading. In those examples we see from close up how intention-utterances work; we see how they function, from within a context of awareness and co-operative interchange, to point to the speaker's future action. How they function in short as "predictions" and not as reports on the inner.

Since, as examples make plain, the job of the intention-utterance is to pick out the end point of the speaker's "project," it is natural that the hearer could not care less about the state of the speaker's soul. He wants to know rather what the speaker will be up to. From the perspective of either speaker or hearer, the point of the utterance is *not* to describe the inner.

My goal, however, is not to produce a dogmatic argument to that effect, nor indeed a knock down argument of any kind. Rather, I accept the idea that what is needed here is a careful and patient examination of actual use. I hope I have made a beginning of examining the use of intention utterances; but of course much remains to do. Among the unfinished tasks is to study various extensions of the language-game, including its incorporation of reason-giving.

Does the language-game admit of doubt? The untroubled and spontaneous making of one of those successful "predictions," in a context like that obtaining in the proto language-game of intention, constitutes an intention-expression. Such spontaneous voicings of one's goal may be falsely construed as cases where one has no doubts. But — despite the dominant picture of the intention as inner — one has no doubts here only in the way that birch bark has no square roots; doubts are logically or conceptually impossible. They have no place in the language-game. It is true we are reluctant to speak of doubting our own intentions. But Wittgenstein would hold that that reluctance is not a consequence of the inner nature of intention but rather derives from the fact that the language-game of intention-stating does not admit doubt.

Doubt has no place in the central cases we have been looking at, of proto and primitive language-games, when the child first comes to the ability to express its intentions. It is no part of those interactions for the child to be able to doubt whether what it indicates or says is its intention is really its intention. When the child subsequently learns to speak of the intentions of others it will also learn that doubts in *such* an instance may sometimes be in place. But it never learns this about its own intentions. At least not about its simple and immediate intentions, like those we have considered. Furthermore, doubt is ruled out for almost all of the subsequent enlargements and complications of the language-game. That is, there is no room for the speaker's doubting his intention-utterance in most of those subsequent uses that share their core functional features with the primitive language-game. And if others doubt the speaker's intention, in such central cases, it can only be on the grounds of doubting his sincerity.

Given what we can plainly observe in the central cases, objections to the idea of the conceptual impossibility of doubting one's intentions would seem to be stuck between two bad choices. One would be to deny the "centrality" of the examples I have given. This is a sorry option, since if the child's "Throw!" and like utterances are not paradigmatic and central intention-utterances (given the supposed context) then what are? The other option will seem more promising, but it rests on a faulty inference. That alternative is to cite cases where we can doubt the speaker's intention-claim, but without doubting his sincerity. In such cases the speaker too can doubt the intention-claim. The faulty inference I referred to rests on a failure to recognize that an utterance has the sense it has because it is made inside the specific language-game operative then and there, at the time and place of utterance. The critic assumes that because we can think of cases where an adult — with mastery of a certain enhanced language-game of intention-stating — can have such doubts, that that in itself shows doubt to be possible in the central cases. The point will become clear if we look at some alleged counterexamples.

A person may learn as an adult to doubt in a case like this, for instance: Doubts about whether she will in fact do what she has said she will do may form the basis for her doubting whether she really does have the intention in question, or whether she truly had it at the time she said it.[19] Someone with all the conviction in the world may tell various people at various time that she will call them, or get together with them, but the calls or meetings *never* materialize. Did she then intend to call when she said she so intended (and this is not meant to question her sincerity)? Our language is certainly loose enough to allow us to say she did not so intend; and similarly loose enough to allow us to speak here of her coming herself to doubt her intentions. But that licence does not carry over to the paradigmatic and simple cases, those that most resemble the initial simple language-game of first person intention-stating. If she calls out to her friend, "I'll get the phone" there is no room for anyone to call this intention into question (without questioning the woman's sincerity); it makes no sense for her subsequently to wonder whether she really intends to do that. Perhaps even here one could construct a story; but what I want for examples are cases where there are no stories — simple plain and ordinary cases of intention-stating. *There* doubt has no place. We never learned how to do it. There is nothing to do. We can no more doubt here than we can move the king into check in chess. And it is no rebuttal in the latter case to say for example that in a certain chess club in Boise, Idaho the game developed in such a way that in certain circumstances the king is allowed to move into check.

Someone might object to my saying that I want plain and ordinary cases of intention-utterance. Doesn't that smack of the fallacy of meeting a counter-example by switching to a different example? The objection misses my point. I grant that in the example doubt is possible. But if one reflects on the idea that there is a centre of variation in common between the primitive language-game of intention utterances and many later, more syntactically proper versions, one will see that very often in everyday life we do exactly what the child Z began to do at age fifteen months or so. We point (verbally) to the future act we will be engaged in, and do so in a context where the hearer of our statement is expected to react in one of the appropriate ways. This is a scenario repeated daily, and in it there is no thought on anyone's part of doubt (unless the hearer suspects the speaker's sincerity).

In those simple language-games, as ancient as childhood and commoner than sin, doubt has no place.

Psychoanalytic theory may also seem to support the construction of counterexamples; but the reply is the same. Here again I grant there are complications or developments of the language-game of intention-utterances wherein doubt on the part of the speaker is possible. Because new rules hold there. It is true, perhaps, that you did not really intend to do X (as you had said) but rather that you intended to do Y (say insult some father-figure); and the criterion for truth will be some complicated rule like: "If you and the analyst agree that the best explanation of a number of things is that you really did intend to insult…, and if that is consistent with your agreed upon interpretations of many other things, including perhaps dreams and slips of the tongue, then you did." That such a (vague) rule holds for the psychoanalytic reading of certain intentions does not imply that anything similar holds for the plain and simple cases as well, when the man tells his wife that he'll get the paper, or lets his secretary know when he'll be back from lunch.

In looking at the simplest cases of intention-utterances it is helpful to compare them with requests. A parent might react to a child's request for something by asking "Are you sure you want that," meaning thereby something like, "You won't really enjoy it," or "It's bad for you," or whatever. But one would not react to what one takes to be the child's intention-utterance by saying "Are you sure you intend that?" And not because inner intentions are easier to observe than inner wants. In neither case is it a matter of something inner. It is rather because the game of intention-stating starts with behaviour (in the same way that the game of requests starts with reaching or other attempts to get things). *Our* behaviourial repertoire includes a pointing by means of words not only to what we want, but to what we are in the process of moving towards doing. These are as it were blind pointings, in that the child just does point, as it just does reach, or just does throw. And in adult life we continue to make the very same moves in the very same language-game, when we say for instance that we'll return the video. The most fanatical Freudian will hesitate to attempt to psychoanalyse every one of our mundane intention statements. Our lives may indeed be wrapped round in fantasy, but there are points of clarity, including those that derive directly from our second year, when we learned full well, once and for all, to make intention-utterances.

In those cases we make our "prediction" and it is invariably accurate — when the special cases are subtracted. There is no room *there* for introducing doubt on the part of the speaker. Doubt cannot get a hold. The language-game does not contain doubt.

Conclusion. Thus my exegesis of RPP I §788. I do not wish to claim that Wittgenstein has proven his point. Its not a matter of proving something, but a matter rather of changing the way one views language. One possibility is to look at language, and hence to look at such attendant phenomena as intention, through the lens of a certain general picture — in particular one that embodies a distinction between inner and outer, subjective and objective, experience and fact, and the like, and embodies also some Aristotelian/Cartesian/Kantian/Tractarian/Chomskian notion that our relationship to the inner is *discursive*, a matter of propositional knowledge. (The ratiocinating mind. Even perception on such a view is propositional; we see that the cat is on the mat. See for example TLP 5.5423.) The later Wittgenstein's alternative view of language is supposed eventually to make it quite clear that that picture, which so dominates contemporary thought, *is* a picture. It is supposed to show us, for example, what really goes on when one states an intention. As I have said, to see that will require an extended investigation of the concept.

I hope the approach I have taken in this paper will be of use in that investigation. I speculate, finally, that such a study as that exemplified here, of this and other concepts, and in general of first language acquisition, will be important also to the social scientific study of humanity, not least because it will help put paid that infamous Cartesian picture we all, and especially the new empiricists, hold so close.

John V. Canfield
Erindale College, University of Toronto

Endnotes

1. He voices those doubts in the passage referred to above (OC §501): "Am I not getting closer and closer to saying that in the end logic cannot be described? You must look at the practice of language, then you will see it."

2. I defend the point in chapter nine of *Wittgenstein: Language and World*. University of Massachusetts Press, Amherst, 1981.

3. For "conceptual investigations" see RPP I §1104 and PI p.213.

4. The point will be misunderstood by those who see Wittgenstein as a (philosophically) conservative thinker who would seek vainly to tie people to the "ordinary use" of words and thus prevent the development of philosophical "theories". Science is not restricted to the ordinary sense of terms like "force" or "energy"; why should philosophers not similarly be able freely to construct theories about such things as intentions or meanings, or what have you? I think Wittgenstein escapes this criticism, but it is a large issue. Some points relevant to its discussion will be made in this paper.

5. RPP II §47.

6. In his *Nothing is Hidden*, Blackwell, 1986.

7. *Philosophia* 6, 1976, 409 — 445.

8. It may be objected that such a study cannot proceed with out consideration of such rival mixes of theory and "data," as those supplied by such writers as Piaget, Bruner, or Chomsky. One salient difference between such theories and Wittgenstein's approach is that they attempt to explain *how* language is learned, whereas his interest is rather in the nature of that which is learned. The Wittgensteinian interest in the customs that constitute language use is rather akin to that of a purely descriptive anthropologist. But suppose for the sake of argument we allow Wittgenstein's unique view of language — his fix, or gestalt on it — to count as theory. That theory nevertheless differs radically from those others; and in addition, "data" is

always informed (or contaminated) by "theory." By these considerations it is legitimate, in an inquiry such as this, to develop a Wittgensteinian view of first language independently of those other approaches.

9. I have made a minor change in Anscombe's translation. She renders the word "Nutzen" in 788c and 788d as "use." Those who read Wittgenstein in English have accepted "use" as one of his chief terms of art, as in "the meaning of a word is its use (Gebrauch) in the language" (*PI* §43). On the other hand Wittgenstein will often employ words from his special vocabulary in ways that are not technical but normal. Thus "picture," for him, may sometimes mean just plain old picture, rather than "metaphysical picture." His practice may be aesthetically preferable, but it can cause confusion. There is no suggestion in 788c that "use" bears the special sense it has in his later philosophy; and in fact *that* "use" cannot go happily into the context, "What ... is the use of my knowing my intention?" One speaks of the use (Gebrauch) of words or expressions or utterances or sentences, but not of the use of knowing. To avoid puzzlement, I have replaced her "use" by "usefulness."

10. Having an intention might be likened to having a Fregean thought, at least in this: One has the thought, and one knows one has it, even though the thought is not necessarily manifest in awareness in the way for example that sense data are. The idea that having an intention may occur without benefit of some particular sort of phenomenal data, or experience, might even be thought by some to be a Wittgensteinian insight. They would be wrong, however; Wittgenstein isn't really in the business of phenomenology.

11. In the present context it is interesting to note Bruner's employment of "intention," which is in keeping with the picture of the intention as inner. It is a basic idea of his that the child can "realize his intentions communicatively" (*Child's Talk*, New York, 1985, p.18). The child's "intent to refer" for example is unlearned, and together with "the recognition of that intent in others" forms the basis or background given which the child learns language (p.122). For, "Some basis for referential intersubjectivity must exist before language proper appears" (p.122). It seems then that I have an intention to refer, and I perceive that you do as well; I somehow pitch my words to that shared aim. How do I ascribe intention to you, since my intention (one presupposes) is internal to me? Bruner's

answer is revealing: "It is a primitive that 'other minds' are treated as if they were like our own minds" (p.122). So once again we see seventeenth century metaphysical views taking a prominent place in twentieth century "empirical" research. I find Bruner's book frustrating, because beneath its "theoretical" veneer of mental intentions and the like one finds a view that is in many places close to Wittgenstein's. One would like to free the facts from the theory.

12. It wouldn't be enough to take the thing one is acquainted with as *evidence* for one's having a certain intention. The acquaintanceship is supposed to result in certainty concerning the intention. If it is argued that it might be nevertheless an inductive certainty, then the question arises of how one establishes the cases that set up the inductive certainty. No, the direct mental relationship must be to the intention itself, not to something which is merely evidence for having the intention.

13. I believe that Kripke gives a wrong impression of this "usefulness." He writes: "... Wittgenstein's general picture of language... requires for an account of a type of utterance not merely that we say under what conditions an utterance of that type can be made, but also what role and utility in our lives can be ascribed to the practice of making this type of utterance under such conditions." ("Wittgenstein on Rules and Private Language." In *Perspectives on the Philosophy of Wittgenstein*. Ed. I. Block. Oxford, 1981, p.286.) This mixes up the question of the role of an utterance in the language-game with the quite different one of the utility to the people (however that is to be decided) of having the language-game. As I believe will become clear in this paper, Wittgenstein's interest is in the former sort of "utility" or, better, "function."

14. See the discussion in my "The Concept of Function in Biology." In *Philosophical Topics*, V. 18, n.2, Fall 1990, pp.29–53.

15. Speaking of wants may be misleading; it makes it look as if there is this single psychological phenomenon, wanting, which may be directed on various things, and which, as so directed, the child learns to express.

16. The ability is not uniquely human, in that chimpanzees can be taught to use symbols in language-games, including, of course, that of requests.

17. PI p.226.

18. Of course the parent need make no overt response, but just display a tacit neutrality in the face of knowing what the child is up to. But in this context such a display is in fact an important form of response; for example, the child may take the parents' neutrality as permission, given the long-standing role of the parent as guardian.

19. I am not speaking here of doubting a past intention on the grounds that possibly I misremember it, or something of the sort. Assume I remember sincerely stating my intention.

CHAPTER II

The Agreement of Thought and Reality

P.M.S. Hacker

Over the last three decades John Hunter has written a large series of essays on Wittgensteinian themes. His mastery of the methods of philosophizing which Wittgenstein taught has grown decade by decade and his writings increasingly display the skill and penetration that can come only from assiduous dedication to the arduous craft of disentangling philosophical confusions. Even when writing directly on passages from the *Philosophical Investigations*, Hunter has not aimed merely at textual exegesis. He has taken to heart Wittgenstein's remark at the end of the Preface to the *Investigations*: "I should not like my writing to spare other people the trouble of thinking. But if possible, to stimulate someone to thoughts of his own." Hence, even in these essays, *a fortiori* in others less closely connected with Wittgenstein's texts, Hunter developed his own distinctive philosophical style. His writings are always thoughtful and thought-provoking, frequently insightful and original. They shed much light not only on Wittgenstein's writings, but also on the problems with which Wittgenstein struggled, often illuminating them from fresh angles. No one who is interested in avoiding the bewitchment by language characteristic of the questions and theories of philosophy, in exposing misconceived answers and in unmasking the illusions of philosophical theorizing can fail to be grateful to John Hunter for his contribution to these goals. The following essay, which *is* exegetical, is offered as a token of gratitude to the author of *Understanding Wittgenstein* and *Wittgenstein on Words as Instruments* from whom I have learnt much.

> §429. The agreement, the harmony, of thought and reality consists in this: if I say falsely that something is *red*, then, for all that, it isn't *red*. And when I want to explain the word 'red' to someone, in the sentence 'that is not red', I do it by pointing to something red.

At first sight this pair of platitudes seems baffling. First, why are they worth saying? Secondly, why is the truism that if I say falsely that something is *red*, then for all that, it isn't *red* held to exemplify 'the agreement, harmony' between thought and reality. Indeed, exactly what *is* this agreement or harmony?

Of course, one may add that if I wish futilely that N. should *visit me* then for all that he does not *visit me*. And if I order N. to *shut the door*, and my order is disobeyed, then what N. fails to do is *shut the door*. Similar moves can be made for belief, expectation, intention etc. But although these transformations generalise the matter, they hardly illuminate it.

To shed light on Wittgenstein's concerns here, we must go back to the *Notebooks 1914-16* and the *Tractatus*. It is evident that the features which Wittgenstein later characterized as 'the harmony between thought and reality' occurred to him already in 1914:

> If a picture presents what-is-not-the case..., this only happens through its presenting *that* which *is* not the case.
>
> For the picture says, as it were, '*This* is how it is *not*' and to the question 'How is it not?' just the positive proposition is the answer (NB 25).

Why should this seem puzzling or extraordinary? One might wonder how a proposition or a thought (which Wittgenstein conceived of as a proposition in the medium of the mind (TLP 3; 3.1)) *can* depict what is *not* the case. For if it is not the case, then it does not exist. And what does not exist is nothing. But to depict nothing is not to depict anything at all, as Socrates argued in the *Theaetetus*. So how *can* a proposition be false? One might also present the problem thus: a true proposition, for example the proposition that A is green, seems to correspond univocally to the fact that A is green. But then to what does the false proposition that A is green correspond? One is perhaps inclined to say that it corresponds to A's *not* being green. But what *is* A's not-being-green? Is it A's being red, or A's being blue, or.... etc? (It might even seem as it did to Schlick that negative propositions such as 'A is not green' are essentially defective because they are ambiguous and hence that they should be banished from logic and science.)

Wittgenstein was not tempted by that thought. He saw very early that one must not confuse p's not being the case with what is the case instead of p, e.g. that if the proposition that this rose is not red is true (since the rose is, as a matter of fact, yellow) the negative proposition does *not* signify that the rose is yellow (NB 94). For 'not-p' does not mean 'everything else, only not p' (NB 95). A negative proposition signifies in a different way from the proposition it negates, for it is parasitic on its sense and *reverses* it:

> One could say that negation must be related to the logical place determined by the negated proposition.
> The negating proposition determines a logical place *different* from that of the negated proposition.
> The negating proposition determines a logical place with the help of the logical place of the negated proposition. For it describes it as lying outside the latter's logical place.
> The negated proposition can be negated again, and this in itself shows that what is negated is already a proposition, and not merely something that is a preliminary to a proposition (TLP 4.0641; cf. NB 26).

The proposition that p determines a logical place irrespective of its truth. It determines what must be the case for it to be true, foreshadowing the fact that would make it true were that fact to obtain. The proposition and its negation correspond to the same reality inasmuch as it is the very same fact which verifies the one and falsifies the other. If it is the case that p, then the fact that p makes the proposition that p true and the proposition that not-p false. If it is not the case that p, then 'p' is made false and 'not-p' true by the same negative fact (NB 94; TLP 2.06).

But if all this is so, how is it possible? How can the proposition or thought *do* this? (Suddenly thought strikes us as extraordinarily mysterious!) Wittgenstein's early reflections revolved around these puzzles:

> The shadow which the picture as it were casts upon the world: How am I to get an exact grasp of it?
> Here is a deep mystery?
> It is the mystery of negation: This is not how things are, and yet we can say *how* things are not (NB 30).

The 'mystery of negation' is none other than the mystery of the harmony or agreement between thought and reality. Its extension to expectation and its fulfilment, command and its execution, wish and its satisfaction occurred to Wittgenstein only in 1929.

The key question seemed to be 'How does the proposition determine the logical place?' or 'How does the picture present a situation, given that it itself is not the situation, which need not obtain at all?' (NB 26). Wittgenstein's early answer prefigured the core of the so-called picture theory of the proposition.

> One name is representative of one thing, another of another thing, and they themselves are connected; in this way the whole images the situation - like a *tableau vivant*.
> The logical connection must, of course, be one that is possible as between the things that the names are representatives of, and this will always be the case if the names really are representatives of the things. N.B. That connection is not a relation but only the *holding* of a relation.
> ...
>
> But when I say: the connection of the propositional components must be possible for the represented things - does this not contain the whole problem? How can a non-existent connection between objects be possible?
> "The connection must be possible" means: The proposition and the components of the situation must stand in a particular relation.
> Then in order for a proposition to present a situation it is only necessary for its component parts to represent those of the situation and for the former to stand in a connection which is possible for the latter.
> The propositional sign guarantees the possibility of the fact which it presents (not, that this fact is actually the case)...
> The picture must now in turn cast its shadow on the world (NB 26f).

In the *Tractatus* this sketch was elaborated into a perfectly general account of the possibility of representation. The pictorial character of any representation whatever, be it a diorama, a picture, a proposition or a thought, consists in an agreement (or harmony as Wittgenstein later put it (PG 142, 163)) of *form* between representation and what is represented. Any representation or picture (*Bild*, model) consists of elements which are representatives of objects in reality. The correlation of the elements with objects is the *pictorial relationship* (TLP 2.1514). The elements of the picture are related to each other in a determinate way, and the fact that they are so related represents (given the appropriate method of projection) that things are related to each other in the same way. The *structure of the picture* is this connection of its elements, and the possibility of this structure, i.e. the possibility that things are related to one another in the same way as the elements of the picture, is the *pictorial form* of the picture (TLP 2.15–2.151). Thus the three-dimensionality of a diorama makes it possible for such a model to represent the spatial relations of objects in a traffic accident in the particular manner in which it does (the two dimensionality of a painting together with conventions of perspectival representation make it possible for a painting to represent the same state of affairs in its different particular manner). The linear spatial ordering of staves in musical notation make it possible for a score to represent the temporal ordering of notes in a musical composition. There must be something identical in a picture and what it depicts to enable it to be a picture *of* that situation; and there must be something different, otherwise the picture would be identical with or a replica of what it depicts. The *representational form* of a picture (e.g. the spatial two-dimensionality of a score) differentiates the picture from what it represents. The pictorial form is what a picture has in common with what it represents, i.e. the possible forms of connection of elements of the picture are identical with the possible forms of arrangement of the things represented. Different kinds of picture with different representational forms may depict the same situation (a diorama and a drawing). They have different pictorial forms too (e.g. three-dimensionality as opposed to two-dimensionality). But what *any* picture must have in common with what it represents, as well as with any other pictures that represent the same situation (including propositions and thoughts) is *logical form*, which is the form of reality (TLP 2.18). A logical picture is a picture whose pictorial form *is* logical form (TLP 2.181). Every picture is *also* a logical picture, although different kinds of picture are distinguished by features of their pictorial and representational forms. A thought, however, is a picture whose pictorial form is, it seems, exhausted by its logical form (TLP 3). What it has in common with the reality it represents *is* logical form. The harmony between thought and reality, according to the *Tractatus*, consists in this agreement of logical form, i.e. identical logical multiplicity (TLP 4.04) in virtue of which the one can be a projection of the other.

This abstract conception was given further elaboration in the *Tractatus* account of the nature of propositional representation. All propositions are held to be truth-functions of elementary propositions (TLP 5). Elementary propositions are logically independent (TLP 5.134). They consist of simple names the meanings of which are simple objects. Names and the correlative objects which are their meanings have the same logical form, and it is this that ensures isomorphism between a proposition and the situation it depicts truly or falsely. The simple objects are sempiternal, a requirement which seemed necessary to avoid reference failure and the dependence of logic, the determination of sense, upon truth, the existence or non-existence of states of affairs (TLP 2.02-2.0272). The connection between language and reality which establishes the pictorial relationship is psychological (NB 99). To be sure, the *Tractatus* is remarkably reticent on this subject. But it is plausible to suppose that Wittgenstein conceived of the correlation of names and the objects that are their meanings (*Bedeutungen*) as effected by acts of meaning (*meinen*), i.e. meaning *this* object by such-and-such a name (cf. NB 70). The intentionality or directedness of symbols is derived from mental acts that one performs in using symbols. It was arguably with his younger self in mind that Wittgenstein later wrote:

> It's beginning to look somehow as if intention could never be recognised as *intention* from outside; as if one must be doing the meaning of it oneself in order to understand it as meaning [*Meinung*]. That would amount to considering it not as a phenomenon or fact but as something intentional which has a direction given to it. What this direction is, we do not know; it is something which is absent from the phenomenon as such (PG 143).

It is striking that Wittgenstein observed in this context that to consider intention as something other than a phenomenon "would make intention reminiscent of the will as conceived by Schopenhauer" (PG 144). For it is probable that he had himself conceived of meaning something by a sign as an act of will performed not by the empirical self (for that would, absurdly, make acts of will phenomena, i.e. something that happens to one) but by the metaphysical self, the willing subject (NB 80).

Hence, incidentally, the point of the mysterious remarks in *Investigations* §§455-7, which gave John Hunter pause in *Understanding Wittgenstein*, essay 19. There Wittgenstein compares meaning something to going up to, or towards, someone — this, he claims, is something we want to say, and he appears to end up (PI §457) endorsing it. What is the temptation, why might one be so tempted, and what exactly is the mature Wittgenstein endorsing? The interlocutor in §454 suggests that what gives 'life' to a mere mark on paper, for example an arrow, what makes it *point* as it were, is its meaning (*Bedeutung*), which is a psychic accompaniment. A venerable tradition conceived of such psychic accompaniments as mental images (or in the contemporary jargon of the still flourishing tradition 'an internal representation'). But only a little reflection is necessary before one realises that the mental image of an arrow can fare no better in this matter than the lines on paper, for it is in effect merely another sign. One might now think of meaning something (*meinen*) as a special kind of *mental process* that accompanies the mental image (the psychic constituents of a thought) *or* the use of the drawn arrow on paper (the propositional sign) and confers intentionality upon it. But this too is of no avail: "For no *process* could have the consequences of meaning" (PI p.218). For example, if I meant you to go *there* ↑ and you went in the wrong direction, I would *correct* you. But how could a mental process, a mere phenomenon, determine a normative consequence? So, finally, we are driven to the conclusion that meaning something is not a process; it is not anything that happens or happens to us (so not a phenomenon) but something we *do* (PG 156) — like going towards someone. This, I suggest, was part and parcel of the psychological hinterland of the *Tractatus*. Part of such a picture is that meaning something is not a phenomenal experience, not something that confronts the subject as an object for a possible description: "The subject — we want to say — does not here drop out of the experience but is so much involved in it that it cannot be described" (PG 156). This is the thought exploited in *Investigations* §456: meaning something is not an experience (which could be described) but an activity of the subject. And the reason it cannot be described is (the Kantian and Schopenhauerian reason) that the self cannot simultaneously engage in an activity and also stand back and observe itself doing so. If one is, as it were, *doing* the meaning, one cannot also watch oneself doing it, for one cannot be both actor and spectator at the same time.

Of course, this is a muddle. Meaning something is indeed not a sensation or sense-impression one has, nor is it having one. It is not an experience of any kind, although it may well be that when one means *this* rather than *that*, one has certain distinctive experiences (RPP I §§226-41). But it is equally misguided to think that meaning something is an activity (PI §693). 'I meant N.N.' refers to a point in time, viz. when I said 'He'll come', but not to any inner act or activity at that time. (Rather, if I had been asked of whom I was speaking I would have replied 'N.N.' (cf. PI §187).) Hence the reason one cannot observe oneself 'doing the meaning' is *not* because it is a very special activity of the mind undetachable from the willing self and incompatible with experience *qua* phenomenon. But it is true that if one is rushing forward, one cannot also stand still and observe oneself rushing forward. That much Wittgenstein dryly concedes in *Investigations* §456, although it would, of course, be absurd to claim that going in a certain direction is not an experience. Indeed, one *can* observe oneself going thither, although of course what anyone sees when he observes himself going is different from what he observes when he observes someone else going (PG 156). In what sense then is meaning something like going towards someone? What is Wittgenstein conceding in *Investigations* §457? - Only an iconographic picture that requires iconological interpretation. Going towards someone has a direction, and we naturally think of meaning Mr. N.N. by the words 'my old friend' as conferring directedness upon the words. It is as if the mind, as it were, makes a connection between the words 'My old friend' and my old friend N.N. - as if an arrow drawing a string behind it is shot by the mind toward N.N. and hits him. This is a fitting emblematic symbol for meaning *this* rather than *that*, for we often explain what or whom we meant by saying 'I meant this ↑' or 'I meant him ↑' and *pointing*. But the emblem is as misleading as any other iconographic representation (Death as a skeleton, Love as a putto with a bow and arrow). For it suggests that the connection between the word I used and the object or person I meant is made by a mysterious inner act of meaning which occurs at the time the word is used. Whereas the connections lie in what I would say if asked whom I meant, in the thoughts that crossed my mind before I spoke, in the photograph of N.N. I might show you, etc.

I have suggested that the harmony between thought, proposition, and reality was explained in the *Tractatus* in terms of a philosophical psychodrama on a vast logico-metaphysical set. In the early 1930s much of Wittgenstein's labour was aimed at undermining this sophisticated mythology of symbolism. I shall briefly call to mind his salient moves. He repudiated his earlier concept of an object as a sempiternal simple, and criticised his idea of facts as constituting the world and as having objects as constituents. He rejected the *Tractatus* notion of a simple name and the conception of an elementary proposition. He denied that all inferential relations depend upon the inner complexity of propositions. Even when an expression can be said to be a name standing for an object, the object it stands for cannot be said to be the meaning of the name. In the sense in which the *Tractatus* conceived of there being a connection between language and reality, Wittgenstein came to think that there is *no* connection between words and world. Rather the meanings of many words are explained by means of an ostensive definition employing a defining sample. But the sample belongs to the means of representation not to a reality which the proposition depicts. It is best counted as a part of grammar, since it functions as a standard for the application of the definiendum. And the ostensive definition that uses the sample neither forges a connection between language and reality in order thereby to determine the meaning of the *definiendum* nor is it a description of how things are. Rather it is a rule for the use of a word.

In the early manuscripts of the 1930s and in polished form in the 'Big Typescript' and the *Umarbeitung*, Wittgenstein turned to criticize his earlier treatment of the harmony between thought and reality. Already in MS 108, p. 196 (written early in 1930) he noted that one cannot present the connection between thoughts and world by reference to the idea that the thought that things are thus-and-so is made true by the fact that things are thus-and-so, *since that says nothing. Investigations* §429 is a precipitate from those reflections.

It was a mistake to conceive of the agreement or harmony between language and reality as an agreement of form. Wittgenstein criticised this as amounting to no more than the claim that every projection must have something in common with what is projected, no matter what the method of projection (PG 163). But that is simply to extend the concept of 'having something in common' to the point at which it is *equivalent* to the general concept of projection. Hence one is relieved of the burden of looking to see whether, if A is projected into B, the two have something in common; rather one holds that a logical condition of the possibility of projection *is* 'having something in common', in which case if B is a projection of A then it *must* have something in common. So now the criterion for having something in common just *is* projectibility.

A related criticism focused on the ambiguity of 'picture'. One can say both that an order is a picture of the action that complies with it and that it is a picture of the action which is to be carried out in compliance with it (PG 212). In the latter sense a blueprint serves as a picture of what is to be made. If we call the way in which a workman makes an artifact in accord with the blueprint 'the method of projection', then one may say that the method of projection mediates between the drawing and the artifact, like lines of projection from one figure to another. But this obscures the fact that the picture together with the projection lines leaves open various methods of application. It suggests that what is depicted, even if it does not exist, is determined ethereally by the picture and its projection lines. In *that* case what we are calling 'the picture' includes both the blueprint and its method of application. But is the method of application something that can be attached to the blueprint? One can perhaps attach a description of an application, but that too has to be applied, in accord with a method of application. One might now ask, in the spirit of the *Tractatus*, how a blueprint can be used as a representation, unless there is *already* an agreement with what is to be made? Wittgenstein turns immediately to a concrete example: how could I play the notes in a score on a piano if they did not already have a relationship to types of hand movement? Here one may concede that such a relationship *sometimes* consists in a certain agreement. But sometimes it amounts only to *having learnt to apply the signs in a certain way*. Comparing the method of projection with the projection lines makes all cases alike; and it misleadingly *conflates* the projection lines with the method of projection.

Likewise it is a mistake to think of the proposition 'If I say falsely that something is *red*, then for all that, it isn't red' as displaying a harmony *between* thought and reality, a harmony which demands an elaborate logico-metaphysical explanation of the essential coordination of language and the world. It is a *grammatical* proposition. The apparent harmony, the harmony the young Wittgenstein thought he saw, is not orchestrated *between* a thought and a situation (which may or may not obtain) or between names and their isomorphic meanings which are sempiternal objects constituting the substance of the world, but rather between *one proposition and another*. For it is a rule of our language that 'It is false that p' = 'Not-p' (PI §136). It is a rule of grammar, not an ineffable metaphysical truth about the relation between language and reality, that if it is false that this is red, then this is *not* red. Indeed it is impossible that there be a language in which what we describe by 'Not-p' would be expressed without using 'p' (PR 69). "Like everything metaphysical, the harmony between thought and reality is to be found in the grammar of the language" (PG 162).

To say that a proposition casts a shadow on the world is just to say that a proposition describes, truly or falsely, how things are. But that merely specifies a grammatical connection between the concept of a proposition and the concepts of truth and falsity that *belong* to it (but do not 'fit' it (cf. PI §136)). To think that the proposition anticipates reality by determining in advance what will make it true is not to plumb any metaphysical depths. It is correct that the proposition that p determines that p must be the case for it to be true, but that statement merely enunciates a rule for signs, viz. 'the proposition that p' = 'the proposition which the fact that p makes true' (PG 161). In a sense, one can indeed read off from the proposition that p the fact that will make it true. But that is no mystery: it is merely *a move in grammar* licensed by this substitution rule. One may be inclined to say, as Wittgenstein once was, that the proposition determines reality save for a *Yes* or *No* (PG 213); and looked at wrongly, that can seem truly amazing. (Even if thought cannot determine what is going to be the case, still it determines the theme of the fact, whether the fact makes the thought true or not (cf. PI §461). And is that not extraordinary?) But what is one amazed at? Not at the fact that in saying or thinking that p one already knows something about reality, for what one says may be true or false. And to know merely that, for example, the assertion 'It is raining' is either true or false is to know nothing about the weather! So one is in effect surprised at being able to say anything at all, truly or falsely; as if merely stating that something is the case predetermines *in some* sense how things are (give or take a *Yes* or *No*). But the mere statement that p, whether true of false, predetermines nothing, and cannot predetermine less than nothing (PG 161, PI §461).

The emphasis in the first sentence of §429 is on the two occurrences of the word 'red', not on the negation. One might rephrase it thus: if I say falsely that something is red, then for all that, what it is *not* is: *red*. The word 'red' occurs in both 'It is red' and 'It isn't red', and one might be tempted to think that the colour red is *the common element* of the two propositions. Of course, this does not mean that if 'A is red' is false (and 'A is not red' is true) then, for all that, A is *in some sense* red, as if A's *not being red* contained as it were the shadow of red. But it suggests that 'the propositional sign guarantees the possibility of the fact it presents (not that this fact is actually the case)' and that it does so in virtue of its component parts representing those of the situation and standing in a relation that is *possible* for the objects represented (NB 27). So, one might say, *thinking* presupposes the elements of a situation, but not its obtaining (cf. PR 67). Hence one might express the problem of the harmony between world and thought thus:

> the thought that p is the case doesn't presuppose that it is the case; yet on the other hand there must be something in the fact that is a presupposition even of having the thought (I can't think that something is red, if the colour red does not exist).

Indeed, the *Tractatus* account of the harmony between thought and reality argued for the *necessary* existence of simple objects as a condition of sense being assigned to sentences. It seemed that for the proposition 'A is red' *and* for its negation 'A is not red' to make sense, red must exist (for present purposes the analysability of red is irrelevant).

But this too is confused. To say that red is a common element in the two distinct state of affairs 'A is red' and 'B is red' is to say that in each something is red. But that obviously *cannot* be said of the pair of incompatible states of affairs 'A is red' and 'A is not red'. If someone nevertheless wants to insist that red *is* a common element in 'A is red' and 'A is not red' then that just means that both *propositions* could be said to be about the colour red, the one asserting it to be a property of A and the other denying it to be so (PG 135).

One might still insist that if both 'A is red' and 'A is not red' are *about* the colour red, then they both *refer* to the colour red, and red *must* exist if these sentences are to make sense. But to say that red *exists* amounts to no more than saying either that something *is* red, or that the word 'red' is meaningful. To say that one could not think that something is red (or that something is not red) if red did not exist is in effect merely to insist correctly that the sense of the proposition only presupposes the grammatically correct use of words (PR 67), not that it presupposes the ineffable sempiternal existence of simple objects. To claim that red *must* exist is just to point out the existence of a red sample *as part of our language* (PG 143), for "What looks as if it *had* to exist, is part of [or — an instrument of] the language" (PI §50). And indeed, the grammatically correct use of 'red' is bound up with the use of samples in explanations of what the word 'red' means and as standards of correct application. "But of course one can't say that our language *has to* contain such a sample; if it didn't contain it, it would just be another, a different language. But one can say, and emphasize, that it does contain it" (PG 143).

The occurrence of the word 'red' in both 'A is red' and 'A is not red' does not indicate the presence of something red (PI §443). Rather the *statement* 'A is red' does that (and its negation, if asserted, denies it). The word 'red' occurs in both sentences with the same meaning, but the senses of the two sentences do not 'contain' the meaning of 'red'. The meaning of the word 'red' is not an object of any kind, let alone the sample pointed at in giving an ostensive definition of the word 'red'. But it is true that if one is asked what 'red' means in the sentence 'That is not red', one would point to a red object, not to one that is *not* red. For there is no such thing as using a green object, say, as a *sample* of red. One could, to be sure, point at a green object and say 'That is not red'. But this would not be an ostensive definition, either of 'red' or of 'not red'. For 'it plays a different part in the calculus from what we ordinarily call "ostensive definition" of the word "red"' (PG 136; PI p.14n.). A green object is not a *sample* for the application of the expression 'not red', for one cannot employ it *as an object of comparison* which will license saying of something yellow or brown or blue or... that it is *not red*. One cannot point at the green object and say of a buttercup 'It is this ↑ colour, so it is not red'.

Just as the first sentence of §429, which explains what the 'harmony between language and reality' really amounts to, is itself no more than a grammatical proposition which determines the correct use of words but does not indicate a 'connection between language and reality', so too is the second. That I explain what the word 'red' means by pointing at something red (use it as a sample) elucidates what we *call* 'an explanation' or 'an ostensive definition' of the word 'red'. And, as we have seen, pointing at a red patch and saying 'That is red' (or 'That colour is red') does not forge a connection between language and reality (which would ensure a metaphysical harmony between thought and world), but employs a red patch as an instrument of grammar. So it is *in language*, not between language and reality, that it is all done (PG 143).

P.M.S. Hacker
St. John's College, Oxford

CHAPTER III

The Autonomy of Language

Robert L. Arrington

"Language," Wittgenstein tells us, "must speak for itself" (PG 40, 63). A name has meaning and a proposition has sense only within a calculus or language-game (PG 190), and the meanings of words are created by conventions (PG 190), by rules (PR 178, 182), by definitions (BB 27), by what Wittgenstein calls grammar (PG 184). The grammatical explanations that create language (PG 143) are not accountable to any reality (PG 184), and yet they establish the connection between language and reality (PG 97) whereby the former can represent and convey information about the latter. "It is in language that it is all done" (PG 143). Giving and explaining sense, justifying usage, and connecting up with reality — all of these are linguistic functions and activities, and they themselves cannot be philosophically explained or justified (PI §§124, 126). Language is "self-contained and autonomous" (PG 97). It will be the task of this paper to elucidate Wittgenstein's notion of the autonomy of language and to trace its implications.

Throughout the ages philosophers have denied that language is autonomous. From Plato's *Cratylus* to the *Confessions* of Augustine, on to Locke's "new way of ideas" and Russell's theory of acquaintance, and right up to the *Tractatus Logico-Philosophicus*, attempts have been made to ground language in something nonlinguistic, something that would explain why language is as it is and that could be appealed to in justification or criticism of specific linguistic practices. If, e.g., language is seen as an expression of thought or sense experience, it can properly be evaluated in light of its ability to express all they contain and only what they contain. If it is viewed as a pictorial representation of facts in the world, it can be required to derive its semantics and syntax from this world. If it is thought of as a pragmatically useful tool, it must be sharpened and cleaned so as to serve our needs as we solve problems and negotiate with reality. In these various ways, language is thought to receive explanation and justification by being related to a foundation that is itself non-derivative, basic, and given. Essences, innate ideas, sense impressions, objects with their possibilities of combination, human drives and problem situations — these are a few of the givens in the history of philosophy that have been thought to do the job in question. The theories appealing to them, in spite of their many differences, may all be said to imply a form of *semantic realism* which treats language as something derivative from and accountable to the nonlinguistic domain. It is in opposition to these realist attempts at explanation and justification, in opposition to the very idea of such an attempt, that Wittgenstein asserts the autonomy of language and claims that language must speak for itself.

A recent example of a realist philosophy of language can be found in what is likely to be an unexpected place, the essays of J. L. Austin.[1] Even if surprising, Austin's semantic realism is clear and persuasive, and it illustrates well a number of realist strategies. In order to understand realism better, let us examine Austin's theory in some detail.

Austin and Wittgenstein are often thought to be the co-founders of ordinary language philosophy, but in point of fact there are some sharp differences of opinion and approach between these two philosophers.[2] And the differences largely pertain to the question of the autonomy of language. Austin, a realist, rejects autonomy. This is apparent in his famous essay "A Plea for Excuses" where he expounds his understanding of the methodology of ordinary language philosophy. As he puts it, this methodology is one of "examining what we should say when, and so why and what we should mean by it."[3] And he goes on to claim:

> When we examine what we should say when, what words we should use in what situations, we are looking again not *merely* at words (or 'meanings', whatever they may be) but also at the realities we use the words to talk about: we are using a sharpened awareness of words to sharpen our perception of, though not as a final arbiter of, the phenomena.[4]

The philosophical study of words, then, tells us something about the nonlinguistic domain. Austin also thinks nonlinguistic phenomena can tell us something about words and meanings — specifically about verbal inadequacies. He warns us that ordinary language is an evolving body of usage which incorporates vestiges of superstition, error, and fantasy. For this reason he is insistent on pointing out the traps and pitfalls that language can set for us, and it is in this spirit that he writes:

> Words are not (except in their own little corner) facts or things: we need therefore to prise them off the world, to hold them apart from and against it, so that we can realize their inadequacies and arbitrariness, *and can re-look at the world without blinkers.*[5] (emphasis added)

It is this unblinkered inspection of the world which may lead us to criticize ordinary language. Such inspection amounts to examining the world without looking at it through language. We are to hold our words "apart from" the things and facts in the world in order to see if the words are inadequate or arbitrary with respect to them.

Let us look more closely at one fault of language Austin mentions, what we might call its incompleteness. We are unable, Austin tells us, "with our limited experience both as individuals and as a race ... (to) anticipate in our vocabularies vagaries of nature which have yet to be revealed."[6] Our vocabulary is incomplete not only in relation to future, unusual experiences but also in relation to the present experience of nature, for although the actual world is "indefinitely various," we possess a limited vocabulary and concern ourselves with no more than "relative similarities" rather than with the minute detail of that actual world.

How is this incompleteness to be overcome? The gap between nature and language will sometimes give rise to a need for "fresh linguistic legislation."[7] Such lawmaking comes in various forms. We may on occasion need only to pass from a stage in which single items in the world define the types designated by our words (or by the senses of our words) to a stage where more formal definitions or conventions serve to relate sense and type. But legislation may also introduce a new name to designate a novel item or distinction.

In these various legislative acts we seem to be establishing what Austin calls the semantics of language, that is to say, the things and situations in the world correctly designated by the words of that language.[8] In light of what we are told in "How To Talk," the semantics of a word is established by a process of ostensive definition in which we assign a name to the type of thing we find in the world "by inspection merely" and, conversely, assign that type of thing as the name's sense.[9] We are to think of name-giving and sense-giving as "involving the selection of a sample or specimen as a standard pattern."[10] The semantics of a term is distinguished by Austin from its syntax, 'syntax' being used by him rather loosely to refer to the relations words have to other words, to the logical rules governing the use of words, and to the grammatical forms and rules of language.[11] Syntax, we might say, involves word-word relations, whereas semantics involves word-world relations.

Austin often derogates syntax because of its tendency to cloud and obscure semantics. His linguistic blinkers, or at least one form of such, can thus be understood as syntactic blinkers. When we are urged to prise words off the world we are in effect being told to examine the semantic referents of words in a vision unfettered by their syntax.

The syntactic rules and characteristics of ordinary language are not in Austin's eyes the only culprits responsible for our failure to see the facts as they are. There is also a way in which our semantic rules serve to blinker our vision. Referring us to "trailing clouds of etymology," Austin argues that many words have historically been associated with pictures and models that are too simple to reveal the complexities of situations to which we apply these words.[12] Here "the model is really distorting the facts rather than helping us to observe them."[13] We need to restrict the application of the model or to abandon it altogether in favor of new models or expanded descriptions which depict the complex facts as they are.

Whether we are dealing with syntactic or semantic conventions of ordinary language, the lesson we receive from Austin is much the same. These conventions can blinker observation and imagination and prevent us from seeing important aspects of the world. They can lead us to misdescribe novel items in terms appropriate to familiar, common, and simple items; they equally are capable of causing misdescriptions of the old and familiar. The inspection of types that allows us to construct language ostensively can also be thought to reveal boundaries and distinctions in nature which were inadequately demarcated, or arbitrarily glossed over, by our semantic and syntactic rules. To correct the errors introduced by syntax we need to investigate directly the semantic referents of our terms, just as we need to look directly at the world to amplify or revise our semantic conventions. In this way ordinary language philosophy will allow us to "straighten out" the ordinary use of words.[14]

If we are aware of the blinkers, the superstition, and the other traps contained in language, we will not want to say that ordinary language is the Last Word on any philosophical issue. But why should we consider it, as Austin recommends, to be the First Word? His answer is:

Our common stock of words embodies all the distinctions men have found worth marking, and the connections they have found worth marking, in the lifetime of many generations: these surely are likely to be more numerous, more sound, since they have stood up to the long test of these survival of the fittest, and more subtle .... than any that you and I are likely to think up in our armchairs of an afternoon.[15]

Or, again, he writes, "If a distinction works well for practical purposes in ordinary life ... then there is sure to be something in it: it will not mark nothing."[16] So we can say that ordinary language, though not a final arbiter of reality, is a well tested, practically reliable guide to it. And Austin appears to take its practical reliability to be a sign of its ontological reliability (soundness) — after all, if a key turns a lock, is this not because it has the same structure as the lock? The philosophical study of ordinary language will in general point us in the direction of reality while at the same time it will reveal ways in which this language occasionally distorts reality.

This discussion of Austin's philosophy of language has been undertaken in order to provide a concrete example of a realist theory and to demonstrate the prominence of semantic realism in contemporary philosophy — even in a place we might not expect it. Austin's realism is also instructive because it illustrates a number of realist strategies, e.g., an appeal to a correspondence (or lack of correspondence) between forms of language and reality, and an invocation of pragmatic considerations in assessing language. Wittgenstein, of course, does not have Austin in mind when he criticizes this kind of theory and promotes the autonomy of language. The likelihood is that in doing so he is criticizing his own earlier philosophy. One of the most sophisticated, but also esoteric and idiomatic, versions of a realist conception of language was developed by Wittgenstein himself in his *Tractatus Logico-Philosophicus*. To understand his later defense of autonomy, we need to see it against the background of his early realism.

According to the famous picture theory of representation contained in the *Tractatus*, a proposition represents a possible state of affairs by being a picture of it (TLP 2.1). Such picturing is the result of the pictorial relationship or correlation which holds between the elements of the picture and things in the world (TLP 2.1514). The elements of the picture are names (TLP 3.202) and the things with which they are correlated are objects (TLP 3.203). An object has what Wittgenstein calls a form, which is the set of possibilities it has of combining with other objects (TLP 2.0141). A proposition pictures a possible combination of objects, i.e., a state of affairs. When two or more objects actually combine in one of the ways open to them they thereby constitute a fact (TLP 2.0272), which is an existing state of affairs. In order to picture a possible state of affairs or an actual fact we must put names together to form a proposition (TLP 2.13, 2.14, 4.031, 4.22). Each name has a certain set of possible combinations with other names, and when two or more names are related in a determinate way their concatenation represents the state of affairs or fact whose objects are related to one another in the same way (TLP 2.15, 3.21). There must be, then, a similarity between the way in which objects can be related and the way in which names can be. A proposition must have something in common with the state of affairs or fact pictured, and what they must have in common is logical form (TLP 2.18). This means that each name in a proposition has to have the possibility of entering into relationships with the other names in the proposition in precisely the same way in which the object it names in the pictured state of affairs has the possibility of entering into relationships with other objects. Such a requirement is satisfied by following the rules of logical syntax. These rules specify the logical form of a name (TLP 3.327), and they permit only those combinations of names that mirror the combinational possibilities of the named objects. Thus a proposition determines a place in what Wittgenstein calls logical space (TLP 2.202, 3.4). This place is a possible combination of objects, that is to say, a possible state of affairs. When this place is occupied, the proposition representing it is true; when it is unoccupied, the proposition is false but nevertheless meaningful, since the possible combination of objects which constitutes this place is sufficient to provide the proposition with a sense.

It is easy enough to see the realist implications of the picture theory. Wittgenstein claims that language is capable of representing the world, either truly or falsely, because its syntactical possibilities mirror the logical space of reality. "I have said elsewhere that a proposition 'reaches up to reality', and by this I meant that the forms of the entities are contained in the form of the proposition which is about these entities" (RLF 36). The possibilities constituting logical space are the source of the logical syntax of language. The requirement that a proposition have logical form in common with the state of affairs it pictures gives rise to the necessity of mapping logical syntax onto the dimensions of logical space. Without such a fit there simply would not be a symbolism capable of picturing reality. It can be argued that Wittgenstein viewed ostensive definition as the means whereby the derivation of logical syntax from logical space is accomplished (TLP 3.263).

Such a realist interpretation of the *Tractatus* can be challenged.[17] Nonetheless, it suggests itself *prima facie* as the most natural reading of the work, and it is the interpretation that Wittgenstein himself seems to have had in mind when he later reflected on that work. In his transitional essay "Some Remarks on Logical Form," he both criticizes and reiterates certain aspects of the *Tractatus*. The object of his criticism is the doctrine that the elementary propositions of language are logically independent. At the same time, he continues to speak of philosophical analysis as being the discovery of logical form and the construction of a language that clearly conveys this structure. As to how best to accomplish this goal, he makes the following suggestion:

> Now we can only substitute a clear symbolism for the unprecise one by inspecting the phenomena which we want to describe, thus trying to understand their logical multiplicity. That is to say, we can only arrive at a correct analysis by, what might be called, the logical investigation of the phenomena themselves, i.e., in a certain sense *a posteriori*, and not by conjecturing about *a priori* possibilities (RLF 163).

It is this investigation of the phenomena which will reveal the necessary logical structure of elementary propositions. For example: "We meet with the forms of space and time with the whole manifold of spatial and temporal objects, as colors, sounds, etc. ... " (RLF 165). Moreover, in the *Philosophical Grammar*, written somewhat later, we find him characterizing his former activity in the following realist manner:

> This is all connected with the false concept of logical analysis that Russell, Ramsey, and I used to have, according to which we are waiting for an ultimate logical analysis of facts, like a chemical analysis of compounds.... (PG 311).

It is not my intention to debate the merits of the realist interpretation of the *Tractatus*. Even if it is not the correct interpretation of that work, it provides us an excellent example of the type of theory which Wittgenstein criticizes later on. That the interpretation serves so well in this capacity is, perhaps, further evidence in favor of it.

The downfall of the picture theory, and of the realist conception of language that it contains or suggests, was no simple matter. The first blow was the criticism leveled against the logical independence of elementary propositions, but this in and of itself was not sufficient to upset the theory. More fundamental were the criticisms developed later on concerning the name-relation and the concept of a picture. And one of the crucial components of the criticism of the name-relation is Wittgenstein's investigation of ostensive definition.[18] In the *Tractatus* the meaning of a name was the object it named (TLP 3.203), and it required an operation like ostensive definition to pin a name on an object and thereby give that name a meaning. A grasp of the nature of the object would yield the syntactical rules governing the name and allowing it to reflect the essential nature of the object. Wittgenstein's later views on ostensive definition show how this instrument is unable to perform the task assigned to it by the realist conception. It is unable to do this because it can explain the meaning of a word only by employing the grammar of language. An ostensive definition does not direct us to an element of reality so that we might read off its logical form and produce a replica of it in the linguistic domain. The components of the definition direct us only in light of the meaning they already have in language, which meanings are a function of their grammar. Hence an ostensive definition does not take us outside of language and inform us of the logical space of the nonlinguistic world. In giving and receiving such a definition, we remain within the grammatical space of language.

This "critical" view of ostensive definition shows us that language cannot be derived from extralinguistic realities. But it must also be shown that language cannot be justified or criticized by an appeal to such realities. In asserting the autonomy of language, Wittgenstein is claiming that the grammar of language can in no way be supported or undermined. There can be no philosophical investigation of the phenomena themselves; we can only describe language systems, games, and calculi. Indeed, "what look like hypothetical assumptions about the logical elements (the logical structure) of the world are merely specifications of the elements in a calculus" (PG 312). Metaphysical attempts at investigating the essences of phenomena or the logical elements of the world are just so many confusions which amount to predicating of a thing what lies in the method of representing it (PI §104). To demonstrate that this is so, Wittgenstein develops a variety of arguments and persuasive considerations, and it will be our task in the remainder of the paper to examine them.

Wittgenstein is keenly aware of the questions and temptations that can lead to a realist view of language. We find him asking in *Zettel*, "Yet can't it after all be said that in some sense or other the grammar of color-words characterizes the world as it actually is?" (Z §331), and again in the *Philosophical Investigations*, "Is there some reality lying behind the notation, which shapes the grammar?" (PI §562). These questions about the foundation and justifiability of grammar are not in his eyes simply to be answered negatively; rather, they must be shown to be confused and meaningless. And one way to do this is to demonstrate that there is no intelligible way of answering them. What do we have in mind when we ask for *justification*? Two paradigms come to mind. First, we justify beliefs by showing that they accord with reality or that they are verified. Second, we justify actions by showing that they lead to desired goals and that they do this better than alternative actions would. Can the grammar of language in principle be justified in either of these two ways? If not, and if no alternative mode of justification can be envisioned, then the very notion of justification is meaningless in this context.

First of all, let us consider the possibility that grammar can be justified by a process of verification.

> One is tempted to justify rules of grammar by sentences like "But there really are four primary colors." And the saying that the rules of grammar are arbitrary is directed against the possibility of this justification, which is constructed on the model of justifying a sentence by pointing to what verifies it (Z §331).

Wittgenstein rejects the justification of grammar by means of its verification by arguing that such an effort is circular.

> Grammatical conventions cannot be justified by describing what is represented. Any such description already presupposes the grammatical rules. That is to say, if anything is to count as nonsense in the grammar which is to be justified, then it cannot at the same time pass for sense in the grammar of the propositions that justify it (PR 55).

To justify the grammar of a proposition by verifying it, one must describe conditions in the world which are the verifying conditions. But in describing these conditions one already employs language, and this language must already have a grammar. If its grammar is different from the grammar of the language one is attempting to justify, the facts one describes by means of it will be irrelevant to the verification or falsification of the part of language in question. They would only be *different* facts, not negating facts, because that which negates must be in the same logical space, have the same grammar, as that which it negates (PR 57, 92). If, however, the grammar of the justification is the same as the grammar to be justified, the question has been begged, for the use of language to describe the verifying facts presupposes the legitimacy of the grammar in question. Hence the purported justification is merely a sham.

Let us consider some examples of the unsuccessful, pseudo-attempt to verify grammar. In ordinary language, physical objects are always describable in terms of their lengths. Whether a particular object can be correctly described as having a certain specific length is a contingent matter, but that it can be correctly described as having a length is not a contingent affair (PI §251). It must be describable as having a length if it is to be considered a physical object. This is a grammatical fact about the way we use the term 'physical object'. If follows that a statement such as "This rod has length" is a grammatical proposition, not a contingent, descriptive truth. We are inclined to think, however, that it is nevertheless true and that its negation, "This rod has no length," is false.

> But this partiality is based on a confusion: we regard the first proposition as verified (and the second as falsified) by the fact "that the rod has a length of 4 meters." "After all, 4 meters is a length" — but one forgets that this is a grammatical proposition (PG 129).

The attempt to justify the grammatical proposition, "This rod has length," by appeal to the contingent fact that the rod in question is 4 meters long begs the question. The description of the rod as 4 meters long already employs the grammar of 'length'. Hence the attempt to justify the grammar of 'length' by appealing to contingent facts in the world is circular; it does not even get started as a justification.

As another example of the question-begging attempt to verify grammar — a rather more subtle example — consider the grammatical fact that in our language we distinguish between colors, shapes, and noises. Aren't these distinctions justified by our experience itself?

> Doesn't one put the primary colors together because there is a similarity among them, or at least put *colors* together, contrasting them with e.g. shapes or noises, because there is a similarity among them? (Z §331)

Don't we just notice similarities among colors on the basis of which we group them together, and doesn't the fact that these similarities do not extend to shapes and noises justify our distinguishing these characteristics in language? Before we follow our inclinations and answer these questions affirmatively, let us pose yet another question. Just what are these similarities among colors which make them different from shapes and noises? One might say that colors are visually detected, but this property, although it might be thought to distinguish colors from noises, does not do so from shapes. Could we say that shapes have geometrical properties while colors do not? Perhaps, but we could equally well say that what has geometrical properties are colored shapes. And as for the suggested mode of distinguishing colors and noises, it seems extremely odd to say that we check out an experience to see if it has the property of being *heard* or *seen* in order to determine if it is a noise or a color. We straightaway see a color; we don't observe that we *see* it and then conclude that it is a color. It soon becomes apparent that no observable properties serve straightforwardly to distinguish colors from shapes and noises. "'The colors' are not things that have definite properties ... " (RC III §127). So if we ask in amazement, "Then might one also take red, green and circular together?" (Z §331), Wittgenstein's answer — "Why not?" — is perfectly apt. There is nothing in our experiences of red, green, and circular which forces us to separate them into different kinds. This should alert us to the fact that when we speak of colors and shapes and noises as *kinds* of things we are using the notion of a kind in a very special way. Wittgenstein warns us of the confusions lurking in this way of speaking:

> The attitude toward the more general and the more special in logic is connected with the usage of the word 'kind' which is liable to cause confusion. We talk of kinds of numbers, kinds of propositions, kinds of proofs; and also, of kinds of apples, kinds of paper, etc. In one sense what defines the kind are properties, like sweetness, hardness, etc. In the other the different kinds are different grammatical structures (BB 19).

Our talk, then, of colors, shapes, and noises is talk of different grammatical structures, there being no observable properties in nature which serve to distinguish them. And if this is so, it follows that no observation of nature could verify and justify the distinctions we draw between these grammatical structures. "Do not believe that you have the concept of color within you because you look at a colored object — however you look" (Z §332), because, as Wittgenstein tells us in *Remarks on Colour*, "Looking does not teach us anything about the concepts of colors" (RC I §72).

This conclusion is very difficult to accept. One wants to say — as Wittgenstein might put it — that there is all the difference in the world between colors, shapes, and noises, and that these differences are noticeable and observable: just attend to a color and see how different it is from attending to a noise. Colors are colors, noises are noises!

To get at the source of both the temptation and the confusion involved in this reply, let us consider at closer range a case of narrower scope, namely the distinctions we draw among types of colors. Is there any sense to verifying that the colors we call by the names 'blue' and 'red' are really distinct? Surely, we may be tempted to say, these colors are not in any way similar. We can *observe* that they are totally different, can we not? Wittgenstein responds as follows:

> What is the distinction, then, between blue and red?
>
> We aren't of the opinion that one color has one property and the other another. In any case, the properties of blue and red are that this body (or place) is blue, and that other is red.
>
> When asked "what is the distinction between blue and red?" we feel like answering: one is blue and the other red. But of course that means nothing and in reality what we're thinking of is the distinction between the surfaces or places that have these colors (PG 208).

It makes sense, that is, to describe something as red and to distinguish that thing from something blue, but it makes no sense to describe red itself (PG 209). For, again, there are no properties that red possesses which distinguish it from the other colors.

It might be objected to this claim that red has numerous relations to other colors, e.g., it is *darker than yellow*. Are these relations not properties? The relations in question, however, are conceptual in nature. We do not observe that as a matter of fact red is darker than yellow, for to do so would presuppose that we might have discovered that it was not darker than yellow. This presupposition does not make sense: if we observed a color lighter than yellow, it would not, by definition, be red. If we are to discover by observation that red has such and such properties, it must be logically possible for red to fail to have these properties. But the conceptual relations we are considering are not like this.

But of course, we want to complain, there are no *other* properties possessed by red which make it distinctive, but what about *the redness itself?* Isn't that something specific and distinctive (Z §333)? Isn't the property of redness itself enough to distinguish it from the other colors?

But what is this property of redness of which we speak? Which among the different colors is it? Surely it is something specific, something we can point to and observe. But which specific color is it? How can we be sure we have pointed to the right thing, to the right color? Wittgenstein shows us that if we point to the specific color red, we have in the very act of pointing begged the question in favor of our color grammar:

> "Red is something specific" — that would have to mean the same as: "That is something specific" — said while pointing to something red. But for that to be intelligible, one would have already to mean our *concept* 'red', to mean the use of that sample (Z §333).

In "That is something specific," said while pointing to something red, the demonstrative is already doing duty for 'that red color', i.e., the concept of red is already in use. Another way of putting it is to note that "That is something specific" makes reference to something that is used as a sample of red, and a sample is a part of language (PI §50). On either reading, we are presupposing something linguistic in saying "That is something specific": the grammar of 'that red color' or the sample of red. Thus in our act of pointing we are already employing the *concept* red (the use of words to designate red or the use of a sample of red) with all the attendant grammar of this concept. It follows that what we observe is defined by our grammar and hence cannot be said to support or falsify it.

There is a related way in which we might bring out the circularity here. If our attempted observation is to be relevant to the goal of assessing grammar, it must be an observation of an entity *correctly* designated by a word in our language. For what we want to find out is whether an entity we correctly call, say, red has a nature that verifies or falsifies the grammar of 'red'. But how do we know what is the correct use of a word? Surely we appeal to its grammar in order to ascertain this — to the rules for its use as reflected in definitions and other explanations of meaning. Let us see, then, what happens when we unpack the grammar of 'red'. What does this grammar tell us about the entities we correctly call red?

It is a conceptual or grammatical fact that the color or objects we call red are not the same ones we call blue — that is, *we never say* "this color (or this surface) is both red and blue." Such a statement is a grammatical absurdity. Moreover, we do not have a color sample which is a sample of red-and-blue. So if the color or colored surface we observe is the one properly called red, it *must* be different from the one we call blue; otherwise it is not the color or surface properly called red. Prior, then, to observing the color, our grammar tells us that red is distinctive, that it is not the same as blue. And without this grammar, we could make no *relevant* observation, namely, no observation *of the color called red* or of *an object correctly called red*. Consequently, an observation could never falsify the grammatical distinction, for if we were to see that "red" and "blue" are similar or that something is both "red" and "blue", it would not be what we correctly call red (or blue).

If observation cannot in principle falsify a distinction, it can hardly verify it either. The very notion of such an observation is a pseudo-notion — the "observation" that a red object is not blue is nothing more than a projection of our color grammar. It is this grammar which is the preconceived idea, the paradigm (Z §331), leading us to group colors together as colors and to distinguish them as red, blue, etc. When we say "Of course red is red and blue is blue — they are quite different," we are really only saying "'red' and 'blue' mean different things in our language." This is a fact of grammar. It is no less a fact for that, however, and it leads us to rebel when we hear someone suggest that red and blue might really be similar. In an effort to refute this suggestion we try to observe the difference between them, and we think we succeed. But our verification of grammar is but a reiteration of that grammar.

Surely the same things can be said of the distinctions we draw in speech between colors, shapes, and noises. "A color is something specific," we think, as we try to grasp that specific quality which is color. We again must turn to grammar (or "logic" or "geometry") to determine what this thing color is that we want to observe, for "isn't it precisely the geometry of colors that shows us what we are talking about, i.e., that we are talking about colors?" (RC III, §86) The quality we observe must be the quality we correctly, grammatically, call a color, and grammatically this quality is precisely the one we may never call a shape or noise. If by chance we say, "This seems similar to a noise" (a very curious remark!), it follows that the referent is not what we correctly call a color — and hence it is not a pertinent item to observe. When we observe the right thing, a color, then of course it is different from a noise or a shape, but this is so, not by virtue of the content of the observation, but by virtue of the fact that we "observe the right thing," namely what we mean by 'color' (and hence not what we mean by 'shape' and 'noise'). "Colors and shapes and noises are really different," then, is a confused way of saying that 'color' and 'shape' and 'noise' have different meanings in our language.

It might be thought that this reduction of the verification of grammar to a reiteration of grammar holds in the cases we have considered only because the terms involved are simple ones which do not admit of definition. Having no properties or parts, redness is such that we have no way to identify it except as the property we call red; and then we are trapped by the fact that the criterion of what we are to examine — what we call or mean by 'red' — already distinguishes it from blue. But what if we consider complex properties, such as circularity and rectangularity? Aren't circles and rectangles different by virtue of their properties rather than by virtue of our linguistic practices? We can specify the properties of circles that render them different from rectangles, whereas we could not do this with color and shape, or red and blue. It may seem plausible, then, to say that observation of these different properties shows us that circles and rectangles are different.

There is a simple argument which shows the cases of circles and rectangles to be no different from those of red and blue. What the properties of circles and rectangles are is given by our definitions of 'circle' and 'rectangle', and what these properties amount to in their turn is given by our definitions of them, e.g., our definition of 'straight line' and 'curved line'. Given that 'straight line' means something different from and incompatible with what is meant by 'curved line', our grammar guarantees that the properties we "observe" are different. We have not examined a case of a circle unless it possesses only what we call a curved line, and it does not possess only what we call a curved line if it possesses what we call a straight line. We have not examined a case of a circle, then, unless what we examine is different from what we call a rectangle. Our observation of the properties of complex entities shows us that these entities are distinct because their distinctiveness is preordained in grammar. In attempting to justify grammar, we once more butt our heads against the circularity of our procedure.

In the discussion above we have operated with a notion of observing those facts in the world that correspond, or fail to correspond, to the grammatical structure of language. In another, related attack on the possibility of verifying grammar, Wittgenstein calls into question the meaningfulness of any talk about the logical form or space of the world which could be said to support and justify grammar. He maintains that there is no way in principle in which this alleged logical space could be *described*. To make this claim is to go beyond the argument from circularity which we have just examined. That argument tries to show that any attempt to describe logical form begs the question in favor of the grammar of language. This further claim proposes that there could be no description of logical form to begin with. We have already noted that color and red, for example, do not have properties such that we might speak of *the fact that* color is F, or *the fact that* red is G. But in a further, *reductio ad absurdum* argument, Wittgenstein shows that even if there were such properties, we still would not be able to describe logical form:

> If I could describe the point of grammatical conventions by saying that they are made necessary by certain properties of the colors (say), then that would make the conventions superfluous, since in that case I would be able to say precisely that which the conventions exclude my saying. Conversely, if the convention were necessary, i.e., if certain combinations of words had to be excluded as nonsensical, then for that very reason I cannot cite a property of colors that makes the conventions necessary, since it would then be conceivable that the colors should not have this property, and I could only express that by violating the conventions (PR 53).

All descriptions of fact, he is claiming, are contingent. Given any fact of nature, it is conceivable that this fact might not exist, that this object or event might not have the property it does have. If then we describe a property of colors by virtue of which we have our grammatical conventions governing 'color', it is conceivable that colors do not have this property. But that this is conceivable is inconsistent with there being a grammatical convention which links our concept of color to the possession of this property, for were there such a convention it would be inconceivable, nonsense, to say that the colors do not possess this property. It is the point of a grammatical convention to permit certain combinations of words as significant and to reject others as nonsense. If these conventions generate a concept of color such that to speak of a color at all is to speak of it as having a certain property, then the denial that a color has this property would not be false but meaningless. The denial would be one of those combinations of words prohibited by the conventions. But I must be able meaningfully to deny that colors have this property if I am meaningfully to describe them as in fact having it. So if I did describe them in this fashion, that would constitute not a justification but a repudiation of the grammatical convention linking the color and the property. Or, conversely, if there is such a convention, there could be no description of a fact that justifies it.

Here we obviously have the expression of a theme that harks back to the *Tractatus*: logical form cannot be said or described.

> What belongs to the essence of the world cannot be expressed in language. ... Language can only say those things that we can also imagine otherwise (PR 84).

No description, Wittgenstein tells us, can ascribe to an object a property that is essential for the very existence of the object (PR 119, 122). Although his justification for this fundamental restriction no longer rests on the distinctive marks of the picture theory, it nevertheless does reflect his abiding conviction that no proper, informative description of reality can be necessarily true. Any description that is to support grammar would have to be necessarily true, for its negation would be ruled out as meaningless by the grammar itself. Hence it would not be a proper description.

What *looks* like a description of some essential connection or internal property, Wittgenstein often warns us, is in reality the expression of a rule or definition that determines a concept (RFM 23; PI §401). We can say of all putative descriptions of logical form what Wittgenstein says of the expression "two negations yield an affirmation," namely, that it contains no assertion (about negation) but is merely a rule for the replacement of one sign by another (PG 53). He consistently makes this distinction between a proper description and an expression of essence. We might properly describe a cube as being red and wooden, but a cube does not have the properties that geometry seems to ascribe to it, for geometry does not describe a cube at all. Rather, "geometry *defines* the form of a cube but

does not describe it" (PG 52–53). If we are looking for a description of
the form of a cube, our only candidate will be a sentence like 'this box has
the form of a cube' (Ibid.), but such a sentence is a contingent description
— of the box! In our attempt, then, to find descriptions of fact that verify
our grammatical rules, what we stumble upon are simply those rules themselves. There are no descriptions of fact of the kind we seek, "for what
belongs to the essence of the world simply *cannot* be said" (PR 85).

This concludes our investigation of Wittgenstein's reasons for rejecting
the first proposed mode of justifying grammar, the mode of verifying it
by comparing it with things or facts in the world. We have seen that this
attempt fails on several counts. Any description or identification of a part
of nature which is relevant to the confirmation of grammar presupposes
the validity of that grammar. Moreover, the very notion of a description
of essence or logical form turns out to be self-defeating. And what appears
to be a description of essence that supports or invalidates grammar turns
out to be a disguised expression of a grammatical rule.

We can now turn our attention to the second realist proposal for justifying grammar, the "practical" justification. The attempt at a practical justification proceeds by arguing that grammar helps us achieve certain goals
we have in speaking. By using language in accordance with a specific set
of grammatical rules, we allegedly are able to achieve these goals in a
more efficient or exact manner than we otherwise would. Perhaps following grammatical rules constitutes a condition of attaining the goals at all.
Natural facts about human beings and their activities, facts independent of
and prior to the use of language, are thought to explain linguistic activity
— as a form of goal-oriented behavior — and to provide the criterion for
the assessment of this activity: success or usefulness in promoting the ends
of action.

Such a view of the nature and justification of language might well be
called pragmatic. Language and its grammar are seen as problem-solving
instruments or as aspects of goal-oriented behavior. Insofar as it is often
suggested that there is a strong pragmatic tendency in Wittgenstein's
philosophy of language, it will be of interest to see just how and why he
rejects this pragmatic justification of grammar. Observing these reasons,
we will be able to say that he charts the "limits of pragmatism" just as in
another context he charts the "limits of empiricism" (RFM 96, 121, 171,
176).

There are, to be sure, textual sources that support the pragmatic interpretation of Wittgenstein's concept of language. After all, he compares language to a set of tools (PG 67; PI §11) and tells us that language and its concepts are instruments (PI § §421, 569). Furthermore, "Concepts lead us to make investigations; are the expression of our interest, and direct our interest" (PI §570). Wittgenstein not only emphasizes the importance of purpose in language use (e.g. in PI §489) but goes so far as to say that the sense of a proposition is its purpose and that the meaning of a word is its purpose (PR 59). If we think of speaking as a form of acting, with ends in view and with words and concepts as instruments, it is natural enough to form a picture of grammar as a set of guidelines for achieving the goals of our speech-acts. But this is exactly what Wittgenstein denies: "Grammar does not tell us how language must be constructed in order to fulfil its purpose, in order to have such-and-such an effect on human beings" (PI §496). What we must understand is how Wittgenstein can stress the purposiveness and instrumentality involved in our language and at the same time reject the notion that grammar can receive a pragmatic justification.

We may begin by noting that there are different senses of 'language'. Wittgenstein distinguishes two different senses in the context of investigating what it would be like to invent a language.

> To invent a language could mean to invent an instrument for a particular purpose on the basis of the laws of nature (or consistently with them); but it also has the other sense, analogous to that in which we speak of the invention of a game (PI §492).

We might introduce a concept into language — that is, a word along with its grammar — because it enabled us to do things we want to do. Here we would be reforming language for practical purposes (PI §132). We might, for example, wish for a notation that stresses a difference more strongly (BB 59). Such a new concept would be advantageous, and it would be justified because of the advantage it brings. Wittgenstein admits that there are concepts of this sort.

> Why do we count? Has it proved practical? Do we have the concepts we have, e.g., our psychological concepts, because it has proved advantageous? — and yet we do have *certain* concepts on that account, we have introduced them on that account (Z §700).

I think that Wittgenstein would grant that there can be a pragmatic justification of the grammar involved in this latter set of concepts. But his main point is that such a set is limited. He gives us no concrete examples of these concepts, and he often brings up the question of their possibility in the context of denying that certain specific concepts fall into this category. Is religious language, e.g. a means to some end (RFM 44)? Do we think (PG 109-19), do we calculate (RFM 178) because it pays? Wittgenstein admits that thinking sometimes, perhaps often, pays (PI §470), but he strongly suggests that this is the *cause* of our thinking, not the reason or justification for it (PI §466). And he denies any interest in language as a means to an end: "Language is not defined for us as an arrangement fulfilling a definite purpose" (PG 190). He is interested only in those concepts (those languages) that are invented in a way a game is invented. And there is no pragmatic justification possible in these cases. Let us see why.

Wittgenstein addresses himself to the cases in which grammar cannot receive a pragmatic justification by contrasting these rules of grammar with rules of cooking:

> Why don't I call cookery rules arbitrary, and why am I tempted to call the rules of grammar arbitrary? Because 'cookery' is defined by its end, whereas 'speaking' is not. That is why the use of language is in a certain sense autonomous, as cooking and washing are not. You cook badly if you are guided in your cooking by rules other than the right ones; but if you follow other rules than those of chess you are *playing another game*; and if you follow grammatical rules other than such-and-such ones, that does not mean you say something wrong, no, you are speaking of something else (Z §320; see also PG 184).

To understand Wittgenstein's argument here, let us introduce a distinction between external and internal ends or purposes. Wittgenstein himself does not employ this distinction, but he lays the basis for it in his discussion of purpose and effect in PG 68–71. The external ends of speaking, we will say, are those effects of speaking which as a contingent matter of fact follow upon a speech-act. The internal ends are those goals that are defined or constituted by the grammar of the speech-act: they are those that are necessarily attained insofar as the speech-act is itself performed. It is to these latter, internal purposes that Wittgenstein refers when he writes, "The rules of grammar may be called 'arbitrary', if that is to mean that the *aim* of the grammar is nothing but that of the language" (PI §497). And it is the internal purpose that he has in mind when he tells us that you can say that the purpose of an order is its sense only insofar as the purpose can be expressed by a rule of language (PG 70). The internal purposes of speaking are the purposes speech-acts have by virtue of rules governing them, rules which define what is done and accomplished in the speech-acts. Such purposes are not to be discovered outside or beyond the language itself. Lying outside of language are its effects, its external purposes. The contrast with cooking and the rules of cooking will make this distinction clear.

The end of cooking is something external to the rules of cooking; it is something that can be identified independently of any appeal to these rules. This end is edible food. Whether or not food is edible is something we ascertain by tasting it, a procedure we can employ without knowing the rules by which the food was prepared. It follows that it is a contingent matter whether or not a certain set of rules produces edible food. It is certainly not the case that 'edible food' is defined as 'food produced by following a certain set of cooking rules'. It is because of the external relation holding between edible food and any given set of cooking rules that we can justify some of the latter by showing that they in fact lead to the former. It will turn out that if we do not follow one of a number of particular sets of cooking rules we could not prepare edible food. Hence the practical justification for using those rules.

Contrast the case of cooking with the case of referring to a horse in saying, for example, "this horse is lame." Is there any way of identifying the aim of this linguistic performance other than by appealing to the rules governing "this horse is lame"? How can we possibly define and determine 'referring to a horse' except by means of those linguistic conventions that specify what it is to use referring expressions? These conventions or rules tell us, among other things, that when 'this horse' is used in subject position we are then referring to a horse. "Subject position" is a linguistic entity; it cannot be understood at all except by means of the conventions of language. Referring, then, is a linguistic activity. One does not use 'this horse' in subject position, etc., and as a contingent matter of fact refer to a horse; using the expression in this way is *ipso facto* referring to a horse. It follows that one could hardly justify the rule prescribing the use of 'this horse' in subject position by arguing that in following this rule, and other related ones, it turns out that, in accordance with the laws of nature, we in fact refer to a horse. It is necessarily the case that we refer to a horse if we use 'this horse' in accordance with these rules, for the rules define what it is to accomplish this linguistic goal. Such a goal is an internal purpose or aim of language.

Hence we are able to confirm the parallel Wittgenstein draws between the rules of a game and grammatical rules. If we do not follow the rules of chess we are not playing chess poorly; we are simply not playing chess. If we do not follow the grammatical rules governing referring expressions, we do not refer poorly; we simply do not refer at all. It makes no sense to say that the rules of chess are justified because they allow us to achieve our goal of playing chess, for the goal of playing chess cannot be identified independently of the rules. The goal is internal to the game itself. Likewise, it makes no sense to speak of justifying the rules governing referring expressions by showing that they allow us to achieve the goal of referring. The goal of referring is internal to language; it cannot fail to be accomplished if the rules are followed. This is a logical 'cannot'. In answer to Wittgenstein's question, "If someone says 'If our language had not this grammar, it could not express these facts' — it should be asked what 'could' means here" (PI §497), we need to stress that it refers to logical or grammatical impossibility. And we might well follow his advice and point out that the matter is better expressed by saying that we *would* not refer if we did not follow the rules of referring than by saying that we *could* not do so (Z §134). We simply would not play chess if we did not follow the rules of chess.

None of this is to deny that the use of "this horse is lame" may have effects above and beyond the linguistic aims of referring to a horse and characterizing it as lame. All sorts of effects may follow: the horse may be shot, he may be purchased for a lower price, he may be treated, the betting on him may drop, etc. But whether or not any of these effects follow from a person's saying that the horse is lame is a purely contingent matter. None of them need of necessity follow. One may know from experience that saying this will cause, say, the betting to drop; one does *not* know it just from knowing the grammar of language. Hence grammar does not tell one how to achieve these effects. And one can hardly justify the grammar of referring by noting that in referring to a horse and characterizing it as lame the betting dropped on that horse. That the betting dropped may in another person's eyes damn the speech act in question, but that hardly amounts to a condemnation of its grammar.

What if we say, however, that in uttering "This horse is lame" the speaker *warns* someone of the horse? This is an effect above and beyond the linguistic aims of referring and characterizing, but it is an effect accomplished by referring and characterizing. Can't the grammatical rules governing referring and characterizing be said to achieve this effect, and can't we say that they are thereby justified because they allow us to do something we want to do (warn someone of a lame horse)? Two things need to be noted in response to this challenge. In the first place, we cannot justify the grammar that turns "this horse is lame" into an expression that refers and characterizes by pointing out that this grammar allows us to warn someone, for the fact that it allows us to do this brings favor upon it only if we approve of the warning, and whether we do is a highly contingent matter. One person may desire to warn someone of the horse; another may desire to keep the lameness a secret. Are we to say then that the grammar of referring and characterizing is justified for the one and not for the other? This makes the whole notion of a practical justification of grammar subjective and idle. But we also need to note, in the second place, that warning is not simply an end external to the linguistic activities of referring and characterizing; it is also a linguistic activity itself, or a linguistic accomplishment. Warning someone requires a certain situation and intention, not as matter of fact, as causal antecedents, but as a matter of grammar. The act would not be one of warning if these conditions did not prevail, because they are internal to what it *means* to warn someone. It follows, then, that if we say "this horse is lame" and have as our purpose in saying this the end of warning someone about the horse, this end is itself defined by the grammar of language. We cannot justify *this* grammar, the grammar of warning, by saying that it allows us to achieve the end of warning. This grammar constitutes warning; it does not as a matter of contingent fact lead to warning. "If we did not use this grammar we could not achieve the end of warning": this only means, if we did not use this grammar we would not achieve this end.

The distinction between the internal goals of language and its external effects allows us to understand §491 in the *Philosophical Investigations*.

> Not: "without language we could not communicate with one another" — but for sure: without language we cannot influence other people in such-and-such ways; cannot build roads and machines, etc. And also: without the use of speech and writing people could not communicate.

Communication is an internal goal of language, defined in terms of the linguistic notions of meaning, stating, affirming, asking, and so on. Using language to build roads and machines is to use it to attain certain external effects. Even using speech and writing allows one to achieve the (to them) external effect of communicating: it is not necessary to speak or write in order to communicate, and one may speak or write with no intent to communicate. Achieving the ends of communication or building roads may justify the means used to do so, but using the speech act of stating in order to communicate does not bestow merit on stating, for this is simply part of what it means to communicate.

Moreover, we must distinguish between pragmatically justifying the use of a concept on a particular occasion and pragmatically justifying the concept itself. Given my purpose on a specific occasion, there may be a point in my using, say, a very precise concept. If I want to build a bridge that will endure I will use an exact mathematical language to describe its structure. Relative to the particular occasion, my purpose would justify the use of this language and its concepts. But it would not justify the concepts themselves. For the use of a vague or ambiguous term in the same family of concepts might equally well be justified if my purpose were different — if, say, I were engaged in sabotage and wanted to construct a bridge that would collapse. In justifying the use of a concept on a particular occasion we make reference to the external effects of our use of language, and these effects are only contingently tied, via variable needs and desires, to grammar. This mode of justifying the use of language is essentially relative, and it does not extend in any way to the grammar of the language.

It might be objected that linguistic practices as well as individual uses of words can be pragmatically justified. Given our normal aims, isn't the practice of measuring by the metric system preferable to the practice of measuring by the ell? Isn't the practice of calculating to be preferred over the practice of counting, given our general aim of arriving at arithmetic conclusions as rapidly and easily as possible? And given the fact that objects normally do not shrink or expand, are we not justified in using stable rather than elastic rulers in measuring these objects?

One problem with this suggestion is that the specification of the standard aims or the conditions in nature presupposes the type of linguistic practice these aims are supposed to justify. What is the fact that objects do not shrink or expand? It is the fact that these objects do not change their dimensions *as measured by stable rulers* (RFM 4). Clearly, then, the type of condition that allegedly justifies the practice of measuring with stable rulers is necessarily connected to this practice, and there is no contingent justification of the practice by reference to the condition. And what is our aim in measuring by the metric system? Can we say more that that it is the aim of obtaining measurements that allow for all the dimensions and all the computations that are possible using the metric system? Thus the aim or end is defined by the very linguistic practice that is alleged to be justified on the grounds that it achieves this end. Finally, counting and calculating are different arithmetic activities that may produce the same result (one more easily and rapidly than the other), but if they do not do so, the results of the calculation, properly checked, will take priority over the results of the counting. Counting is subordinate to calculating in the arithmetic language-game, and the latter needs no additional support from the external fact that if often yields "faster", less cumbersome results.

Wittgenstein gives the example of another tribe's way of selling wood — not, as we do, by the volume, but by the area covered by the wood (RFM 44). If we say that our way is to be preferred because the alternative way would be absurd given the standard interests involved in buying and selling wood, it seems likely that these standard interests already are framed in terms of our practice of buying and selling wood. To say that our practice therefore satisfies these desires and that the alternative practice does not would be simply a matter of begging the practical question.

Wittgenstein's conclusion, then, is this: to the extent that the end of speaking is external to the language involved, there is no pragmatic justification of the grammar of that language; and to the extent that the end of speaking is internally defined by grammar, this grammar cannot be justified by appealing to its ability to achieve this end, for such is a pseudo-ability. To say that grammar allows us to attain the goals that grammar itself creates is a practical form of begging the question. It is a projection of the grammar of language onto the ends of action.

So much for the explicit arguments that Wittgenstein presents on behalf of his claim that language is autonomous. There remain to be considered some general attitudes toward language which Wittgenstein frequently expresses and refers to in elaboration of his theme of autonomy. These attitudes are summed up in the notion of conventionalism. Our study of Wittgenstein's arguments for the autonomy of language will help us better understand Wittgenstein's conventionalism.

Conventionalism affirms the independence of language from the world by maintaining that meaning is a creature of arbitrary, conventional rules. A "full-blooded" conventionalism — sometimes attributed to Wittgenstein — also expresses the independence of any one linguistic utterance from any other, a doctrine which seems to some to follow from Wittgenstein's considerations with regard to following a rule.[19] Insofar as we are concerned only with the independence of language from reality, we will consider only the first aspect of Wittgenstein's conventionalism.

We have noted in passing that ostensive definition does not provide a word with a meaning by pinning it onto a meaning-entity in the world. Rather, an ostensive definition is a purely linguistic rule, and its use presupposes the grammar of its component terms. The meanings explained by ostensive definitions are not already there in the world, predetermined is some way. Words have the meanings they have because people decide to use them in certain ways:

> But let's not forget that a word hasn't got a meaning given to it, as it were, by a power independent of us, so that there could be a kind of scientific investigation into what the word *really* means. A word has the meaning someone has given to it (BB 28).

Wittgenstein is not expressing here the platitude that what words we use is a conventional and arbitrary matter, e.g., that we use 'red' to talk about red rather than using 'der' for that purpose. Such a platitude is consistent with the view that meanings are things that are given, predetermined, and independent of the use of words, and that we (arbitrarily) choose a word to mark one of these meanings. It is this latter view that Wittgenstein is rejecting. There is nothing that already is a meaning prior to the establishment of rules. This being so, there is nothing beyond the rules with which they can be compared.

> Grammar is not accountable to any reality. It is grammatical rules that determine meaning (constitute it) and so they themselves are not answerable to any meaning and to that extent are arbitrary.
>
> There cannot be a question whether these or other rules are the correct ones for the use of 'not' (that is, whether they accord with meaning). For without these rules the word has as yet no meaning; and if we change the rules, it now has another meaning (or none),

and in that case we may just as well change the word too (PG 184; see also PI p. 147).

Thus the set of grammatical rules that create meaning is like a "free-floating calculus" (PG 313), and a sub-set of these rules, like mathematics, is similar to "a celestial body floating free in space" (PG 297). There can be no foundation for the distinction between sense and nonsense (PG 126–7), for rules cannot be given a justification (RC I §74; III §91).

Wittgenstein likes to compare rules of grammar with standards of measurement (PG 185, 192). For the purpose of illuminating the doctrine of conventionalism, such a comparison is helpful. Surely it is true to say that *we decide* to measure something in terms of yards or meters; we decide what is to count as a yard or a meter; and we could have decided, without being accountable to any reality, to adopt different standards or none at all. It makes no sense to say that facts in the real world, the properties of space, determine how long a yard really is, and that we can compare our yardstick with these properties. There is no sense to the notion that our yardstick is either true or false to the facts (PG 185). We can speak of true or false measurement *only* after we have decided upon a standard of measurement. Grammar or logic, Wittgenstein tells us, is antecedent to the correspondence between statement and fact "in the same sense ... as that in which the establishment of a method of measurement is antecedent to the correctness or incorrectness of a statement of length" (RFM 45). We use a yardstick to determine if a statement of length ("this object is three and a half yards long") is true, and it serves in this capacity because it tells us what our word 'yard' means. Likewise, grammatical rules tell us what our words mean, and these grammatical rules can be used in ascertaining if the statements we make with these words are true or false: "What belongs to grammar are all the conditions (the method) necessary for comparing the proposition with reality" (PG 88). That which is arbitrary — the yardstick, the grammatical rule — allows us to make judgments of truth or falsity which are not arbitrary. The antecedent measure or rule is not itself true or false (RFM 4), and different measures or rules cannot be evaluated in terms of their comparative truth or falsity. As Wittgenstein puts it:

> The thing that's so difficult to understand can be expressed like this. *As long as* we remain in the province of the true-false games a change in the grammar can only lead us from *one* such game to

another, and never from something true to something false. On the
other hand if we go outside the province of these games, we don't
any longer call it 'language' and 'grammar', and once again we
don't come into contradiction with reality (PG 111).

The grammar of a language-game constitutes the measure of truth and falsity within this language-game, and these terms of evaluation have sense
only with respect to this grammar. A different grammar would yield a new
sense of 'true' and 'false'. But the grammar itself cannot be judged true
or false. What would constitute the measure of the measure? What sense
is there to such a notion? Our grounds or evidence for making certain
judgments must live up to our standard of good grounds — "but the standard has no grounds!" (PI §482).

It is important to realize exactly what Wittgenstein means when he
characterizes the rules of grammar as being conventions and as being arbitrary. Such talk easily leads to an assimilation of conventionalism to sub-
jectivism or simple social-rule relativism. There is no hint of these odd
theories in what Wittgenstein himself has to say. He speaks as if the fact
that grammatical rules are arbitrary and conventional simply follows from
the arguments demonstrating the autonomy of language. He writes, for example, "I do not call rules of representation conventions if they can be
justified by the fact that a representation made in accordance with them
will agree with reality" (PG 186). We have seen how he has shown that
these rules cannot be justified in this fashion by virtue of the circularity
involved in the attempt and for other reasons as well. And again: "The
rules of a game are 'arbitrary' means: the concept 'game' is not defined
by the effect the game is supposed to have on us" (PG 192). We have seen
that many concepts are not defined in terms of their effects. Given Wittgenstein's frequent insistence that the sense of a proposition is conveyed
by the means of verifying or proving it (PG 81; PR 200; PI §353), we
should conclude that the sense of "grammatical rules are arbitrary conventions" is given by the various arguments demonstrating autonomy. This is
important. 'Arbitrary' and 'conventional' are slippery terms, and we must
take care not to read more into them than Wittgenstein intended. In his
usage they signify only that language cannot be understood as the semantic
realists suggest. Language is neither derived from nor justifiable or criti-
cizable in light of language-independent realities. Language is autonomous.

Robert L. Arrington
Georgia State University

Endnotes

1. J.L. Austin, *Philosophical Papers* (Oxford: Oxford University Press, 1961).

2. For a direct criticism of Austin's views from a Wittgensteinian perspective, see my "Can There Be a Linguistic Phenomenology?" *The Philosophical Quarterly*, Vol. 25, No. 101 (October, 1975), pp.289-304.

3. Austin, op.cit., p.129.

4. Ibid., p.130.

5. Ibid.

6. Ibid., p.194.

7. Ibid.

8. Ibid., p.25.

9. Ibid., pp.182-83.

10. Ibid., p.184.

11. Ibid., p.25.

12. Ibid., p.149.

13. Ibid., p.150.

14. Ibid., p.181.

15. Ibid., p.130.

16. Ibid., p.133.

17. See H. Ishiguro, "Use and Reference of Names," in P.Winch (ed.), *Studies in the Philosophy of Wittgenstein* (London: Routledge and Kegan Paul, 1969), pp.20-50.

18. For a discussion of Wittgenstein's critique of ostensive definition, see my "'Mechanism and Calculus': Wittgenstein on Augustine's Theory of Ostension," in C.G. Luckhardt (ed.), *Wittgenstein: Sources and Perspectives* (Ithaca: Cornell University Press, 1980), pp.303-338.

19. See Michael Dummett, "Wittgenstein's Philosophy of Mathematics," *Philosophical Review*, LXVIII (1959), pp.324-348.

CHAPTER IV

Suspicion

Alan R. White

There is what H.H. Price correctly characterized as "the traditional view" of belief according to which "a rough scale of assent can be constructed, ranging from suspecting or surmising at the bottom end, to absolute sureness or conviction at the top end, with various degrees of opinion in the middle". This view of belief as something which possesses degrees is at least as old as Locke, who, like Price in this century and Cardinal Newman in the previous, frequently discussed belief under the name "assent" and Newman's book was called *A Grammar of Assent*. The view that belief has degrees is standard among twentieth century philosophers, such as Ramsey, Keynes, Braithwaite, etc. One of the few opponents of this view is Newman who in chapter six of his *Grammar of Assent* vigorously criticised Locke's arguments.

Philosophers have rarely paid any attention to the notion of suspicion. Those who have even mentioned it adopt the view advocated by Price, namely that it is "the lowest degree of belief". Even the OED defines suspicion as "partial or unconfirmed belief".

The exact nature of suspicion and the question whether or not it is a degree of belief is, at present a live and practical issue in English law. The problem set by section 22 (1) of the Theft Act 1968, is whether evidence that an accused suspected that the goods was handling were stolen is sufficient to make him liable under that section to the charge of "knowing or believing" that they were stolen. In the case of Atwal v. Massey the then Lord Chief Justice gave a ruling which seemed to hold that it did. And this view was followed in Archibold's standard *Criminal Pleading, Evidence and Practice*. It was, however, rejected by later courts such as R. v. Griffiths in 1975 and R. v. Hall in 1985.

Despite the philosophical tradition, the dictionary, and some legal decisions, I want to try and show, first, that belief does not have degrees, secondly, that even if it did, suspicion is not a degree of belief, and, thirdly, what exactly suspicion is.

There are various reasons for denying that belief has degrees. First, a belief cannot be increased or decreased in amount nor become more or greater, less or smaller, in the way that, for example, either heat, weight, length and pressure or anger, joy and pride can. I do not believe that p, e.g. that London is the capital of the U.K., more than I believe that q, e.g. that Lima is the capital of Peru. Nor is this inconsistent with the fact that belief in a person or his word, as contrasted with the belief that p, can increase or decrease, be more or less, great or little, and that one can believe one person more than another. For such belief is akin to faith or trust.

What has mislead philosophers into the view that belief has degrees is the fact that a belief can vary in various respects which do admit of degrees. A belief can be more or less faint, firm, obstinate or unwavering, obsessive or tentative, confident, hesitant or unquestioning; it can be half-hearted or whole-hearted. But these are not degrees of belief; they are degrees of conviction, confidence, or tenacity with which the belief is held. Certainty is not the highest degree of belief, but of conviction, confidence or lack of doubt.

A clear example of this confusion occurs in Locke who assimilates his so-called "degree of ascent" to "assurance", "confidence", "unavoidability" on the one hand and to "conjecture, guess, doubt, wavering, distrust, disbelief, etc." on the other hand. Thus he says of one of his groups "in this case, our assent has a sufficient foundation to raise itself to a degree which we may call confidence". Similarly, it is sufficient that Price frequently, even commonly, alternates between talking of "degrees of belief" and talking of "degrees of confidence" with which one can hold a belief and between regarding suspicion as a very low degree of the former and regarding it as a very low degree of the latter. He even suggests, without making clear how far he agrees, that some people may actually define "degrees of belief" in terms of degrees of confidence and himself asserts that the latter is necessary to any "tolerable analysis" of the former. Newman, on the other hand, clearly recognizes this mistaken assimilation when he points out that "this increase or decrease of strength does not lie in the assent itself, but in its circumstances and concomitants, for instance, in the emotions, in the ratiocinative faculty, or in the imagination".

A second reason for denying that belief has degrees is the fact that whereas qualities which can have degrees, whether it be heat, weight, length and pressure, or anger, joy or pride, can usually also be expressed adjectivally, e.g. as hot, heavy, long, pressing, or as angry, joyful, proud; there is no adjective corresponding to the noun "belief". It is further significant that the nouns for such conditions as confidence, conviction or certainty — with which Locke and Price have confused belief — which all have degrees, have also got corresponding adjectives.

Thirdly, these other conditions, such as confidence, conviction, or certainty, with which belief has been confused, are something we can feel. But we cannot feel belief. Fourthly, what may have contributed to a false assimilation of belief with these feelings with which we can hold it is the fact that, e.g., confidence, conviction and certainty that p imply a belief that p and, conversely, a belief that p may imply at least a minimum of each of these.

Having concluded that belief does not have any degrees, our next task is to show that, even if it did, suspicion could not be a degree of belief. First, suspicion, unlike belief, does have degrees. One can be more or less suspicious, a little or very suspicious; one's suspicions can increase or decrease, grow or fade away, be added to or lessened. I can not only suspect one person more than another, I can also suspect that p, e.g., that the butler stole his employer's jewels, more than I suspect that q, e.g., that he also murdered his employer. In this respect, suspicion is more akin to those accompaniments of belief, such a confidence, conviction or certainty, than it is to belief itself. Secondly, the noun "suspicion" has, again like those for confidence, conviction and certainty, but unlike that for belief, an adjectival form "suspicious". Thirdly, suspicion, like these accompaniments but unlike belief, is something one can feel. Finally, to suspect that p does not imply believing that p. Even the strongest suspicion need not involve even the faintest belief. Suspicion may be a step on the road to belief, but it need not ever reach it. Suspicion may lead or give way to belief, but it need not. I can quite consciously suspect equally, but not believe equally, both that p and that not p.

Even if alleged degrees of belief are wrongly, as we have seen they sometimes are, equated with belief or varying degrees of confidence, suspicion could not be the lowest degree of even of this latter, since for the reasons just given, a suspicion that p not only lacks many of the characteristics of a belief that p, it does not even imply it.

If then suspicion, which can have degrees, is not a degree of belief, which can not have degrees, what is it?

Suspicion is, I think, related in some way to belief. This is why, like belief, it has grounds, reasons and evidence, confirmation, verification, and justification. It is also why, though suspicion is not a degree of belief, the ground or evidence for one's suspicion are a less degree of the same kind as those for one's belief. Suspicion is, as even those who regard it as a degree of belief suppose, something weaker than belief.

I can think of only two views, both of which were rather inconsistently expressed or at least hinted at in Newman's *Grammar of Assent*, of the nature of suspicion. The first is that to suspect that p is to believe that it may (or might) be that p; the second is that to suspect that p is to be inclined (or have an inclination) to believe that p. It is clear that on neither view would suspicion be a degree of belief. And both views have the virtue that they allow, as any correct theory must, that a suspicion that p — whether this is an inclination to believe that p or an actual belief that it may be that p — does not imply even the slightest belief that p. They both allow that suspicion is something weaker than belief.

Let us first consider the view that to suspect that p is to believe that it may (or might) be that p. A weak suspicion is a belief in a low probability that p and a strong suspicion is a belief in a high probability that p. The hints of this view in Newman occur in his classification of suspicion, together with Locke's other items of conjecture, doubt, wavering, etc., as examples of "opinion". Such opinions, he says, are "assents to the plausibility, probability, doubtfulness, or untrustworthiness, of a proposition". The same view has also been advanced, though later overturned by a higher court, in English law.

Plausibility is given to this view by the fact that most philosophers, including both those, like Locke and Price, who accept degrees of belief, and those, like Newman, who deny them, agree that either the degree of confidence, conviction or certainty with which one holds a belief that p or one's alleged degree of belief that p is correlated with the degree of probability which one believes that p has. As Locke, whose chapter on "Degrees of Assent" follows immediately on his chapter on "Probability", said, "as they [sc. the grounds of probability] are the foundations on which are assent is built, so are they also the measure whereby its several degrees are, or ought to be regulated". Modern advocates of so-called "subjective probability" seem even to equate degrees of probability with degrees of (rational) belief.

This analysis of suspicion has, however, several difficulties. First, though there is, I think, a correlation between a suspicion that p and a belief that it might be that p has some probability, this is not in itself an equation of the two. Indeed, if the latter is the foundation or the case of the former, it cannot be the same as it. Moreover, such an equation would be inconsistent with the Locke-Price view that suspicion is a degree of belief, since a belief that it might be that p is not any degree of a belief that p, but a belief in something other than p. Similarly, a correlation of degrees, e.g. weak or strong, of a suspicion that p with a belief in degrees of probability, e.g. might possibly be or very probably is, that p is not an equation of degrees of suspicion with a belief in degrees of probability.

Secondly, and similarly, although changes in the character of one's suspicion are plausibly correlated with changes in the character of what one believes - so that a mounting suspicion, for example, is correlated with a belief in mounting probability - the former are not the same as the latter. One's suspicions can be raised, aroused, excited, or calmed, allayed, set at rest, conquered, overcome, or dispelled; but none of these can happen either to one's beliefs or to the probabilities in which one believes.

Thirdly, one can not only suspect that p but also suspect that it might be that p. But on this analysis the latter would amount to the dubiously intelligible belief that it might be that it might be that p. Fourthly, what one suspects when one suspects that p is not what one suspects if one believes that it might be p. Nor does what verifies, confirms or justifies the former verify, confirm or justify the latter.

The second view, namely that to suspect that p is to be inclined (or to have an inclination) to believe that p, has also earlier inclinations in Newman's Grammar of Assent. Though he only mentions suspicion in passing, he seems to lump it with what he calls "opinion", with "half-assent" or with "prima facie assent". In these one is "inclined to believe", one has "an inclination to assent", one "feels drawn towards assent".

The inclination present in suspicion is the inclination which is akin to a readiness or a temptation, not that which is akin to a proneness, tendency or trait. It is an inclination one can feel as one can feel suspicious. Hence, unlike a tendency, it is an inclination which only the animate can have. Unlike a tendency, it is an inclination to something particular rather than a general kind of thing. One can have a feeling inclination to hold a specific belief or perform a specific act as contrasted with a tendency-inclination to hold a type of belief or perform a type of act. Whereas one cannot have a tendency-inclination to such and such an attitude or deed which is never manifested, one can quite easily feel inclined to do what one never in fact does. So we can feel inclined to believe, as we can suspect, what we do not in fact believe and, *a fortiori*, what we have no tendency to believe.

This second view of suspicion, like the first, also allows for a correlation between suspicion and belief in probability, since one's inclination to believe that p can, and usually will, vary proportionately with the degree of probability which one believes p to have. One will be more or less inclined to believe that p the greater or smaller is the believed probability of p.

But, unlike the first view, it also explains the normal characteristics of suspicion. For an inclination to believe can, like a suspicion, have degrees; one can be more or less, a bit or very, faintly or increasingly, suspicious or inclined to believe. An inclination to believe that p can, like a suspicion that p, be raised, aroused or excited, and overcome, dispelled or got rid of. It can mount or subside. It can be momentary or sustained, come on suddenly or gradually.

Moreover, what one suspects when one suspects that p is what one is inclined to believe when one is inclined to believe that p; it is, as we saw, not what one actually believes when one believes that it might be p. Similarly, what verifies, confirms, substantiates or justifies one's suspicion that p is the p which one is inclined to believe, not the possibility or the probability of p which one actually believes in.

I must admit, however, that parallel to the dubious iteration which the idiomatic "I suspect that it might be that p" poses for the first theory, namely that suspecting that p is believing that it might be that p, there is a different dubious iteration which the idiomatic "I am inclined to suspect that p" poses for the second theory, namely that suspecting that p is being inclined to believe that p.

A difference between "being suspicious" (or "having a suspicion") and "suspecting" is that the former seems to carry a hint, which the latter does not, that its object is something untoward. Such a difference between a verb, on the one hand, and its corresponding verbal adjective or verbal noun, on the other, is not uncommon. It has different explanations in different cases, but none of these shows a difference in meaning. Thus one who is obliged or required by force of circumstances, unlike one who is morally or legally obligated or who is required by regulations, is not "under an obligation" nor is he faced by any "requirement". A soldier who is ordered to pick up his rifle, unlike one who is ordered to search every visitor, is not "under orders"; nor is suspected foul play, unlike a suspected butler, "under suspicion".

CHAPTER V

Act, Content and the Duck-Rabbit

Roderick Chisholm

Die Gefahr, die darin liegt, Dinge einfacher sehen zu wollen, als sie in Wirklichkeit sind, wird heute oft sehr überschätzt. Diese Gefahr besteht aber tatsächlich im höchsten Grade in der phänomenologischen Untersuchung der Sinneseindrücke. Diese werden immer für viel einfacher gehalten, als sie sind.[1]

Wittgenstein

Introduction

This paper is concerned with the philosophical problem of the duck-rabbit. The problem is a difficult one that Wittgenstein took very seriously, and I shall take it as seriously as he did.

The problem pertains first of all to *sensation* or *appearance* and, indeed, to *visual* sensation or appearance. Its proper treatment, Wittgenstein thought, would throw light upon many other activities — for example, it would tell us something about the nature of language.[2] But I shall discuss just the problem of the duck-rabbit; and I will try to fit Wittgenstein's treatment into what I believe to be a traditional philosophical perspective. This is one of the many aspects under which, in 1989, we can and should view Wittgenstein as a philosopher.

In the *Philosophical Investigations*, he reminds us of what it is to see a picture as a picture of a duck and to see the same picture *as* a picture of a rabbit. And then he puts this question: If I describe such a phenomenon, am I describing "my sense-impression [*Eindruck*]" or am I describing my own "attitude or point of view [*Stellungname*]" with respect *to* the sense-impression? A traditional formulation would be: Am I describing the *content* of experience or the *act* of experiencing?

The picture that Wittgenstein provides for us is reproduced in Figure 1:

87

I shall propose a way of dealing with the philosophical problem that Wittgenstein has formulated. What I say will involve a description of what it is to *attend* to a feature of a sensation or appearance, and it will involve an analysis of the ways in which attending is logically related to sensing and to interpreting.

What I shall say is inconsistent with some of the things that Wittgenstein says. But it is also suggested by other things that he says. And, I believe, it is adequate to the wealth of philosophical data that he has provided for us.

Seeing

To formulate the problem, let us begin, as Wittgenstein does, by considering the nature of seeing. The statement "*I see a picture*" provides us with a simple and straightforward example.

It has features not shared by *He sees a picture* or by *You see a picture*. Putting the matter the way that Austrian philosophers prefer, I will say that the statement expresses several quite different "moments" of seeing. Four such moments may be summarized as follows.

If I can truly say that I see a picture before me, then: (i) there is a picture before me; (ii) the picture presents a certain appearance; (iii) I judge that what is presenting such an appearance is a picture; and (iv) it is evident to me that there is a picture before me.

The situation involves, therefore: the *object* of the visual perception (the physical thing that is seen); the *subject* of the visual situation (the one who sees); the *sensible content* that is presented (the sensation or appearance); the psychological *act* of the subject (his judging); and the *propositional content* of that act (what it is that the subject judges).[3]

The situation also involves an *epistemic* moment. If I can truly say "I see a picture before me," then my judgment that there is a picture before me is epistemically justified. The traditional term for the appropriate level of epistemic justification is "evident." Fortunately, this epistemic moment, although it is essential to seeing, is not our present concern.[4]

These are among the things that take place, then, when one can truly say, "I see a picture."[5]

And what if the picture is one that can be seen as a picture of a duck or as a picture of a rabbit? The question seems to pose a dilemma.

"Half Impression and Half Interpretation"

What is it that changes when, as we say, there is a change of aspect — for example, I begin to see the picture *as* a duck?

The picture itself, of course, is not the thing that changes. Nothing need happen to the physical object on the wall when one ceases to see it as a rabbit and begins to see it as a duck. This fact seems to confront us with two undesirable options. We might say that what changes is the *sensation or appearance* that is produced or called up by the picture. Or we might say that what changes is the *judgment* that is made about that sensation or appearance. And so Wittgenstein asks: "What is different: my impression? my interpretation?" (195e)

The dilemma is this. If we consider the sensation or appearance and ask whether *that* is the thing that changes, we are led to conclude that what changes is the interpretation. But if we consider the interpretation and then ask whether that is the thing that changes, then we are led to say that what changes is the sensation or appearance. And there seems to be no third possibility.

Appearances

The problem has to do with the *appearance*. And, as almost every philosopher since Aristotle has known, the concept of an appearance means trouble. Wittgenstein had obviously thought these things through. In his *Remarks on Colours*, he makes the following observation.[6]

Don't we just *call* brown the table which under certain circumstances appears brown [*braun erscheint*] to the normal-sighted? We could certainly conceive of someone to whom things seemed [*schienen*] sometimes this colour and sometimes that, independently of the colour they are (III 97).

He warns us against assuming that our concern is with some "*inner* picture" that is produced by the outer picture — an inner picture which, like the outer picture, has lines, shapes, colours and perhaps even an organization. Such an inner picture, he says, would be a "non-thing," an "*Unding*" (196). Yet we cannot deny that the outer picture *is* appearing in a certain way and that this fact is central to our problem.[7] What Wittgenstein is telling us is that the sense in which a *physical thing* can be said to have such properties as colour and shape is *not the same* as that in which a *sensation* or *appearance* can be said to have such properties as colour and shape.

Attending

That there is a kind of psychological activity that falls between having a sensation and making an interpretation is, of course, nothing new to philosophy and psychology. The traditional term is *attending*. Wittgenstein uses the word "notice" when he formulates the problem: "I call the experience the noticing of an aspect" (193e). It is one thing to perceive an object and it is another thing to notice or attend to the features of the appearance of that object.

Wittgenstein says this about the problem: "Here it is *difficult* to see that what is at issue is the fixing of concepts [*dass es sich um Begriffsbestimmungen handelt*]" (204). Yet that is what is at issue. What I will now try to do, therefore, is to fix the concept of attending. I will do this by singling out five features of the concept.

I will begin by saying this:

> (1) There is an act of the subject — namely, that of *attending* — that falls between having a sensation (sensing an appearance) and the act of making an interpretation.

This, of course, is a paraphrase of what Wittgenstein says. But I say that attending is an "act of the subject," while Wittgenstein writes that the dawning and continuation of an aspect involves a certain occupation [*Beschäftigung*] with experience. The English translation uses the personal pronoun: "I should like to say that what dawns here lasts only as long as I am occupied with the object in a particular way" (210e). But, in the original German, Wittgenstein avoids the personal pronoun by using the passive voice: "so long as a certain occupation with the observed object endures [*als eine bestimmte Beschäftigung mit dem betrachteten Objekt dauert*]" (210). He is reluctant to say, "*nur so lange stehen bleibt als ich mit dem Objekt beschäftigt bin.*"

As Wittgenstein makes clear, *what* we can attend to has to be something that is *there*. Only certain pictures can be seen as duck-pictures or as rabbit-pictures. "I cannot see the schematic cube as two interpenetrating prisms" (212e). Sensations, like everything else, have indefinitely many characteristics. But only some of these characteristics can become objects of attention. Which features of an appearance are *there* to be attended to?

Wittgenstein has two technical philosophical expressions that will help us here. The first is the adjective "*internal*," which he introduced in the *Tractatus* (4.123). He wrote: "This blue colour and that stand in the internal relation of brighter and darker..."

The second philosophical expression is "direct," as used in "*direct* description." Wittgenstein writes: "I ought to be able to refer to the experience directly, and not only indirectly. (As I can speak of red without calling it the colour of blood.)" (p.194e).

The *internal* properties of a sensation or appearance are those that I would be referring to, if, in Wittgenstein's terms, I were to describe it *directly*.[8] There is no problem at all in finding those internal properties of a sensation that one can describe directly. They are among the properties that the sensation or appearance has *necessarily* — for example, the properties of being-brown, being-speckled and being-bright. These are the internal properties of sensations that Wittgenstein is concerned with in his *Remarks on Colours*. The red picture on the wall is not necessarily such that it is red. But the *sensation* that it presents is necessarily such that it is red.[9]

We may add a further point, then, about attending:

(2) One may attend to internal properties of sensations (appearances).

One of the striking features of the duck-rabbit phenomenon may now be put by reference to attending. You may be able to see the picture as a duck and to see it as a rabbit, but you cannot do both at once. This feature of attending had concerned earlier psychologists and philosophers. Wundt, for example, had said that, to the extent that attending makes one feature clearer, it results in "the inhibition" of other features.[10]

But now a general question arises: *What* features of a sensation are such that attending to those features precludes attending to others?

Spatial Wholes as Objects of Attention

As Wittgenstein makes abundantly clear, the duck-rabbit sensation is not the only type of visual sensation that involves "seeing as" and the dawning of an aspect. Some of the other types are simpler in that they do not involve the factors of association and "being reminded" that seem essential to the problem of the duck-rabbit. I suggest that the proper procedure is to begin with the simpler examples.

Let us consider, therefore, another example that Wittgenstein provides for us — the "double cross" of page 207 of *Philosophical Investigations*.

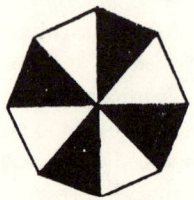

Here there is an octagon having diagonals that form eight equal triangles, four of which form a black cross and four of which form a white cross. One may attend to that whole which is made up of the four black triangles, in which case the picture will be seen as a black cross; or one may attend to that whole which is made up of the four white triangles, in which case the picture will be seen as a white cross. This type of example is more simple than that of the duck-rabbit, for it need not involve "being reminded" of any other thing.

I had asked: What features of a visual sensation may be such that attending to those features precludes attending to others? The answer is clear. Certain *spatial* features of the duck-rabbit sensation are such that attending to those features precludes our then attending to other spatial features of that sensation. If we attend to a certain part (or "figure") within a sensation then (a) that part may be said to become "foreground" and (b) the spatial whole surrounding that part may be said to become "background." But the terms "foreground" and "background," though useful, are not themselves needed in formulating our suggestion.[11] We will say this:

(3) One can attend to spatial parts of a visual sensation but only to
    one such part at a time.

Attending to the spatial parts of a visual sensation should not be confused with *fixing* the eyes upon the physical thing that is the object of that sensation. In an ocular examination one may be asked to fix upon a certain object and then to report upon what is in one's periphery of the visual field. In such a case, one fixes upon one part of the external object while attending to a part of the sensation that is produced by another part of that object. One then attends to a part of the sensation falling outside of the part produced by the object one is fixing upon. A similar thing happens when one tries, surreptitiously, to observe something "out of the corner of the eye" and fixes upon something other than the object of interest and attention.

What spatial features of a visual sensation can become objects of attention? Those spatial parts of an appearance that can be attended to are themselves wholes that contain further spatial parts. Hence principle (3) tells us that, if we attend to a spatial part of a sensation, we cannot at the same time attend to any of the *parts* of that part, and we cannot then attend to any whole of which that part may be a part.[12]

Now we may formulate some particular questions about the duck-rabbit. *What* features of the sensation produced by looking at the picture of the duck-rabbit are involved in seeing the picture as a *duck*, and just *how* are they so involved? And *what* features are involved in seeing it as a *rabbit*, and just how are *they* so involved? The latter two questions are the most difficult "phenomenological" questions that the problem of the duck-rabbit involves. But one cannot pretend to solve the problem without at least attempting to answer them.

What we have said about attending to the spatial features of a sensation suggests this. There are certain spatial features of the sensation which are such that attending to those features is essential to the discovery that the picture can be seen as a picture of a rabbit; and certain other features are essential to the discovery that the picture can be seen as a picture of a duck.

In order to single out the relevant features, let us say that, when we attend to a spatial whole within a visual sensation, then any parts of the sensation that are outside of, but continuous with, it become "appendages" to that whole. My suggestion about the duck-rabbit sensation produced by Figure I may be put by reference to those parts of the picture that one might call the "ear-bills." If I make these parts mere appendages, then I am in a position to discover that the picture may be seen as a picture of a rabbit. In other words, if I attend to any whole that is composed of "the eye" and the lines above and to the left of it, with the result that the "ear-bills" are outside that whole and therefore mere appendages to it, then I will be in a position to see the picture as a picture of a rabbit. And if I attend to a whole which contains "the eye," the lines above and below it, and also the "ear-bills," with the result that the latter are parts and not mere appendages of the whole that is attended to, then I will be in a position to see the picture as a picture of a duck.

Once one has found the rabbit in the picture, or the duck, *then* one may, sometimes only with effort, see *any* part of the picture as a part of a rabbit or as a part of a duck. But, according to the hypothesis here proposed, only certain spatial parts of the picture are such that attending to those parts leads to the discovery of a rabbit; and only certain other spatial parts are such that attending to those parts leads to the discovery of a duck.

I have said that when *I* attend to one part, then I first think of a rabbit and not of a duck, and that when I attend to another part then I first think of a duck and not of a rabbit. And, of course, the situation may be different in your case. Perhaps *you* are such that, when you attend to the former part you first think of it as a rabbit and not as a duck, and when you attend to the latter part you first think of it as a duck and not as a rabbit. The question "*Why* should it be one way with you and a different way with me?" *is* a causal question that the philosopher or descriptive psychologist is not in a position to answer. What I am here suggesting is not an answer to such causal questions. I am suggesting that attending to certain *spatial* features of the sensation is an essential part of the "*dawning of an aspect.*" This point is clear in the case of the black and white crosses (Figure 2). This case, unlike that of the duck-rabbit (Figure 1), does not involve "being reminded" of anything.

It is in this way, then, that I would answer the "what"-questions formulated above. As I have said, any adequate solution to the problem of the duck-rabbit, must provide answers to these questions. And I would add that, so far as I know, no alternative answers to the three questions are available.

Attending as a Subdeterminate Way of Sensing

Wittgenstein's question about the duck-rabbit may now be put as a question about *attending*. Is attending a matter of having a sensation or a matter of interpreting a sensation?

The answer may be found by considering the relation that *attending to a sensation* bears to *having a sensation*. The relation is one that W. E. Johnson called that of *subdeterminate* to *determinate* — or *subdeterminable* to *determinable*.[13] I will put this fact as follows:

(4) Attending-to-a-sensation is a *subdeterminate way* of having-a-sensation.

Before presenting a formal definition of this concept, I will illustrate its logical properties.

The clearest examples of the subdeterminable relation may be found within the sphere of the psychological. I will cite three: (1) the relation of judging to thinking; (2) the relation of joyfully anticipating to expecting; and (3) the relation of being red to being coloured. The logical properties of the relation of subdeterminate property to determinate property may best be seen by considering the third example — the relation of being red to being coloured.

The example, which is taken from Brentano, will serve our purpose, provided that we take the words "red" and "coloured" in their ordinary senses and therefore in the way in which Wittgenstein uses them in our citation from the *Remarks on Colour*. The relation of red to colour may seem to be no different logically from the relation of *red horse* to *red* and from the relation of *red horse* to *horse*. But there are logical similarities and logical differences between the two types of relation. This may be seen by describing three features that the property of being red bears to the property of being coloured.

(1) The property of being red implies the property of being coloured. (2) The property of being coloured does not imply the property of being red. In these first two respects the relation of red to colour is like that of red horse to horse and like that of red horse to red. But the relation of colour to red is also different from that of red to red horse and from that of horse to red horse. One does not *add* anything to colour to get red — at least, not in the sense in which one may be said to "add" the concept red to the concept horse in order to get the concept of red horse. Consider any property which is such that, the conjunction of that property conjunction with the property colour will yield a property that is equivalent to red. Examples are: (i) being red; (ii) being either non-coloured or red; and (iii) being either red or both non-coloured and round. Each of these three properties is conceptually dependent either upon the property red or upon the property colour. That is to say, one cannot *conceive* any one of these properties without thereby conceiving either the property red or the property colour. The third point, then, is this: (3) Red is not a conjunction of two conceptually independent properties one of which is equivalent to colour.

Our definition of the subdeterminate relation, therefore, is this:

D1   R is a *subdeterminate way* of being C $=_{df}$ R is
necessarily such that whatever has it has C; C is not
necessarily such that whatever has it has R; and any
property P which is such that C-and-P is logically equivalent
to R is necessarily such that whoever conceives P conceives
either C or R.

The pair of variables, "R" and "C", are satisfied, respectively, by the
following pairs: red and colour; judging and thinking; joyfully anticipating
and expecting; and attending to a sensation and having a sensation.

The Way That Attending Is Related to Interpreting

And what of the other side of the story? How is the act of attending
related to that of making an interpretation? The answer is that attending
is like making an interpretation — and unlike the mere having of a sensation — in the way in which it is "subject to the will." Indeed, this is
Wittgenstein's way of putting the matter. He compares *seeing an aspect*
— what we are now calling "attending to an aspect" — with *imagining*
something and he says that both "are subject to the will [*unterstehen dem
Willen*]" (213).

To understand the point, we should remind ourselves, that there is *one*
clear sense in which the visual sensation is *also* subject to the will. For I
can change my visual sensations "at will." I have only to turn my head or
move my eyes. But Wittgenstein is not denying this. In *what* sense, then,
can we say that the visual sensation, unlike the act of interpreting, may *not*
be subject to the will?[14]

Wittgenstein's own expression, "directly," will help us once again. The
visual sensation that I have, unlike my turning my head or moving my
eyes, and unlike my act of interpreting, is not something I can aim at *directly*. What is it to aim at a thing directly? I can aim at bringing about a
thing *directly* when I can aim at bringing it about without thereby aiming
at bringing about some *second* thing *for the purpose* of bringing about the
first thing. In other words, an act is *directly* subject to the will provided
that I can undertake it without undertaking some other thing for the purpose
of bringing it about.

(5) Attending to the features of a sensation is something that can be aimed at directly (it is something one can aim to do without aiming to do anything else in order to bring it about).

St. Augustine was aware of the significance of this concept.[15] He reminds us of the strange talent that a few favoured people happen to have — namely, that of being able directly to wiggle one's ears. Most of us, if we need to wiggle our ears, have to undertake something else in order to get our ears to move. The simplest thing is to reach up and move them with our hands. But the fortunate few can do it *directly*: they do not have to undertake some *other* thing in order to get their ears to move.

Wittgenstein was wholly aware of this distinction and its significance. He points out that our desires, although they may not be directly subject to the will, are indirectly subject to the will. His example is the desire to swim. He writes:

In the sense in which I can ever bring anything about (such as stomach-ache through over-eating), I can also bring about an act of willing. In this sense I bring about the act of willing to swim by jumping into the water (p.159e).

Proposed Solution to the Problem

Since, as I have said, our problem is one of descriptive psychology or "phenomenology," it is essential to note exactly what undefined psychological and philosophical concepts are needed to express the solution. In the present instance, the terms are those expressed by: (1) "x exemplifies y"; (2) "x is necessarily such that it is F"; (3) "sensation" (or "appearance"); (4) "x attends to y"; (5) "x is part of y"; and (6) "x conceives being-F." (The letter "F" in "being-F" may be replaced by any English predicate, in which case the resulting expression is a term.)

And so I will summarize my proposed solution to the problem, a solution that involves a philosophical analysis of the psychological concept of attending to a sensation.

One can attend to the spatial parts of a sensation. These parts are themselves spatial wholes; and they are such that attending to them precludes then attending to other spatial parts of the sensation.

To see a picture *as* a rabbit-picture is, in part, to attend to one of the spatial features of the appearance presented by the picture; and to see the picture as a duck-picture is, in part, to attend to another one of the spatial features of the appearance presented by the picture. And I have tried to suggest just *what* these features might be.

The concept of *attending* to a feature of a visual sensation or appearance is not a concept that is *added* to that of *having* the visual sensation in the way in which one might add the concept of an auditory sensation to that of a visual sensation. Attending to a feature of a visual sensation or appearance is a *subdeterminate way* of having that sensation or appearance, just as joyfully anticipating is a subdeterminate way of expecting.

Attending is like interpreting and unlike the mere having of a sensation in that it may be directly within one's power. To attend to a certain feature of what is appearing, once one knows what to look for, one has only to *act with the intention* of attending to that feature — to *aim* at attending to it. One need not act with the intention of doing some other thing that will then bring it about that one is attending to it. When we act with the intention of attending to what it is appearing, then, as Wittgenstein says, we will interpret what we see "and *see* it as we *interpret* it" (193).

Here, then, is one way of removing the philosophical puzzlement from the assertion that seeing the picture as a duck or as a rabbit is "half visual experience" and "half thinking."

Wittgenstein's Objections

But Wittgenstein seems to have objections to some of the points that I have just been making. And he also, inadvertently perhaps, tells us how to answer the objections.

The objections are suggested by the familiar passage:

One doesn't *take* what one knows as the cutlery at a meal *for* cutlery;
any more than one ordinarily tries to move one's mouth as one eats.
Or aims at moving it (195e).

The passage is inconsistent with *two* of the points that I have been trying to make.

It is inconsistent with my account of what it is for attending to be "subject to the will." For I have characterized being "directly within one's power" in terms of the *aims* or *intentions* that one has. And what I have said implies, contrary to what Wittgenstein suggests, that ordinarily when I eat I *do* aim at moving my mouth or *act with the intention* of moving my mouth.

And the first part of the quotation from Wittgenstein — "one doesn't *take* what one knows as the cutlery at a meal *for* cutlery" — is inconsistent with what I have tried to say about the nature of seeing. For in describing seeing, I said that when I can truly say that I perceive a picture, then the picture is appearing to me in a certain way and I judge that what is appearing to me in that way is a picture.

This means that, if I am at the table and say truly that I see a fork there, then there is a fork there that is appearing to me in a certain way, and I *judge* that the thing that is appearing to me in that way *is* a fork. And this, I'm sure, is a case of *taking* what one knows as a piece of cutlery at the table *for* a piece of cutlery — something that Wittgenstein denies that we normally do.

Why does he deny it? He is impressed by the fact that ordinarily one would never say that one is doing these things. And it is, of course, true that I am not likely to say to my companions at meal-time that I am taking something to be a fork or that I am about to act with the intention of moving my mouth. But is the fact that I wouldn't make these statements a reason for concluding that they would be false if I *were* to make them?

If you ask me what I am now seeing, I am not likely to reply, "I see a lady who is less than 9 feet tall." But my reluctance to say this is not due to the fact that the statement is *false*. If the statement is made in a situation like the present one, it is so obviously trivial that it isn't worth making. Moreover, when time is short, trivial statements prevent us from saying the things we ought to be saying. If the King has just died, one doesn't make an announcement to the effect that someone has recently passed away. But such an announcement would be true if it were to be made.

Or does Wittgenstein have a better reason for denying that I *take* the fork to be a fork and that I *act with the intention* of moving my mouth? If he does, I have no idea what it might be. And, in fact, as I have said, Wittgenstein himself gives us a reason for not accepting what he says in the passage about knives and forks and trying to move one's mouth.

It is true that one does not ordinarily try to move one's mouth when one eats — if "to try" means to experiment and to make an effort. And one doesn't *aim at* moving it — if "to aim" is to put oneself in a position and concentrate upon the object of one's act. But on ordinary occasions, one moves one's mouth *intentionally*; one acts *with the intention* of moving one's mouth.

And why do I say this? Wittgenstein gives us the answer:

> Let us not forget this: when 'I raise my arm', my arm goes up. And the problem arises: what is left over if I subtract the fact that my arm goes up from the fact that I raise my arm? (161e)

The answer to Wittgenstein's question is this. What is left over if I subtract the fact that my arm goes up from the fact that I raise my arm, is the fact that I have acted *with the intention* of moving my arm.

Wittgenstein's question about raising one's arm has its analogue in the case of perceiving there to be a picture. We may put it this way:

> Let us not forget this: when 'I perceive a picture before me', there is a picture before me. And the problem arises: what is left over if I subtract the fact that there is a picture before me from the fact that I see a picture before me?

What is left over is the fact that I *take* something to be a picture.

To those of you, if there are such, who think that there are no problems here for philosophers, I would call attention to Wittgenstein's own conclusion in *Philosophical Investigations* (p.212): "We find certain things puzzling, because we do not find the whole business of seeing puzzling enough."

Endnotes

1. Ludwig Wittgenstein, *Philosophische Bemerkungen* (Oxford: Basil Blackwell, 1964), p. 281.

2. The general background of the problem is discussed by Kevin Mulligan in "Seeing As and Association," Brentano Studien, Band I (Dettelbach: Verlag Josef F. Röll, 1989), pp. 129-152.

3. It should be noted that Wittgenstein says in one place that seeing is a *condition* [*Zustand*] and that interpreting is an act [*Handlung*]. See *Bemerkungen über die Philosophie der Psychologie* (Stuttgart: Reclam, 1984), Part I, Paragraph 1. This way of putting the matter presupposes that what is thus called "seeing" does not include interpreting; hence it would seem to be using "seeing" in the way in which Wittgenstein elsewhere uses having an impression. Compare Joachim Schulte, *Wittgenstein: Eine Einführung* (Stuttgart: Reclam, 1989), p.206.

4. This epistemic element enters into of the first-person statement "I see a picture," in a way that it does not enter into the third-person statement, "He sees a picture." If I say that *he* sees a picture, my statement has no implications about the beliefs or evidence that he happens to have. It implies that there is a picture that he sees, but it doesn't imply that he has any beliefs about pictures or that he is justified in having any beliefs about pictures.

5. There is also the *causal* relation that the object of sensation — the picture — bears to that psychological experience which is the having of the sensation (the sensing of the appearance). If one is to see a picture, then there must be such a causal relation. But in order to see a picture, the perceiver need not know anything about the details of the causal relation or about stimulus objects or physiological processes. And, as Wittgenstein says, it is not the causal relation that interests him when he discusses the duck-rabbit. He writes: "Here we are not asking ourselves what are the causes and what produces [*hervorruft*] this impression in a particular case" (201).

6. Ludwig Wittgenstein, *Remarks on Colours* (Oxford: Basil Blackwell, 1977). I have discussed these remarks in "What Are Wittgenstein's

Remarks on Colour About?", in *Proceedings of the 12th International Wittgenstein Symposium* (Vienna: Hölder-Pichler-Tempsky, 1988), pp.290-295.

7. In one of his earliest writings on the subject, Wittgenstein presented it as being as pertaining to "the phenomenological investigation of sense-impressions [*der phänomenologischen Untersuchung der Sinneseindrücke*]." See the quotation from Wittgenstein's *Philosophische Bemerkungen* at the beginning of this paper. This work was written in 1930.

8. Elsewhere he cites a different example of an indirect description. "Someone tells me: 'I looked at the flower, but was thinking of something else and was not conscious of its colour.' Do I understand this? I can imagine a significant context, say his going on: 'Then I suddenly *saw* it, and realized it was the one which . . .'" (211e). What he came to realize was the truth of a certain *indirect* description of the colour of the flower.

9. Meinong emphases the *a priori* nature of such statements in his "*Bemerkungen über den Farbenkörper und das Mischungsgesetz*" (1903); see Meinong's *Gesamtausgabe*, Band I, ed. Rudolf Kindinger and Rudolf Haller (Graz: Akademische Druck- und Verlagsanstalt, 1964), pp.497-526; esp. 502-3.

10. See J. M. Baldwin, ed., *Dictionary of Philosophy and Psychology* (New York and London: The Macmillan Company, 1901), vol. I, p.61.

11. These are terms that are used in psychological studies of these questions. See, for example, Evan L. Brown and Kenneth Deffenbacher, *Perception and the Senses* (Oxford University Press: New York and Oxford, 1979), Chapter Ten, "Perception of Visual Form," pp.322-355.

12. A related question that is not strictly relevant to our present problem is this: Can we attend to those wholes (if there are such) which are parts of the sensation and which are themselves *scattered objects* — for example, that whole (if there is such) composed of the "eye" of the duck-rabbit and one of the "ear-bills"? It would seem not. If we attend to any whole containing these two wholes, then that whole will also contain something that falls between the two inner wholes.

13. See W. E. Johnson, *Logic*, Vol. I (Cambridge: The University Press, 1921), p.176. Franz Brentano seems to have been the first to point out the importance of this concept. See his discussion of "one-sided detachability," in *Versuch über die Erkenntnis* (Hamburg: Felix Meiner Verlag, 1979), p.29. The relevant essay was written in 1903.

14. We should not, of course, be mislead by the substantival expression, "the will." The point is not that my acts of interpretation are usually under the control of a certain faculty that I have and that may appropriately be called "the will." The point is, rather, that my acts of interpretation are usually under *my* control and in a way in which my sensations are not under *my* control.

15. See *The City of God*, Book XIV, Ch. 24.

CHAPTER VI

Why Can't a Baby Pretend to Smile?
(*PI* §249 and Something Else)

Eike von Savigny

"Are we perhaps over-hasty in our assumption that the smile of an unweaned infant is not a pretence?" *PI* §249

In Wittgenstein's view, the smile of a baby is genuine by virtue of the rules of our language games that prevent babies from pretending to smile. This is due to the fact that to babies, we do not grant the position of a person who can guarantee us anything. Our conventions for treating babies are such that we do not hold them responsible; the genuineness of babies' smiles is, therefore, a conventional fact. This kind of conventionality, in the *PI*, extends to any psychological fact whatsoever. And that's the real point of what I am going to suggest as an interpretation of §249.

1. The introductory sentence of §249 conceals a 'grammatical sentence'[1] in Wittgenstein's sense. This is a fact about it which is virtually obvious, given its context, viz. §§247–252, which are apparently unconnected both with the question preceding them in §246 (Who is in the better position to know about my pain - myself or others?) and with the question that follows in §253 (Can others have my pains?). These later questions have a clear role in the overall context of the private language argument; thus the sequence running from §247 to §252 acquires the sharp outline of a spot that has spoiled a fine pattern, and becomes as coherent as a spot might possibly be.

What is the sequence about? This is easy to tell from §248, which also defines the author's intention in spoiling the pattern, and from §251. §248 tells us that the sentence, "Sensations are private", is comparable to a sentence that, unless it is imagined to be uttered in far-fetched circumstances, strongly calls for being used in a definition-like explanation, viz. of a certain card game called "patience". And §251 introduces the sentence, "Every rod has a length", as an example clearly intended to clarify the character at least of the sentence, "I can't imagine the opposite", and gives a definition-like translation: "we call something (or *this*[2]) 'the length of a rod' but nothing 'the length of a sphere'." Leaving aside the question as to whether the example does justice to the nature of what it is intended to illustrate, we may note that Wittgenstein's procedure shows that in this context, he uses sentences like "I can't imagine the opposite" as examples of statements about what we call such and such (at least as far as what we are concerned with are statements where our power of imagination could not possibly be increased by learning from new experiences).

In using the words "the picture attaching to the grammatical proposition" in §251 e, Wittgenstein explicitly refers to "this picture, in connexion with this proposition" in §251 d, where the "proposition" is: "Every rod has a length." Thus what he calls a grammatical sentence is a sentence primarily suitable for explaining one or several key words occurring in it; it may even be assumed - consistently with the whole text of the *PI* - that a sentence is called a grammatical sentence only when it is actually being used for this explanatory business. (Wittgenstein does not pay very much attention to the possible distinction between the meaning of a sentence and the meanings of utterances of it.) In §251 b the words "I can't imagine the opposite" are characterized as "a defence against something [...] which is really a grammatical [proposition]". This grammatical sentence is not stated explicitly; plausible formulations that draw on the examples in §251 a might be: "My images *cannot* be other than private", or: "Only I myself *can* know whether I am feeling pain." (The latter example is a quotation, of course, except for the fact that the italics are mine.)

The next piece of direct evidence for the assumption that our sequence is about grammatical sentences is, of course, the first one occurring in it, viz. the opening sentence of §247: "Only you *can* know if you had that intention." (Italics mine.) It shows that a grammatical sentence need not simply be used as an explanation of words; for although Wittgenstein himself comments: "One might tell someone this when one was explaining the meaning of the word 'intention' to him", he goes on to state that when being used in such an explanation, the sentence "means: *that* is how we use it." This step from explaining the meaning to explaining the use would be completely insignificant with Wittgenstein of all people, if he himself had not gone on to explain, in the bracketed sentence that follows, why the reminder is important at this place: "(And here 'know' means that the expression of uncertainty is senseless.)" That is to say, if the circumstances are such that the sentence "Only you can know if you had that intention" is being used as an explanation of the meaning of the word "intention", then the person addressed is being told that she is not to express uncertainty while telling anybody what her intention was because it is part of the use of the word "intention" that a person who explains what her intention was must not do so with uncertainty. (I interpret "the expression of uncertainty" as meaning "manifesting uncertainty", viz. while explaining one's intention; this is possible, at least as far as the German text is concerned.) Thus what Wittgenstein says here is that in explaining a word by using a grammatical sentence, one may inform the addressee about facts about its use such as what authority a speaker can claim in using the word.

Thus it seems plausible, and perhaps not in need of further argument, that "*Only* such and such *can* ..." or "Such and such *cannot* ..." sentences, in the sequence under consideration, figure as grammatical sentences in the sense explained above. This assumption throws some light on the opening question of §250: "Why can't a dog simulate pain?" Going on the assumption that this is a "grammatical question" (for this term see *PI* §47), i.e. a question calling for being answered by a grammatical sentence, and given that the question clearly presupposes that a dog cannot simulate pain, we may assume that for Wittgenstein, the sentence "A dog cannot simulate pain" is a grammatical sentence. If so, it ought to be usable for explaining a word occurring within it; because of the question immediately following it, "Is he too honest?", I take it that the word to be explained is "to simulate". The suggestion has been made that what is being explained is the word "pain"[3]; but although this interpretation could possibly be made to fit in with the overall private language argument context, it seems to be excluded by the statement in the section's last sentence that the dog's behaviour cannot be *real simulation*, rather than that it cannot simulate *real pain*. (The reason why this is so, viz. that the necessary surroundings are missing, will be discussed in section 2.)

Now given the assumption that, placed among the sections considered so far, §249 ought to conceal a grammatical sentence, possible candidates are: "The smile of an unweaned infant *cannot* be a pretence"; "we *know* that the smile of an unweaned infant is not a pretence"; "it is not an *assumption* of ours that the smile of an unweaned infant is not a pretence". Furthermore, given the fact that the bracketed sentence refers to lying and that the grammatical question introducing §250 is likely to concern the word "simulation", I take the likeliest word to be explained in using one of those grammatical sentences to be the word "pretence";[4] Wittgenstein's reason for holding that it is a matter of the use of language that an unweaned infant cannot pretend to smile I shall try to outline in sect. 2. There is also the possibility that what is at stake are, rather, questions concerning learning capacities ("Lying is a language-game that needs to be learned", §249; "Perhaps it is possible to teach him", §250); with this I shall deal in section 3.

2. Since in §249 the German for "pretence" is "Verstellung", we may assume that what a baby cannot do is pretend to smile in the sense of smiling dishonestly; pretending in the sense of stage-acting does not come into play, then, and can all the more be disregarded in what follows because if it were accepted as a possible interpretation, my point could be argued even more easily. Now pretending to do some special thing in a sense akin to lying, i.e. akin to pretending to give true information, is parasitic on actually doing this very thing in the same sense as lying is parasitic on giving true information. By "parasitic", I mean a particular state of affairs; let me explain this by beginning with explaining part of what is involved in informing people, given Wittgenstein's overall view of language-games. To a certain extent this explanation is reconstructive; it represents an attempt to make sense of what Wittgenstein means when he is saying that an expression derives its meaning from its use, function, or role in language-games, that understanding and meaning an expression manifest themselves in rule-governed ways of dealing with them (be it in the position of the speaker or of the addressee), and in particular that making a note (§260), giving descriptions (§§290, 291), and asserting (§486 a) have functions which *behaviour subsequent to the utterance* is important for. The reconstructive proposal is restricted to a necessary condition: If a speaker *S* informs an addressee *A* that *p*, then *A* may, at the expense of *S*, rely on its being the case that p.[5]

It is immediately obvious that and why Wittgenstein would never have subscribed to such a formula: It is very general, and anyone who wants to go by it is forced to accept very strained interpretations of "relying on some fact at the expense of some person". A very formal instance is that of a clerk in a bank office who informs a customer that the latter can buy certain shares at a certain price; if the customer then sells other shares at an unfavourable rate in order to avail himself of the money he needs for the first transaction, and if it turns out that the clerk had reported a too low price, then the bank has to pay the customer's loss. A very informal instance: If I inform you that the public swimming pool is open, and if going there you find it closed, I have to "pay up" for your loss of time by accepting your scolding. However, general as our formula may be, Wittgenstein himself asks us to consider under what kind of circumstances we would say that people in a newly discovered country had a language that contained orders (*PI* §206), and this is just one example; reports are on the same footing, as §207 b shows. Thus even if our necessary condition is rather general, it may well give us the correct general idea of what circumstances to look for if we wonder whether certain noises mean that people are informing each other.

If we accept the condition for the sake of interpretation, we can easily see why an unweaned infant could not possibly inform us about any fact: We simply would not hold him responsible if what he had said turned out to be wrong; therefore, we should not rely *at the baby's expense* on what the baby had said, even if God had endowed him with miraculous linguistic capacities. In such a case we might, of course, rely on his utterance because previous experience had taught us that his utterances usually turn out to be true; but this would mean relying on a natural sign, a symptom or an indicator, at our own risk. We should treat the baby like a Pythia whom we may rely upon without, however, being in a position to complain if she is wrong. In order to be an agent in the language-game of informing, people must have access to the position of a person who has to pay up for damages. Babies haven't, and that's why they cannot inform us. We simply do not give them the opportunity.

In this respect, we treat babies like dogs. "Why can't a dog simulate pain?" (§250) Because if a dog howls on certain occasions, his way of howling being indistinguishable from when he howls because his tail is jammed in the door, and if the veterinarian finds out that everything is o.k. with him except for the fact that some mischievous person has trained him to howl that way on such occasions, we do *not* deduct the veterinarian's bill from the money we normally spend on the dog's food. True, we have been taken in; but we do not blame him. Poor dog — we do not take him seriously; "the surroundings which are necessary for this behaviour to be real simulation are missing". (§250) The necessary surroundings would consist of people who took him seriously. Note that we could be people who blamed their dogs; but we aren't.

We need not stick to the necessary condition stated above for informing. All we need is, firstly, that for someone to be in a position to inform another person, the former must be subject to some rules or other, and secondly, that an unweaned infant is not subject to these rules. He cannot, then, be a participant in the language-game of informing. Thus, my interpretation can also be accepted by someone taking a Gricean stance on informing,[6] provided he requires that the operative intentions be conventionalized (as they are with Lewis, Schiffer, and Bennett[7]). Without such an element which safely places informing in a network of rule-governed behaviour, my interpretation will not do. Note, however, that a purely intentionalist construal of informing, lying, and pretending is no good for an exegesis of our passage; for *in the text, there is not even the faintest hint* at the point (which might otherwise be quite sound) that an unweaned infant cannot have iterated intentions. In contrast, the conventional element is signalled, in the closer context, by two verbal parallels in §250: Its first sentence, "Why can't a dog simulate pain?", asks a question almost identical with the opening question of §268, "Why can't my right hand give my left hand money?", and the word "surroundings" clearly refers to a social system in §584 (on which see below, section 4).

P.M.S. Hacker *(ad loc.)* gives no reason for his claim that "surroundings" refers to a wider scope of the dog's individual behaviour; "Umgebung" would be a peculiar word to refer to such a thing. Be this as it may, Wittgenstein observes, in the *PI*, a consistent use of "surroundings" ("Umgebung"). Besides §250, there are five further sections where the word is used other than to designate a physical scenery; in all of them, the word denotes a socially defined situation. The most salient case of §583, 584 will be discussed in section 4. Here are the remaining ones: According to §412, uttering the sentence, 'THIS is produced by a brain-process!' in surroundings different from, say, those of being a subject in a psychological experiment, means uttering it "in the surroundings" different from those "in which it would have an everyday and unparadoxical sense". In §535, the "surroundings" relevant for the character of a smile are different where the smile is being directed either at a playing child or at a suffering enemy. And §540 says: "'Isn't it very odd that I should be unable — even *without* the institution of language and all its surroundings [singular in the German text!] — to think that it will soon stop raining?'" The interlocutor's question is rhetorical from Wittgenstein's point of view.

I have relied on the parallel between a pretence and a lie because Wittgenstein hints at it himself. However, it waits to be substantiated: Are there rules for smiling such that whoever wants to be in a position to pretend to smile has to be subject to these rules, and such that babies are not subject to them? True, we hold each other responsible for what we say; but do we do so for our smiles? The answer is clearly yes. If I spoil my hostess' tablecloth with red wine and look at her in despair, then if she smiles kindly she accepts the obligation not to blame me; if her husband, in contrast, smiles mockingly, he thereby accepts the potential challenge to be able to show that I was at least clumsy. If *A* has to run an errand for *B* in a specific way but does it differently, then in reporting this to *B* he may smile in a way clearly asking for *B's* excuse, thus accepting that *B* might justly blame him; and if *B* then smiles back in a way manifesting that he puts up with it, he commits himself to not blaming *A* any further. In the course of a conversation, by reacting to a suggestion with an embarrassed smile, one warrants the speaker's expectation to still have something to say about it. And a mutual smile may of course, under suitable circumstances, be nothing less than an outspoken agreement.

I wonder whether such observations are in any way surprising when connected with observations on truth-telling and lying; if so, it may well help to recall the outlines of plausible ethological explanations. Social animals have to adapt their behaviour to each other, and in order to do so, they must rely on the most diverse kinds of cues in each others' behaviour. As far as they learn to do so, and as far as providing such cues is learnable, too, they will reach an equilibrium of what to expect on account of cues, and when to provide them: viz. to provide them only when prepared for the resulting expectations. Such equilibria are likely to be stabilized by those unkind reactions that are probable in cases where expectations are disappointed. Now smiling, with humans, is one of the most important cues of all. E.g., in suitable circumstances, it rouses the expectation that the smiling person is pleased; therefore, if she smiles although she is not pleased, she has to expect to be treated as if she were.

3. Thus according to my interpretation, a baby cannot pretend to smile because we simply refuse to count as a cue, to be answered for by the baby, whatever he might do. This interpretation, I agree, is not the most obvious one; for in §249 b Wittgenstein says: "(Lying is a language-game that needs to be learned like any other one.)" And the same thought recurs in one of the last sentences of *PI* II xi: "A child has much to learn before it can pretend." (p. 229) The stress on learning seems to point in a different direction: It might be the case that in order to acquire certain advanced competencies, the learning person has to take advantage of more basic ones. The capacity to pretend to do *x* may in this way presuppose the capacity to do *x*; or at any rate, the capacity to pretend to smile may presuppose the capacity to smile.

Now although I seriously doubt that one can attribute to the *PI* any learning theories at all, let us concede the point about acquiring the capacity of pretending to smile. Then in order for the sentence "An unweaned infant cannot pretend to smile" to be established as true, we have to assume further that since the baby can smile (not from birth, but babies learn it within some weeks), there is a specific obstacle for his learning to pretend to do so as long as he is still an unweaned infant. There may be one; however, *it is not hinted at in the text*. And note that not just any obstacle whatsoever will do; the obstacle must be such that it acquires its role as an obstacle from the rules of our language-games. Again, there may exist such obstacles; however, *they aren't hinted at in the text,* either. Thus even if it were the case that a person needed much more experience in social behaviour than a baby can conceptually have had (e.g. because he will no longer count as a baby as soon as he begins to actively participate in social transactions), the interpretation would lack a textual basis. On the other hand, the interpretation given above makes sense of the direct juxtaposition, with §249, of §250. And on the general level, the way indicated above of interpreting the sentence quoted from *PI* p.229, is at least put into doubt by II iv. For the rhetorical question in §249, "And on what experience is our assumption based?", has an obvious parallel in the sentences: "Do I also *believe* that he isn't an automaton? [...] I am not of the *opinion* that he has a soul." (p.178.) For this point, the history of how the other person has learnt does not matter at all; what matters is: "My attitude towards him is an attitude towards a soul." (Ibid.) Our attitude towards a baby is not an attitude towards a responsible person.

A related, although slightly different, answer to the opening question in §249 might be found in the distinction Wittgenstein draws, in §244, between natural and acquired expressive behaviour.[8] Let us disregard the fact that babies learn to smile (a fact Wittgenstein may well have been unaware of); then he might be taken to mean that an unweaned infant's smile, being a piece of natural expressive behaviour, cannot be a pretence *if this behaviour is actually used,* in §249, *as an example of natural as distinguished from acquired* expressive behaviour. This, however, is extremely doubtful in view of the context: According to §250, the dog's howling would not be simulation although he has been trained to howl. Furthermore, §249 would be misplaced within a sequence on grammatical sentences; for it can hardly be a rule of language that none of a baby's expressive behaviour can be acquired. Are we perhaps over-hasty in our assumption that the 'Ouch' of an unweaned infant is not a pretence?

Lastly, the stress on learning is not at all at odds with the interpretation given in sect. 2; we just have to remember that at all places in the *PI* where Wittgenstein makes learning his subject matter he relates it to the idea of the learner's acquiring the competence *to follow certain rules*, or of *becoming initiated into a language-game*. It is only after initiation that the learner counts as a person that the rules apply to; on this interpretation, the baby's disadvantage is essentially the same one.[9] (I am referring to learning in the sense in which it is used in §249 and on p. 229, i.e. in the sense of acquiring capacities, be it by way of training or instruction or without any intentional assistance, i.e. in the only sense of "lernen" in German; I am not referring to learning in the sense of coming to know. In §246 b, Wittgenstein twice uses "lernen" in the latter sense; this is one of his more salient anglicisms.) That is to say, although of course learning means acquiring competences, what Wittgenstein is interested in in this connection is a special competence, viz. that of rule-following. Learning one's native tongue is the most frequent example; next in number come the cases of learning how to follow algebraic rules. (These passages comprise all entries in Kaal-McKinnon's concordance[10] not explicitly referred to in the following.) At §137, the rule to be learned is an explicitly formulated rule of syntax; §156 discusses learning how to read. §535 asks: "What happens when we learn to feel the ending of a church mode as ending?"; as placed in its context, the answer is the same as the one given on p.208: "The substratum of this experience is the mastery of a technique." §§9, 159, 160, and p.180 refer learning by heart; if what is learned by heart is still corrigible behaviour, this does not contradict my point, and if it isn't it is not relevant for learning to pretend. §§52, 89, 340 and 413 are comments on what the philosopher has to learn. On p.174, as well as possibly in §386 (where it otherwise would refer to language learning), "lernen" is misused in the same anglicizing manner as in §246 b; and in §308 it occurs as part of "näher kennenlernen", something like "coming to know more about", which is out of the question in §249.

The only real difficulties might be presented by the repeated references to learning, toward the end of *PI* II xi, where what is to be acquired is knowledge of human nature of a kind that provides one with "a 'nose' for" the genuineness of an expression. But even if the explicit references, in this very context, to correctness and rules on p.227 are played down, the context teaches us something very interesting. It begins right after the famous lion aphorism on p.223, and, running through to the end of *PI* II xi, it discusses different types of certainty. One fact about the sequence is remarkable, given the style of the *PI* in general: It states the thesis which it is going to establish in explicit form, viz. on p.224 — "The kind of certainty is the kind of language-game." I think the meaning is pretty obvious: Different language-games differ by their rules; different rules may provide speakers with different kinds of safeguards against attacks. This is why the kinds of certainty are different, e.g., in mathematics, in talk about colours, or in the assessment of other people's feelings; certainty with respect to the conviction a person expresses is likened to social security. What a person has to learn, in order to be able appropriately to give expression to certainty within these language-games, is to recognize whether or not she actually is in a safe position — safe with respect to the rules of the respective language-game. Therefore, learning, here as elsewhere, means learning to master rules.

It is a conventional fact, then, that the baby's smile is not a pretence. As is the case with all conventional facts, this one could possibly be different, too. If our babies acquired many of their capacities much more quickly than they in fact do, we might possibly treat them differently. E.g., if three-week old babies were very much like six-year-old children in those respects which are relevant for our practice of requesting honesty from children and blaming them for lies, then it might be the case that we should treat the babies in the way we treat older children. We might then rely on them and punish them when disappointed. If our conventions are actually different, this is because it belongs to "certain very general facts of nature" (p.230) that unweaned infants are very much unlike six-year-old children.

4. In its context, §249 has no function over and above that of providing just another example of a grammatical sentence;[11] however, the more interesting fact about it is that it foreshadows Wittgenstein's treatment of *non-linguistic expressive behaviour* on the model of *linguistic utterances*. This in turn means that just as a person can *mean something* with a given *linguistic utterance* only insofar as others are prone to deal with this utterance in a way appropriate to this meaning, so no *mental fact* can obtain about a person unless others are prone to deal with her *expressive behaviour* in a way appropriate to this mental fact.

How a person can mean something definite in using a linguistic expression is stated in a remarkably explicit form in the *PI* §190. (It is only one of many strange facts about the sham discussion relating to Wittgenstein's alleged meaning-scepticism that the book which staged the discussion does not even mention this section in passing.) Having worked out, in §189, the point that if an unknown algebraic formula is to determine its applications, it has to be explained by reference to a formula which has got an established use, Wittgenstein then goes on to state, in §190: "*That* is, therefore, how meaning something can determine the steps in advance. " (Wittgenstein's italics.)[12] He is distinguishing two cases there. By meaning something in using an expression one can either go along with the established way of using it; then the steps to be taken in accordance with how the sign is meant are determined by the established way of using it. Or else one is using a sign which has either not got an established way of being used or is being used in a way different from the established way of using it; then in order to use it while meaning something in using it, one has to adapt oneself to the established way of using some other sign; in a way, one is implicitly committing oneself to this latter way which will, then, determine how the expression is to be applied. That is to say, whether or not the psychological fact that a person means something actually obtains depends on the existence of established customs; it is a conventional fact.

The generalization to any psychological fact whatsoever which is foreshadowed in §249 is the main topic, or at least one of the main topics, of the second half of part I of the *PI*, roughly §§316-693. I shall content myself with two examples, viz. those of hoping and imagining, because I can make use of two fairly concise texts to illustrate my thesis. (It cannot, of course, be *established* by such sporadic evidence.) The first is taken from a sequence, running from §571 to §587, which is designed to establish how the expression of a psychological fact determines the latter's nature:

583.   [...] Could someone have a feeling of ardent love or hope for the space of one second — *no matter what* preceded or followed this second? — What is happening now has significance — in these surroundings. The surroundings give it its importance. And the word "hope" refers to a phenomenon of human life. (A smiling mouth *smiles* only in a human face.)
584.   Now suppose I sit in my room and hope that N.N. will come and bring me some money, and suppose one minute of this state could be isolated, cut out of its context; would what happened in it then not be hope? — Think, for example, of the words which you perhaps utter in this space of time. They are no longer part of this language. And in different surroundings the institution of money doesn't exist either.

A coronation is the picture of pomp and dignity. Cut one minute of this proceeding out of its surroundings: The crown is being placed on the head of the king in his coronation robes. — But in different surroundings gold is the cheapest of metals, its gleam is thought vulgar. There the fabric of the robe is cheap to produce. A crown is a parody of a respectable hat. And so on. "

The message is obvious. Just as whether a certain performance "is the picture of the pomp and dignity" depends on the conventional significance of its surroundings, so whether or not *my present state is one of hoping* that N.N. will come and bring me some money depends on the fact that *my behaviour is expressive of hope in our form of life*, whereas it could count as expressing something different in surroundings where socially established customs were significantly different.

Although the message is obvious, the argument is less so; for the possible conventional modifications Wittgenstein is referring to in §584 a relate firstly to linguistic expressions and, hence, do not go beyond what we learned about meaning from §190, and secondly to money. Now everyone will agree that hoping for money is conventional insofar as what is hoped for is conventional; establishing the conventional character of psychological facts ought to show this also for hoping that the rain will cease and things like that. This is why I turn to my second example, imagining, where Wittgenstein hints at an argument which is suitable to show that for any p, "x imagines that p" is a conventional fact about x. The example is that I imagine people to be concealing frightful pain:

391. [...] And if I imagine this — what do I do; what do I say to myself; how do I look at the people? Perhaps I look at one and think: "It must be difficult to laugh when one is in such pain", and much else of the same kind. I as it were play a part, *act as if* the others were in pain. When I do this I am said for example to be imagining, ..." (Italicized "*als ob*" for "*as if*" in the German original.)

I do not wish to attribute to Wittgenstein the general *theory* that imagining that p is a kind of stage performance of p; but the idea is clearly present, and if we pursue it we arrive at the conclusion that whether or not my behaviour expresses my imagining that p depends on whether or not it comes close enough to a stage performance of p. And what counts as a stage performance of p in different civilizations is, of course, a conventional matter.

In the *Philosophical Investigations*, general arguments of this kind are to be found for several psychological facts besides meaning something, hoping and imagining. Understanding, in its dispositional sense, is on par with meaning something; it is expressed in correct application (see e.g. §§145-150), where correctness is a matter of social guarantee (§§145, 185). On the relevance, for pain, of suitable social reactions see §§284, 286, 287. In the second half of part I, further salient passages, on mental facts other then meaning, include §§319 ff., where thinking a thought is compared with writing it down, the consequence for correctness being highlighted in §§325 b, 337f.; §§445, 452, where linguistic and non-linguistic expressive behaviour play identical roles[13] in determining what a person is wishing, planning, or expecting; §581, where expecting x is linked to a situation that warrants the expectation; §§628-632, where 'willing' an action is related to being master of its execution (mastering something is socially determined in the same way as is rule following).[14]

I suggest there is, in these arguments, a common pattern: A given psychological fact obtains about a person P only if P exhibits a pattern of behaviour expressive of that fact (where the pattern covers long stretches of time, and where it includes patterns of suppressing and the like); and a given pattern of behaviour is expressive of a certain psychological fact only if it is placed within social surroundings of reacting to it which are such that they characterize the behaviour as being expressive of just this fact. This, then, is the way in which the argument on a baby's smile being genuine is universalizable.

Endnotes

1. "Grammatischer Satz" is translated as "grammatical proposition" by Prof. Anscombe. I keep this usage only when quoting her text.

2. All italics in quotations from the *PI* are Wittgenstein's unless stated otherwise.

3. G. Hallett, *A Companion to Wittgenstein's "Philosophical Investigations"*, Ithaca, N.Y., Cornell U.P., 1977; *ad loc.*

4. P.M.S. Hacker, in his *Analytical Commentary on the Philosophical Investigations, Vol. III, Wittgenstein: Mind and Language*, Oxford, Blackwell, 1990 assumes (*ad loc.*) that the baby example connects with 244. Then why did Wittgenstein place it here than next to §244? Arrangement of context is a master clue to identifying threads of PI arguments, and the §§247–252 sequence is conspicuously coherent. As regards content, any affinity of §249 to §244 is only superficial because of the proximity of §250; on this, see p.111.

5. If this condition is essential for an utterance to constitute an undertaking that *p*, then it is identical with John Searle's "essential rule" for statements; see his *Speech Acts*, Cambridge, Cambridge U.P., 1969, p.66.

6. David Pears and Ernst Tugendhat (in discussion) have pointed out the possibility that Wittgenstein might be up to an unweaned infant's being conceptually incompetent to form higher-order intentions.

7. *Convention*, Cambridge, Mass., Harvard U.P., 1969, esp. pp.154-159; *Meaning*, Oxford, Clarendon Pr., 1972, ch.V; *Linguistic Behaviour*, Cambridge, Cambridge U.P., ch.7.

8. This point was raised, in discussion, by Brian McGuinness.

9. Lying, *pace* Wittgenstein, is not a language-game; it relates to reporting, informing, promising, and to many other language-games as cheating relates to playing a game. The last sentence of §249 had better be expressed on the model of the quotation from p.229, and in the light of the fact

that learning to follow a rule means becoming initiated into a language game, it would read: "A child has to be initiated into a language-game before it can cheat in playing it."

10. Hans Kaal, Alastair McKinnon, *Concordance to Wittgenstein's Philosophiche Untersuchungen,* Leiden, Brill, 1975.

11. Since what Wittgenstein wants to show is that sentences like "Sensations are private" are grammatical sentences, we should only expect that some of his instances of grammatical sentences are sentences that contain psychological predicates. What matters is what he uses his instances as instances of.

12. I have modified Prof. Anscombe's translation, which seems to me to suggest a guarded statement; in the German text, I find no sign of noncommittal expression.

13. In his thoroughgoing interpretation of §445 and context, Robert Arrington attributes the content-defining role of expressions of psychological states to linguistic expressions only. However, §445 must not be read in isolation from §452 where it is said explicitly that the expression of expectation can be *seen.* See R. Arrington, 'Making contact in language: the harmony between thought and reality', in *id.* and H.J. Glock eds., *Wittgenstein's Philosophical Investigations: Text and Context,* London, Routledge, 1991, pp.175-202.

14. On the exegetical details, see my *Wittgenstein's "Philosophische Untersuchungen": Ein Kommentar für Leser,* Frankfurt a.M., Klostermann, Vol. I 1988, Vol II 1989.

I wish to thank Glenn W. Most for correcting the English text.

CHAPTER VII

Playing With Language:
Language-Games Reconsidered

Bernd Frohmann

I

The metaphor of language as music occurs in several places in Wittgenstein's writings. One example is the parenthetical remark in this passage from the lectures on the foundations of mathematics:

> Let's suppose a tribe which liked to decorate their walls with calculations. (An analogy with music.) They learn a calculus like our mathematicians in school . . . they use the calculus solely for the purpose of decorating walls.[1]

Another example occurs in the *Philosophical Investigations*:

> §232. Let us imagine a rule intimating to me which way I am to obey it; that is, as my eye travels along the line, a voice within me says: "*This* way!" ... I teach ... some way of hearkening, some kind of receptivity.
> §233. It would also be possible to imagine such a training in a sort of arithmetic. Children could calculate, each in his own way as long as they listened to their inner voice and obeyed it. Calculating in this way would be like a sort of composing.

The following remarks are not intended as an interpretation of these passages for I want to use them simply to motivate a piece of "anthropological science fiction"[2] of my own, in which mathematics is compared to musical composition, in order to show how a specific reading of the role of language-games can be elicited from Wittgenstein's trope, and to comment upon some more general issues of interpretation of his text.

Suppose a tribe which, like the mathematical wall decorators, also likes to use mathematical symbols for aesthetic purposes. These people might be called "mathematical composers". They use mathematics, first, in practical applications, just as we do (this is a point of disanalogy with Wittgenstein's wall decorators), for example, to balance their bank statements, to calculate the results of engineering problems, to figure out the date of their vacations, to play the odds at the race track, and so on. But there is also a highly educated group among them who use mathematical symbols much as composers in our culture use musical notation. A mathematical pattern is pursued because it is pleasing, or because it is thought to express something not otherwise expressible, or as a display of virtuoso talent, or as an expression of an "avant-garde" sensibility, that is, for a wide variety of reasons analogous to those for which our composers write music.

For the mathematical composers, the rules governing correctness and incorrectness of calculations in practical life simply don't apply to their compositions. They all learn mathematics in its everyday applications, just as everyone else does, and they are just as concerned as the others in calculating the right bank balance. But they differ from the rest because they have at some point in their lives been struck by the beauty and profundity of various patterns that can be created with mathematical notation. They study their "old masters", pioneers of magnificent "mathematical concepts" and deep "mathematical theorems", who first elaborated extremely compelling mathematical patterns over 2,000 years ago, perhaps under the influence of such questions as "what *is* a number?" or "what is equality, addition, multiplication?", to which their "moderns" have contributed similar concerns regarding, e.g., differentiation, topology, and set theory. Their responses to these questions take the form of generating mathematical patterns, the precise point of which is that they are not subject to the rules of practical calculation. If someone points out that the pattern is "incorrect" by appeal to school mathematics or to how children learn to calculate, they thereby betray a misunderstanding of what the mathematical composers are at. (Of course, there may be a "realist school" among them which argues against "artifice" in mathematical composition, and which claims to see as much value in the practical rules of mathematics for their compositions as some of our musicians see in folk melodies for musical composition, but these "realists" are no more able to clinch their arguments by appeal to "correctness" when it comes to mathematical composing, even if they express themselves by means of that concept, than can our corresponding "realist" musicians when it comes to composing music.)

Even though the mathematical composers are not bound by the rules of practical mathematics, it would be as wrong to say that they are not bound at all, as it would be to say that *any* sequence of notes is acceptable as a musical composition. Unlike practical calculators, who all go on in the same way when given, for example, the formula $y = x^2$, the mathematical composers are not constrained by *those* rules, yet their compositions are not *random*. There is such a thing as education in what they do, and such a thing as naive versus expert, even profound, composition. Their compositions are grouped into "schools" and "styles", and people with their higher mathematical education (and there may be talented amateurs) feel attracted to one or another of these, feeling more at home in one style than in another, and better able to freely compose, to demonstrate mastery, virtuosity, and a flair for independent "thinking", in one style rather than in another. Some may be "converted", perhaps in their maturity, from their youthful style, just as the work of their great composers may exhibit an "early" and a "late" period, while others show only a gradual "development". Thus, although their "goings on" from formula to formula will not be "correct" by their school mathematics, they nonetheless do *go on* in patterned ways.

The mathematical composers believe, and it is accepted in their culture, that something great, deep and serious is expressed in their mathematical compositions. The ability to compose in a manner acceptable to the coterie of advanced composers (sometimes acceptance comes late, even after death) is taken as the demonstration of penetrating insight into the meaning of mathematical concepts. Their culture includes, of course, those ubiquitous cynics who belittle all but practical activities, but their complaints carry as little weight in their culture as analogous complaints carry in ours.

Now a philosopher appears among them, leaving an obscure but powerful book called *Mathematical Investigations*. He promotes a new method, forcing a distinction between "philosophical" and "ordinary" uses of mathematical symbols, by means of ingenious comparisons between mathematical composition and practical calculation. He encourages comparisons between uses of mathematical symbols and simple "games" that might be played with them, sometimes presenting these as ways in which a child might be taught arithmetic. Many of his games involve objects and actions directly, for example, the game of addition in which three nuts are placed next to two others, and a technique of counting is described, whereby a use of the expression "2 + 3 = 5" is described. He claims that genuine mathematics, that is, meaningful rather than nonsensical uses of mathematical expressions, is actually made up of atomistic, heterogeneous "mathematical games", similar to those offered in his book. He says that "a perspicuous representation" of these ordinary, everyday, practical mathematical games, will relieve the "confusion", the "mental cramp", which he says is at the root of the motivation to compose in mathematics. For the mathematical composers, he claims, do not practice *mathematics* at all, but produce *nonsense* instead. Comparisons between mathematical compositions and the simple, ordinary, practical "games" which make up the "civil life" of mathematics, reveal that in compositions, mathematical expressions are employed outside their "natural homes", thus becoming unhinged from their connections to the world, which are required for *sense*. Once returned from their "philosophical" uses of mathematical notation to "ordinary" uses, the composers will find peace from their intellectual torments and conceptual confusions.

II

How much resemblance is there between my imaginary *Mathematical Investigations* and the *Philosophical Investigations*? I would like to press some disanalogies, in order to identify a reading of language-games which will, I hope, connect in a useful way with some general interpretations of Wittgenstein's text.

PI §527–534 is a useful place to begin, because there, Wittgenstein's metaphor of language as music is in full flower:

§527. Understanding a sentence is much more akin to understanding a theme in music than one may think. What I mean is that understanding a sentence lies nearer than one thinks to what is ordinarily called understanding a musical theme. Why is just *this* the pattern of variation in loudness and tempo? One would like to say "Because I know what it's all about." But what is it all about? I should not be able to say. In order to 'explain' I could only compare it with something else which has the same rhythm (I mean the same pattern). ...

§531. We speak of understanding a sentence in the sense in which it can be replaced by another which says the same; but also in the sense in which it cannot be replaced by any other. (Any more than one musical theme can be replaced by another.) In the one case the thought in the sentence is something common to different sentences; in the other, something that is expressed only by these words in these positions. (Understanding a poem.)

§532. Then has "understanding" two different meanings here? I would rather say that these kinds of use of "understanding" make up its meaning, make up my *concept* of understanding. For I *want* to apply the word "understanding" to all this.

§533. But in the second case how can one explain the expression, transmit one's comprehension? Ask yourself: How does one *lead* anyone to comprehension of a poem or of a theme? The answer to this tells us how meaning is explained here.

§534. Phrased like *this*, emphasized like this, heard in this way, this sentence is the first of a series in which a transition is made to *these* sentences, pictures, actions. (A multitude of familiar paths lead off from these words in every direction.)

These passages provide a particularly striking example of the cohabitation in Wittgenstein's text, of two very different kinds of language use. On the one hand, simple, strict language-games, but on the other, as in this case, a more or less free play with language, in which the strict rules of the typical, strict language-games are relaxed, and where, as in music, creativity, virtuosity, and the construction of *unique* patterns are not only permitted, but are the *point*, of this use of language. In these passages, his comparison is between poetry and music, but there are countless examples of non-poetic uses of language, where his metaphor of paths leading off from words in every direction, but along which we can be guided by others, reminds us that descriptions of such uses, should we for some reason ever be inclined to provide them, can reveal agreement in patterns of language use, rather than merely individual, random, and isolated utterances. Our uses of language may not always be, and in fact rarely are, as strict as Wittgenstein's "clear and simple language-games" (PI §130). Yet a looseness in agreement does not prevent us from *understanding* creative, virtuoso uses of language. Thus, unlike the *Mathematical Investigations*, the *Philosophical Investigations* provides a space for virtuoso verbal or written performances, even though they are not cases of ordinary, simple, and practical language-games. They are not *ordinary*, but rare, they are not *simple*, but full of nuance, capable of alternative interpretations, and require talent, and they clearly are not *practical*. Nor do they feature that direct involvement with objects and actions which is so characteristic of the *Philosophical Investigations*'s typical language-games. Yet, they are not *meaningless*: "I *want* to apply the word 'understanding' to all this."

There are many other passages which support the possibility of free play with language. In PI §42, for example, Wittgenstein imagines a playful variation of the builder's language-game. His response to the question "But

has for instance a name which has *never* been used for a tool also got a
meaning in [the builder's game]?" is, "well, even such signs could be given
a place in the language-game, and B might have, say, to answer them ...
with a shake of the head. (One could imagine this as a sort of *joke* between
them.)" This joke is a good example of a creative use of a kind of expression which has also got an ordinary, practical, "civil" application. One could
not insist that joking and practical uses are unconnected, atomistic, heterogeneous language-games, without obscuring the joke. Explaining the meaning of a name which has never been used for a tool, involves describing
it as a joke on the ordinary use. PI §41—42 thus undermines attempts to
draw a hard and fast distinction between ordinary, practical, object-action
language-games, and creative, playful, non-practical, extraordinary uses
of language. A complete description of uses of names in the builders' language-game would include both the joking and the practical, and their connections. One of the lessons of PI §41—42 seems to be that when there is
some customary pattern, or *some* agreement in a use of language, an explanation of meaning can get a foothold.

Another example occurs in PI §295, where, in considering the statement
that we know from our own case what pain is, Wittgenstein says:

> Suppose everyone does say about himself that he knows what pain
> is only from his own pain. — Not that people really say that, or are
> even prepared to say it. But if everybody said it — it might be a kind
> of exclamation. And even if it gives no information, still it is a
> picture, and why should we not want to call up such a picture? Imag-
> ine an allegorical painting taking the place of those words.

A strange use of "know", and certainly not an ordinary, simple, everyday, practical use, but not, according to this passage, a prohibited use, if
only there is *some* agreement about *something* to be done with it. Wittgenstein on many occasions exhibits extraordinary talent in imaging possible
roles for odd constructions; here, he imagines a use of "I know ... only
from my own case" as a kind of exclamation. His further suggestion, comparing a possible role for it to the role of an allegorical painting, prefigures
PI §401, where he responds to the insistence, "But when I imagine something, or even actually *see* objects, I have *got* something which my neigh-
bour has not" (PI §398) by saying:

What you have primarily discovered is a new way of looking at things. As if you had invented a new way of painting; or, again, a new metre, or a new kind of song.

Allegorical paintings, new metres, new kinds of song — all these are analogous to the products of the imaginary mathematical composers. Such products are not random, but exhibit structures of styles, movements, themes, and variations. A teaching and an understanding is possible, because there are *patterns*, or *some* agreement on how to "go on". The comparisons between language and music, and language and painting, underwrite a tolerance for a free play with language in which expressions escape the imperatives of simple, atomistic "language-games", forming patterns which can be taken up for longer or shorter duration, by a larger or smaller number of speakers. It would betray a serious failure of imagination, for example, to insist that the expression "married bachelor" never makes sense, on the grounds that its two constituent terms are verbal truants, gone AWOL from their "natural language-games".[3]

Throughout his text, Wittgenstein tries to show the significance of the fact that human beings *agree* in uses of language, without being guided by mental contents, whether concepts, images, representations of rules, or any other objects of consciousness. He also constantly inveighs against attempts to draw hard and fast conceptual boundaries where none exist, and against the analytical imperative of strict definitions, rules which "never let a doubt creep in" (PI §84), exact explanations, and demands for essence, by his insistence upon family resemblances and continuous series of cases. All of this suggests tolerance for any expression, or set of expressions, which passes smoothly between speakers in customary patterns.[4] There is no reason whatever for supposing that the degree or kind of agreement in uses of language must take only the form of well-defined, atomistic "language-games". At the one extreme, there indeed may be a few uses of language which are sufficiently policed to resemble Wittgenstein's clear, simple, "frictionless" (PI §130) language-games (there are probably many more today, introduced into our language by Wittgensteinians, than before Wittgenstein's writings became known). But "agreement" in language use is a family resemblance concept; there are different kinds of agreement, arranged along a series, from strong to weak. Among them are those wherein language is the object of play, talent, creativity, and imagination. In such cases, agreement may be restricted to a select few,[5] but as long as there is *some* agreement, some customary pattern, talk about sense and meaning can obtain a foothold. Explanations of meaning can, of course, extend no *further* than descriptions of agreement in the practice with an expression. Thus the "meaning", in PI §42, of a name never used for a tool, extends no further than its role as a joke on the ordinary use. But if there is *some* pattern, then *some* role is available for description; there is something to be taught, and something to understand, so an explanation of meaning can get off the ground.

Whether there is enough resemblance between uses of language in which there is very loose agreement and Wittgenstein's simple "language-games", such that the former even deserve the name, is of little consequence, except for a philosophical theory which would wish to use a claim that language consists of a collection of atomistic, heterogeneous language-games, in order to situate verbal compositions analogous to the imagined mathematical compositions (especially those classed as "philosophy" in our libraries) outside the bounds of sense. If this claim is to have any content, it cannot use Wittgenstein's way of deflecting the objection, "You talk about all sorts of language-games, but have nowhere said what the essence of a language-game, and hence of language, is" (PI §65). As objects of comparison, Wittgenstein's language-games perform their function without requiring any strict criteria of identity. But if uses of language in which there is very loose agreement are pronounced nonsense by a philosophical theory of language, on the grounds that they are not *language-games*, then it is not enough to say what language-games are by a gesture towards some very simple and highly regulated examples, accompanied by the rider "and others like these", without begging the question of whether those to be excluded *are* "like these".

The theory that language consists of language-games might be thought to find support in the claim that language is rule-governed. The claim that language consists of a collection of atomistic, heterogeneous language-games might then be given content by the theory that language-games are rule-governed. Uses of language too loose, too shifting, too lacking in the rigour required for unanimous (or near-unanimous) judgments of correct and incorrect application, are on these grounds declared nonsense, just as the *Mathematical Investigations* condemns mathematical composition as nonsense on the grounds that the notion of rules doesn't apply to an agreement of this sort. It is only in the practical, everyday, ordinary applications, in the "civil life" of an expression, that meaning can be found, because it is only there that the notions of *rules*, of *criteria* governing judgments, and of the "natural home" of expressions, can get a grip.

In this respect too, there are disanalogies between the *Philosophical Investigations* and the *Mathematical Investigations*. In deflecting the demand to state the essence of language-games, Wittgenstein makes it quite clear that not even all games are governed by rules. And the upshot of the demolition of the fantasy of rules as hidden forces, guiding our patterned activities, whether they be playing chess or talking sense, is to demystify rules, with the consequence that they are rarely involved in language at all. The insistence on "rules of language" can find no more support, in the absence of spoken or written rules actually involved in teaching or in a specific use of language, than the possibility of describing a language use *as if* rules were actually involved. But, given the enormous variety of uses of language, especially their conflicts and the varieties of connections with one another, there is no reason to believe that *all* of them must be sufficiently rigorous to be capable of such description. The philosophical theory that language consists of language-games would find support in Wittgenstein's remarks on rules only on the misunderstanding that uses of language must be rule-governed.

Thus the *Philosophical Investigations* distributes sense and nonsense differently than the *Mathematical Investigations*. In the imaginary case, the sense/nonsense opposition matches the oppositions of (i) ordinary vs. "philosophical" uses of language, (ii) strict, rule-governed uses vs. "free play", or uses with very loose agreement, and (iii) language-games, i.e. uses of language with identifiable rules, vs. "language on holiday", where expressions migrate from the language-games which are their "natural homes". But the *Philosophical Investigations* does not distribute the distinction between sense and nonsense in this way. In it, sense and nonsense matches the opposition between social vs. individual. The target is not customs of language use too loose to be rule-governed, or too loose to be considered language-games (in the sense required by a philosophical theory that language consists of language-games), but utterances which are not part of *any* shared pattern, any custom, or any social exchange. The attack is directed against the fantasy that life is breathed into language by mental representations associated with it. The problem, for example, with the private diarist's writing "S" in the face of a sensation (PI §258–261), is not that this action is part of a pattern with too loose an agreement to call a "language-game", or too loose to permit a description in terms of rules which, as it were, are followed, but that a purely individual act of writing a scribble or making a noise does not have sense conjured into it by some mental accompaniment. One way of dramatizing this point is to imagine utterances isolated from *any* patterned, shared practices, in contrast to simple, strict, rule-governed language-games with clear agreement in the application of an expression. Wittgenstein often emphasizes that mental representations do not breathe life into language, by imagining the most fanciful uses of expressions, driving home the point that as long as the expression has *some* circulation, which may be described, or taught, or understood, it has thereby *some* sense.

III

Passages like PI §527–535, which admit "free play" with language, suggest to me the following three consequences for interpretations of Wittgenstein's text.

(1) "Language-game" functions far more often in his text as indicating a philosophical method than as an expression which refers to actual uses of language, and never as a part of a philosophical theory, according to which language consists of language-games. The latter point is made quite unequivocally:

§130. Our clear and simple language-games are not prepatory studies for a future regularization of language, as it were first approximations, ignoring friction and air-resistance. The language-games are rather set up as *objects of comparison* which are meant to throw light on the facts of our language by way not only of similarities, but also of dissimilarities.
§131. For we can avoid ineptness or emptiness in our assertions only by presenting the model as what it is, as an object of comparison, as, so to speak, a measuring-rod; not as a preconceived idea to which reality *must* correspond. (The dogmatism into which we fall so easily in doing philosophy.)

One of the legacies of Wittgenstein's writings is to make available an enormous suspicion of reifications or totalizations of language by general theories of its essence, or theories of that in which it consists. The reader learns to distrust claims which imply a single, unified referent of the term "language". The claim that language consists of language-games falls into the dogmatism decried in the passage above. When we look at actual uses of language, we do not see atomistic, isolated, heterogeneous language-games, but something which is in constant flux ("If we look at the actual use of a word what we see is something constantly fluctuating"[6]). We see an agonistic field of conflicting uses, of some uses strictly controlled, of others spinning off in all directions, of new uses developing and old ones dying off, of uses related to one another in a wide variety of ways, of some people favouring some uses and others favouring alternatives. Actual language is not an achievement, not something settled and accomplished, but more like a project, or field of possibilities. The analogy with music is apt, for indeed much of our talk *is* like music, since there are no strict rules for the transition from one sentence to another, and in the vast majority of cases, there is no question of violating or conforming to a "criterion" of an expression's correct application, because *that* kind of rigor is not required. Most of the time, the "correctness" of the use of an expression consists of little else than its *accepted position* in a stream of discourse. There are no "applications" anything like those very clear cases imagined by Wittgenstein, involving objects and actions directly, since, for the most part, our talk connects with just more talk. When someone begins to speak, we join in, replying, embellishing, questioning, arguing, admiring; we tell stories, develop hypotheses, recount reminiscences, laugh, cry, get angry, or make jokes. Or we sit and listen to the radio, or watch television, taking it all in without any, or very little, verbal response. Patterns of words are produced, evoking others, just as one musical theme replies to another, and at no time need there be a single exchange so object-and-action oriented as "Pass the salt", much less like Wittgenstein's "Block!". Yet, and I take this to be one of the points of the comparison to music, there are patterns, and these can be described. Although there may be no verbal moves subject to rules of "correctness" and "incorrectness" as strict as those governing the expansion of the +2 series, there are at least structures of appropriateness, of deviations not tolerated, and of virtuoso performances applauded. Speakers *agree*, and even their disagreements are most often part of a larger pattern, since they are rarely *random*, just as a piece of music can be described as a "confrontation between themes."

If we take absolutely seriously Wittgenstein's statements that he is making propaganda against an *illusion*, then we can better appreciate the methodological role of language-games. Wittgenstein considers it an illusion to think that "meaning" is a mental content associated with a word. Since the illusion is something conjured up, it takes a conjuring trick to remove it. Language-games offer ways of looking at language in which the mentalist illusion of meaning is conjured away, in which, as Wittgenstein puts it,

"No such thing [is] in question here" (PI §1). Simple, clear, and ordinary language-games are imagined, not because they represent the only legitimate uses of language, but because they are uncontroversial and unobjectionable. Objections to "language on holiday" are not to uses failing to conform to simple, rule-governed cases, but to utterances thought to have meaning only because images, or other "mental contents", are associated with them:

> PI §38. Naming appears as a *queer* connexion of a word with an object. And you really get such a queer connexion when the philosopher tries to bring out *the* relation between name and thing by staring at an object in front of him and repeating a name or even the word "this" innumerable times. For philosophical problems arise when language *goes on holiday*. And *here* we may indeed fancy naming to be some remarkable act of mind, as it were a baptism of an object.

Forcing comparisons with strictly rule-governed cases is one way of highlighting the radical isolation of such utterances from any kind of shared pattern of use. The apparatus of criteria, symptoms, rules of language, logic, and grammar, all belonging to the notion of language-games, are devices enabling relevant comparisons with actual uses, which are not, in fact, rule-governed at all. They are not terms of a theory of language proposed as a rival to a "mentalist theory".

(2) The relationship between the *Philosophical Investigations* and the philosophical canon is not analogous to the relationship of the *Mathematical Investigations* to the classics of mathematical composition. For we can, in trying to understand the writings of a philosopher, or of a school of philosophy of a particular historical period, bracket the meaning of its propositions,[7] and try instead to see the patterns in the text, much as I have supposed patterns could be discerned in the work of the mathematical composers. We take note of the text's repetitions, its methods of transforming, linking, accepting, and excluding statements, and the patterns of circulation of its primary assumptions, motifs, and metaphors. In short, we try to describe what Foucault has called the "economy" of its discourse, but without any preconceived criteria of meaning, according to which one part of a text makes sense whereas another does not. We simply take the text as given, and attempt to describe the patterns we find there. We treat it, again in Foucault's terms, as a *monument*.

Suppose that this analysis of philosophical texts reveals regularities. Not, to be sure, the strict regularities constituting, e.g., the "correct" and "incorrect" expansion of the +2 series,[8] but more like "the case where we play and make up the rules as we go along" (PI §83). The analysis reveals a custom, an institution,[9] because competent speakers simply "go on" in patterned ways, making distinctions between acceptable and unacceptable philosophical discourse. They "compose" with words that have other, practical applications, just as the imaginary mathematicians compose with the symbols of arithmetic. It would be difficult to tolerate the joking use described in PI §42 as a legitimate "language-game", while banning, say, patterns in the uses of "the transcendental unity of apperception" among Kantians. (Some interpreters of Wittgenstein might allow circulation of *this* expression only as a kind of joke.)

While our imaginary text's specific targets are compositions analogous to our philosophical canon, the *Investigations*, as is well known, rarely cites any philosophers by name, and hardly ever includes anything which might even be mistaken for an analysis of their work. At the most, Wittgenstein's writings may be inspired by questions arising from the work of others, as we know it to have been in *On Certainty*, by Moore's "Proof of an External World", but even then his contribution does not consist of anything like an analysis of another's text. Whatever is meant in the *Philosophical Investigations* by "philosophy" in its pejorative use, there is little ground to interpret the target as the champions of our tradition, and even less to suggest a critique aimed at showing that no customary patterns are to be found there. On the contrary, passages like PI §527–535 suggest that a post-Wittgensteinian reading of philosophical texts would have more in common with Foucauldian discourse analysis than with positivistic dismissals of them as nonsense. It takes little effort to treat any philosophical text as if it were a radically isolated utterance, and to force comparisons with "Bring me a block". It takes somewhat more effort to discern patterns of language use in larger segments of philosophical writing. But the mentalist illusion also operates in philosophy to prevent reading a philosophical text as anything but the outering of a radically individual inner conception, rather than, as Wittgenstein's remarks might lead us to suspect, as much a social practice as continuing the +2 series.

(3) Wittgenstein's demolition of the notion of a *foundation* of language, whether it be mental representations, rules, or logical structure, clears the post-Wittgensteinian philosophical terrain for descriptions of language uses which include accounts of their mode of existence, their operation, and

their maintenance. In this respect too, Wittgenstein can be read as a companion to Foucault, because Wittgenstein's writings are compatible with Foucault's insight that large areas of language use, or what he would call "discursive formations", are maintained only by specific relations of power. In addition to uses of language in which we all, or almost all, agree, almost as a reflex, there are others in which agreement is clearly the product of culture and socialization, and yet others in which it is the effect of explicit power relations, introduced, maintained and enforced for specific and identifiable ends. Once Wittgenstein's aim of exorcising the mentalist illusion is accomplished, his emphasis on language as a technique, or, in his special sense, on language as a *practice*, together with his notion of philosophy as description, encourages pursuit of more detailed descriptions of actual uses of language, aiming to show in detail the specific interests served by particular discursive formations, as well as the conflicts between opposing uses of language.

Wittgenstein's emphasis on the arbitrariness of grammar also has the consequence that confrontations between discourses are political struggles. If someone invents a game, something like chess, but in which the *king* moves two squares at a time, it is no use for me to justify our game by insisting, perhaps in the face of my mental representation of what a king, in *essence*, is, that a king moves only one square at a time. There are two games here, and which one we will play depends, often, on who has more power. In the same way, no more than rhetorical purposes are served, for example, by arguments that the *essence* of humanity must be universal, in opposing uses of "human" according to which the term is not applied to blacks, women, gays, Jews, Arabs, or any of the many other groups attracting our blood-lust, or in which "murder" is so differentially applied that it simply doesn't make sense to say a white person *murdered* a black person.[10] The conflict between uses in which "human" is applied equally to all of woman born, and those in which it is differentially distributed, is political. But to point out that language is not founded on thought is not, as some critics of Wittgenstein have insisted,[11] to favour a quietist, conservative political stance, where, for example, references to 100,000–200,000 Iraqui dead as "collateral damage" are situated beyond criticism. On the contrary, the Wittgensteinian position is a prolegomena to political action, because it encourages close attention to actual uses of language, thus offering the benefit of a clearer understanding of the deployments of expressions in the real world.

(4) Wittgenstein scholarship is itself a prime example of "free play" with language. It has also, more than 100 years after Wittgenstein's birth, achieved the status of a philosophical *monument*. Before the *Philosophical Investigations*, no philosopher ever used the term "language-game". Now, "a multitude of familiar paths lead off from these words in every direction." Smart thinks the expression is confusing and obscure[12]; Specht analyses it as a "model-concept in Wittgenstein's theory of language";[13] Rhees expresses skepticism about its usefulness in answering "the question of what it is to have a language or what it is to speak";[14] Canfield says both that Wittgenstein "does not think that language *is* a game or series of games with fixed rules", and that "language is a collection of language games, governed by criterial rules[15]; Sellars's reflections on language-games are expressed in terms of "syntactical metalanguages".[16] The *Philosophical Investigations*, like any other text, offers a field of discursive possibilities. It invites comment: admiration, agreement, disagreement, defense against attacks, expressions of disgust, support for its detractors, inspiration for one's own thinking. As in music, patterns emerge, solidify, shift, and pass away, to be replaced by others. The monument can be described. But it would be a vain hope to suppose that the term "Wittgenstein" refers to a unified, but elusive, subjectivity which, if we could only grasp it, would resolve all the ambiguities of the text, and would bar all but one of those paths now leading off from it in so many directions. The closest to a "natural home" for the term "language-game" will always be Wittgenstein's text, and it, like any other, is not governed by rules which would make any one of the many readings grafted onto it as obviously correct as 1,002 is the correct continuation of 1,000 in the +2 series. There are many paths in Wittgenstein's text, leading off from the term "language-game". This paper gestures towards just one of them.

Endnotes

1. *Wittgenstein's Lectures on the Foundations of Mathematics: Cambridge, 1939*, Cora Diamond (ed.), Ithaca, N.Y.: Cornell University Press.

2. I borrow this term from John V. Canfield's "Anthropological Science Fiction and Logical Necessity," *Canadian Journal of Philosophy* 4 (1975): pp.467-79.

3. I owe this point to Marilyn Randall.

4. The existence of disagreement and controversy is not sufficient ground to condemn a discourse as "idling language", since controversy may itself be patterned, as in philosophy.

5. Especially when restricted to writing, since, by some recent estimates, 25% of the population of the United States is functionally illiterate.

6. *Philosophical Grammar*, §36.

7. In so doing, we perform what Hubert L. Dreyfuss and Paul Rabinow identify as an essential part of Foucault's early methodology of discourse analysis, in their *Michel Foucault: Beyond Structuralism and Hermeneutics*, Chicago: University of Chicago Press, 1983.

8. Historical investigation may reveal that some schools of philosophical thought initiate their members with no less rigour than that applied by the most Draconian public school teacher to enforce the rules of arithmetic.

9. If the Foucauldian analysis were carried out according to the methods of his later thought, revealing the connections between a particular discursive economy and its uses by specific social institutions, the characterization of discursive regularities as customs or institutions gains even more force.

10. Tom Sharpe provides a savage parody of such a "language-game" in the opening of his black comedy, *Riotous Assembly*, London, 1973.

11. E.g. Russell Nieli, *Wittgenstein: From Mysticism to Ordinary Language* Albany, New York: State University of New York Press, 1987, and Nicholas N. Gier, *Wittgenstein and Phenomenology*, Albany, New York: State University of New York Press, 1981.

12. H. R. Smart, "Language-Games," *Philosophical Quarterly* 7 (1957): pp.224-35.

13. Ernst Konrad Specht, *Foundations of Wittgenstein's Later Philosophy*, Manchester: Manchester University Press, 1969.

14. Rush Rhees, "Wittgenstein's Builders," *Proceedings of the Aristotelian Society* 60 (1960), pp.171-86.

15. John V. Canfield, *Wittgenstein, Language and World*, Amherst, Mass.: University of Massachusetts Press, 1981.

16. Wilfrid Sellars, "Some Reflections on Language-Games," *Philosophy of Science* 21 (1954), pp.204-28.

CHAPTER VIII

Transfinite Numbers

Alice Ambrose

When Hilbert protested against Cantor's opponents that he would not be driven out of the paradise Cantor created, it is evident that both he and Cantor's opponents supposed their disagreement was over the existence of a created, or newly discovered, set of entities — infinite numbers, which numbered the set of integers, the set of points in space, and possibly other sets with magnitudes in between. Philosophers have concerned themselves with the question as to what it comes to to claim existence for any of the familiar numbers, let alone that of a number which numbers the infinite. Further, if there exists an infinite number of anything, say of natural numbers, there will always *be* unnamed elements. And what does *this* come to? It is clear that these are the same kind of questions disputed about through the centuries, which exercised the supporters and detractors of the Platonic theory that there are abstract entities. About numbers, which are the prime examples of such entities, "these, if anything", said Theaetetus, " have real existence". "We renounce abstract entities[1]" said Goodman.

In this paper for the volume in honour of Professor J.F.M. Hunter I wish to consider questions in this area of philosophy, and in particular, what certain investigations by Wittgenstein contributed to them. As a guide concerning procedure, I shall try to use his own guide: that to find our way among these questions, confusions engendered by our use of language have to be got round, the aim being "*complete* clarity" which "simply means that the philosophical problem should *completely* disappear"[2]. When one considers the many centuries of controversy over every philosophical thesis, without resolution, and seemingly without hope of resolution, it would seem that the failure to come to truth indicates that a different approach to the disputes is necessary.

Before embarking on a discourse on method we should have before us several statements about infinite totalities made by disputants during and since the time of Cantor. According to Hilbert, "we meet with the true infinite when we regard the totality of numbers 1,2,3,4,... itself as a completed unity, or when we regard the points of an interval as a totality of things which exists all at once".[3] Paul Bernays brings in omniscience to describe this meeting with the infinite: "If we conceive of the idea of a divine omniscience at all", he says, "then we would certainly ascribe to it the attribute of being able to survey at *one* glance a totality of which every single element is in principle accessible to us".[4] He allows that even a divine mind could not *effectively* calculate all the terms of an infinite sequence any more than it could trisect an angle with ruler and compass. Bertrand Russell, on the other hand, does not concede this, and instead maintains that a completed infinity of operations is, in his words, only medically, not logically, impossible.[5] He describes how anyone could, in principle, count off the infinity of natural numbers: Supposing one takes one minute to count the first number, by quickening one's pace one could do the second number in 1/2 minute, the third in 1/4, the fourth in 1/8, and so on, finishing the whole series at the end of two minutes.[6]

This account does not bear scrutiny; it covers up a *petitio*. For it presupposes that an infinite series of time intervals, $1 + 1/2 + 1/4 + 1/8 + \ldots$, and so on is summed up at time $t = 2$, that is, that it comes to completion. If there is a question about the possibility of enumerating all the natural numbers, there is the same question about the possibility of completing the series $1 + 1/2 + 1/4 + 1/8 + \ldots$. There is nothing theoretically objectionable about the hypothesis that a person does each operation in half the time of the preceding one. What is disputable is the argument that because $1 + 1/2 + 1/4 + 1/8 + \ldots$ has the sum 2, all the operations are completed at the end of two minutes.

Maintaining that this series can be grasped at one glance, or that it can be run through, of course implies that there can *be* such a totality. Cantor said that "The whole numbers seem to me to be constituted as a world of realities which exist outside of us with the same character of absolute necessity as the realities of Nature".[7] And he goes further: Both separately and collectively as an infinite totality, the natural numbers "exist in the highest degree of reality as eternal ideas in the Intellectus Divinus".[8] For transfinite numbers nothing more than consistency is required for their existence, inasmuch as what is consistent is possible, and an omniscient God could comprehend every possibility, and not only this, He could realize it *in concreto*. As for ourselves, just as we arrive, by abstraction of particular qualities from finite sets of elements, at the concept of any finite number, so we arrive at the concept of a transfinite cardinal by abstraction of particular qualities of any infinite set *taken as a whole* (Cantor's emphasis). Just as $\sqrt{2}$ has a "material verification" in the diagonal of a 1 x 1 square, so transfinite numbers are exemplified by the aggregate of the constituents of matter. Once the existence of infinite totalities was established, the existence of numbers to number them was assured. No one could reasonably accept the existence of irrationals, which are defined in terms of infinite sets and by similar procedures, and reject transfinites. It is quite clear that, leaving aside Cantor's falling back on God for the existence of transfinite numbers, his arguments are transparently analogical.

An air of paradox hangs about the arithmetic of transfinite numbers which Cantor developed, and also about what he took to be the essential property of the aggregate of the natural numbers. $\aleph_0$, so named by Cantor for the cardinal number of all natural numbers, was such that $\aleph_0 + 1 = \aleph_0$, $\aleph_0 - 1 = \aleph_0$, and $2 \times \aleph_0 = \aleph_0$. The essential property of the totality of natural numbers was its 1-1 correlatability with a proper part of itself. (E.g. the numbers in the sequence 2,3,4..., in the sequence of squares, 1,4,9..., in the sequence of primes 1,3,5,7,11... etc. correlate 1-1 with 1,2,3,4...) It is significant that Leibniz and Cantor used this feature to arrive at opposite conclusions, the one that infinite numbers are impossible, the other that there are infinite sets which are distinguished from finite sets by this property. The storm of controversy which Cantor's papers aroused is well known. We know that some mathematicians — Kronecker, for example, denied the existence of a class of elements, in extension, with the number $\aleph_0$ — the class Cantor thought of as "the consummated infinite". Present-day finitists (or intuitionists, or constructivists) are aligned against those classical mathematicians who joined with Cantor in viewing his opponents as holding that there are only finite numbers. Statements which Wittgenstein made in *Philosophical Grammar* and in *Philosophical Remarks* are often taken to align him with the finitists, e.g. "There is no such thing as 'the cardinal numbers', but only 'cardinal numbers' and the concept 'cardinal number'"[9], and "You can't talk about *all* numbers, because there is no such thing as *all* numbers".[10]

I do not wish to go into the question whether such statements classify Wittgenstein as a finitist nor whether there are inconsistencies between various things he has said (e.g. in *Philosophical Remarks*, "Of course we may not and cannot deny the existence of anything"[11]). I am going to make use of a procedure in which he engaged again and again in dealing with a philosophical theory, and about which he was explicit. In *The Blue Book* he said his investigations had best be thought of as an "heir" to what is traditionally called philosophy. For they are directed to the language by which a theory is expressed rather than to the truth of what it expresses. Traditionally philosophers picture themselves as seekers after truth. The indicative form of speech in which they state a view is the same form as that by which a scientist, or the common man, asserts a fact. Wittgenstein said in lecture that to treat philosophical problems as though they concerned questions of fact rather than questions about language is to treat them "perfectly hopelessly". "Your questions", he said, "relate to words, so I have to talk about words."[12]

I am aware that this approach is in as serious disagreement as any philosophical dispute to which it is applied. Michael Dummett contends, as he says, "for a more traditional characterization of philosophy than Wittgenstein's, a view namely that accepts it for what it appears to be, a sector in the quest for truth".[13] Those who disagree over the existence of infinite totalities conduct their disagreement as though their words express truths — that not language, but the truth of what language expresses, is at issue. Here the disagreement will be looked at as due to "troubles arising from a particular use of language".[14] More specifically, the dispute between Cantor and his opponents will be viewed as a dispute over the language of the infinite, rather than over what the language refers to — but without the disputants being aware that they are supporting or objecting to a convention.[15] The source of the philosophers' use of language Wittgenstein described as, in general, "the wish for a notation which stresses a difference more strongly, or for one which uses more closely similar forms of expression...".[16] This description I am taking to apply to mathematicians' use of language to express their philosophical views. Its application here is to the language in which "infinite", "totality", etc. figure.

Wittgenstein raised the question, "What harm is done, e.g. by saying that God knows *all* irrational numbers? Or: that they are already all there, even though we only know certain of them? Why are these pictures not harmless?" His reply: "They hide certain problems."[17] He did not specify at that point in the *Remarks on the Foundation of Mathematics* which problems were hidden by this way of talking. But it is not difficult to surmise what some of them are. One is the philosophical question whether there can be an infinite whole, which in turn raises the question whether $\aleph_0$ is the name of a number — a huge number — which measures a magnitude. Another question concerns what is shown by the 1-1 correlatability of an infinite set with a proper part of itself. As is obvious, the opposing answers to these questions are put forward as *a priori*; and as is well known, Wittgenstein characterized *a priori* propositions as "rules of grammar". This description suggests that they are in some way about terminology. His idea was that it is the special use of language in the expression of philosophical theories which both creates and hides philosophical problems under the appearance of being *a priori* truths. One of the basic tasks to which he addressed himself was to bring into the open what language tends to conceal, in the present case, *differences* as well as similarities between talk about the finite and the infinite.

We have already noted Cantor's analogical reasoning for the existence of infinite numbers. The charm of the infinite lies in the imagery which it is natural to associate with the sequence of natural numbers, and with the real numbers correlated with the points of a line segment. It is true, but misleading, to contrast the following pairs as to size: the infinite sequence of natural numbers 1,2,3... and the partial series 1,2,3; the expansion of π and the expansion of π to the 10th place; the sum of the addends $1 + 2 + 3$ and the sum $1 + 1/2 + 1/4 + 1/8$ ...; the number of cardinal numbers and the number of trees in a row. In each case there seems merely to be *more* elements in the one collection than in the other: more numbers in the infinite sequence than in the partial series, more elements in the geometric sum than in the sum of the addends $1 + 2 + 3$, more cardinals than the trees in a row. And at any given time the numbers will outstrip the numerals (the written signs). The linguistic analogies between the members of these pairs carry with them imagery which tempts us to minimize their difference by treating it as merely quantitative.

It is useful here to cite Wittgenstein's extended remarks from his 1934-1935 lectures:

> We always think of the infinite as something very huge or very tiny. The idea of converging to a point is the idea of convergence on something infinitely small. But the infinite has nothing to do with size. ... There is a constant temptation to picture an enormous extension when we find the remainder in a division equal to the dividend. We take this to be the criterion for infinite periodicity, and we say the result can be infinitely repeated. And it looks as though some superhuman being might survey the infinite extension even though we cannot. The greatest puzzle is that in some queer way what has not been done, say, division to the 17th place, seems as though it has been done, as though the whole extension has been given. ... If this picture of an enormous extension is given up, we see the infinite is on a totally different level from the finite... I do not mean by this that the infinite is "unreal". The word "infinite" has its uses; for

example, that there is no 6 in the infinite development of 1/7 means that it is not in the period; and that is all.[18]

The following excerpt from The Yellow Book[19] reinforces the point:

> Given the series 1, 1 + a, 1 + 2a, ... and so on, where "and so on" trails off into saying silently four additional numbers, what one has is a series that comes to an end: three numbers said aloud, followed by four numbers trailing off. This idea of "trailing off" makes us fail to realize the difference in grammar for "and so on". It creates the illusion that we have done the counting and not done it. We behave as though the numbers which trailed off were *meant* though unsaid... We in fact have three numbers and "and so on", each with their own grammar.

When we write "and so on, ad inf." that expression gives the picture of numbers *trailing off* in the distance too far for one to see, for in the back of our minds we have the idea that "infinite" or "transfinite" means huge, only more.[20]

It is possible to trace the source of this idea. For one thing, "There are infinitely many primes" and "There are ten primes between 1 and 30" both are answers to the question "How many?". What Euclid proved, to put it in Cantor's way, was that there are $\aleph_0$ primes. The number of primes altogether, and the number of primes between 1 and 30 are, respectively, $\aleph_0$ and 10.

But are the symbols "$\aleph_0$" and "10" on the same footing? Are both of them names of numbers? That their usage is in some ways similar is evident, apart from their being similar parts of speech. The fact that we have a technique which, as Wittgenstein said, "there is a certain justice in calling 1-1 correlation of two infinite series"[21], seems to put $\aleph_0$ on the same footing with 10, which is a property of a sequence 1-1 correlatable with the fingers of my hands. It was suggested to me by Morris Lazerowitz that Cantor and his opponents were opting for different conventions for the use of these symbols — the one treating "$\aleph_0$" as the name of a number, the other refusing. It is clear that Cantor was motivated by the philosophical view that there is a reality corresponding to truths about numbers. What intuitionists say can be construed as acceptance of the opposite philosophical view. But one need not come down on one side of the other, on either Platonism or its denial, if one looks at the controversy as a concealed effort to alter or fend off changes in mathematical notation. Cf. Wittgenstein's comment in *The Blue Book* that "we sometimes wish for a notation which stresses a difference ... or one which uses more closely similar forms of expression".[22]

We have already detailed some of the similarities and differences in the use of "$\aleph_0$" and of numerals naming numbers such as 2 and 3. Although it is tempting to say that $\aleph_0$ applies to sets whose correlation with the integers we cannot carry out, the important difference is that going through the process of correlating 1-1 all the integers, say, with all the primes is logically impossible, i.e. finishing the correlation of two arrays that have no end. There is no logical impossibility of correlating two rows of trees whose ends we cannot see. The reason for the former impossibility is not that "sequence having $\aleph_0$ members" has a huge array as its extension. "Having $\aleph_0$ members" functions in a different way in our language from "having a huge number". If we look outside mathematical language to the use of numbers which function both inside and outside, the difference is clear: $\aleph_0$, unlike 10, is not a number we use in counting. Wittgenstein noted that if we characterize a person as having learned to do $\aleph_0$ multiplications, we can mean nothing more than that he has learned to multiply, whereupon the imagery of his having mastered a huge task disappears. Further, we see that "1,2,3,...and so on", unlike "a,b,c,... and so on", is not *an abbreviation*. Also, questions about extensions, such as whether there is a 6 in the infinite development of 1 divided by 7, can be answered by citing a *rule*, here the rule of periodicity, as well as by not finding a 6 in the course of development.

These considerations suggest that "$\aleph_0$" is not used to denote a property of an extension as is "2" for denoting a property of a couple. If we call it a numeral, it is by courtesy, in virtue of its similarity to 2, 3, etc. This point is reinforced if we express such a theorem as "There *is* an infinite number of primes" as "There is no greatest prime". The fact-stating, indicative mode of speech emphasizes the similarity of this statement to "There is no largest planet", and conceals an important difference. The opposite of the latter is clearly conceivable: there could be two different planets of the same size which are larger than all others. But the opposite of "There is no greatest prime" is inconceivable, since the theorem follows by *reductio ad absurdum* from "There is a greatest prime". The sentence, "There is a greatest prime", expresses a logical impossibility. This verbal fact entails and is entailed by the fact that "greatest prime" does not have a use to describe a number. Note that the logical fact that it is impossible for there to be a greatest prime is not the *same* as the verbal fact that "greatest prime" has no use. But what we know in knowing the logical fact is something verbal. In a concealed form the proposition that it is impossible for there to be a greatest prime makes a linguistic claim.

The account here of a specific necessary proposition is an application of the general account of necessary propositions put forward and supported in detail by Morris Lazerowitz.[23] Put very briefly, the import of a necessary proposition is verbal, although it is not itself equivalent to a verbal proposition. To illustrate, the fact that the English sentence, "Lions are feline", expresses a necessary proposition is equivalent to the verbal fact that "feline" applies to the class that the word "lion" applies to. Note that this exhibition of the connection between a necessary proposition and a verbal fact avoids the pitfall of conventionalism: equating a (nonverbal) necessary proposition with a contingent proposition about English usage. It is the assertion that a sentence expresses a necessary proposition, not the proposition, which is equivalent to a verbal proposition. The fact that a proposition is necessary rests on convention but it makes no assertion about a convention.

Disputes over the truth of a mathematical proposition are usually disputes in which the conventions for the use of words are accepted by both sides. But there are disputes in which it is the convention itself which is at issue, however well concealed this may be. The history of mathematics provides numerous examples where such expressions as the following came to be accepted: "surface having only one side", "points (at infinity) where parallel lines meet", "curve formed by infinitely small straight-line segments", "$a°$", "roots of the equation $x^2 = -1$". Justifications for introducing these expressions were usually given in the idiom more natural to justification: the language of proving truth. E.g. the proof that $a°=1$.

The point at which classical mathematicians and intuitionists disagree indicates the point at which the dispute becomes a question about a new convention. Both of these disputants agree that not only cardinal numbers but infinite sets of real numbers between 0 and 1 can be constructed. By the latter, intuitionists mean constructing by the diagonal process a number which is not in the array of decimals already constructed. And the set already constructed is not a totality, but an unending sequence each of whose elements can be computed separately. Where the disputants part ways is over the claim that the self-contradictoriness of enumerating all decimal sequences shows that there is a *non*-denumerable totality of decimal sequences. Some axiom sets contain a "power set axiom" which asserts the existence of a set of all sub-sets, e.g. that all the decimal sequences form a set. Cantor asserted the existence of such a set, the set of all real numbers. He held its number to be $2^{\aleph_0}$, a number greater than the number of denumerable sequences of decimal fractions. $2^{\aleph_0} > \aleph_0$ he took to be a necessary truth, justified by the diagonal process. Intuitionists took the diagonal process to show only that the enumeration of all real numbers is impossible, and that it merely gives the means of constructing a real number not in any array of decimal fractions. As for $2^{\aleph_0} > \aleph_0$, this they held to be nonsense.

If we look at the verbal import of the necessary truth Cantor claimed it to be, it must be admitted that he was opting for a new convention rather than appealing to already accepted conventions. Sometimes the language of mathematicians indicates their awareness that a convention is being introduced. R.L. Wilder, for example, remarks that $\aleph_0$ can "come with practice to have the same significance for us as the number 15".[24] And N.J. Lennes commented as follows on the geometric series $1 + 1/2 + 1/4 + 1/8 \ldots$, which does not have a sum in the arithmetical sense of "sum of addends": "If this series is to be regarded as having a sum at all, it must be defined in a new way."[25] When Russell describes counting the terms of that series in two minutes, he is not stating a truth about what is possible for a superhuman mind, but is capturing the infinite by the semantic device of re-defining the term "sum".

What I have said in this paper is intended to make the point that the controversy over transfinite numbers is only apparently about a realm of existents, that what is at issue is the acceptance of a new convention. Viewed in this light the dispute disappears, for the "paradise that Cantor created" is no longer relevant. We can perhaps understand Wittgenstein's question, "Where does our investigation get its importance from, since it seems to destroy everything interesting, that is, all that is great and important?"[26]

Alice Ambrose
Smith College

Endnotes

1. Nelson Goodman, "Steps toward a Constructive Nominalism", *Jour. of Symbolic Logic*, Vol. 12 (1947), p.105.

2. *Philosophical Investigations*, p.51.

3. "On Infinity", in *Philosophy of Mathematics*. Selected Readings, eds. P. Benacerraf and H. Putnam, p.139.

4. "Comments on Ludwig Wittgenstein's *Remarks on the Foundations of Mathematics*", Op.cit., p.520.

5. "The Limits of Empiricism", *Proc. of the Aristotelian Society*, Suppl. Vol.XXXVI, p.143.

6. Ibid.

7. Letter to Hermite, Nov. 30, 1895, quoted from J.W. Dauben's *Georg Cantor, His Mathematics and Philosophy of the Infinite*, p.228.

8. Ibid, p.228.

9. *Philosophical Grammar*, p.187.

10. *Philosophical Remarks*, p.146.

11. Ibid., p.261.

12. *Philosophical Investigations*, p.49.

13. *Truth and Other Enigmas*, p.456.

14. *Wittgenstein's Lectures, Cambridge 1932-1935*, from the notes of Alice Ambrose and Margaret Macdonald, p.13.

15. *The Blue Book*, p.57.

16. Ibid., p.59.

17. *Remarks on the Foundations of Mathematics*, p.195.

18. *Wittgenstein's Lectures, Cambridge 1932-1935*, pp.189-190.

19. Op.cit., p.189. The Yellow Book consists of notes taken by Margaret Masterman and Alice Ambrose in the intervals between dictation of The Blue Book.

20. See *Wittgenstein's Lectures on the Foundations of Mathematics, Cambridge 1939*, from the notes of R.G. Bosanquet, Norman Malcolm, Rush Rhees, Yorick Smythies, ed. Cora Diamond, pp.170–1.

21. *Remarks on the Foundations of Mathematics*, p.59.

22. Ibid. p.59.

23. *The Language of Philosophy*, Ch. I.

24. *Introduction to the Foundations of Mathematics*, p.97.

25. *College Algebra*, p.113.

26. *Philosophical Investigations*, p.48.

CHAPTER IX

RELIGIOUS BELIEF

John W. Cook

Although Wittgenstein did not write at length about religious belief, one can find in his writings many scattered remarks on the subject. It is easy enough to understand why he should have felt obliged to comment on religion, for it provides a good test case, so to speak, for his views about language. For, to judge by what religious believers actually say, it certainly looks as though they believe in transcendent beings and that in their prayers, sermons, creeds, hymns, and tracts they are constantly speaking of something beyond experience. But is that possible? It was axiomatic with Wittgenstein that "one cannot use language to go beyond the possibility of evidence" (PR 55). Consequently, he was obliged to insist that "it isn't possible to believe something for which you cannot imagine some kind of verification" (PR 89). It might seem, then, that Wittgenstein ought to conclude that religious belief is impossible, that what look like beliefs here are only so much nonsense. This was the conclusion drawn by other positivists, such as A. J. Ayer. Wittgenstein, however, saw the matter differently, for he had at his disposal two other ideas about language: his idea that language may contain 'misleading forms of words' and his 'use' theory of language. What we need to consider in this chapter is the role these two ideas play in his treatment of religious belief.

To show what their role is, and how they came to play that role, I will set forth what I take to be the steps in Wittgenstein's thinking. I will then undertake to confirm this account with quotations from his writings. In order to refer back to these steps in his thinking, I will number them.

(1) It isn't possible to believe something for which you cannot imagine some kind of verification, i.e., not possible to believe anything about transcendent beings.

(2) If "God" were the name of a transcendent being, then where this word comes into prayers, sermons, creeds, etc., we would not have sense but only nonsense.

(3) On the other hand, if "God" is *not* the name of a transcendent being, then religious beliefs are not nonsense, but also they are not really *beliefs*,

and in that case creedal statements, such as "I believe in God the Father, maker of heaven and earth ...," are misleading forms of words.

(4) If, in choosing between these alternatives, we were to opt for (2) rather than (3) — as Ayer does, we should then have to conclude that the meaning of an expression is *not* its use in the language, for prayers, sermons, creeds, and the like certainly have a *use*, i.e., they have a place in human activities. Whereas, if we opt for (3), then we can invoke the formula that the meaning of a word is its use in the language and proceed to investigate the meaning of religious utterances.

(5) If, like Ayer, we were to take the view that religious utterances are meant to be about transcendent beings and are, for that reason, nonsense, we would be opening ourselves up to the following charge of inconsistency: if you are going to adopt that view of (i.e., a Realist interpretation of) religious utterances, then in the name of consistency you should adopt the same view of what the plain man says about material things and 'other minds,' namely, the view that all of those propositions are nonsense, too.' In other words, it is hardly consistent to adopt a Realist view of religious language and brand it as nonsense while dismissing Moore's Realist account of material things and other minds in order to avoid the conclusion that most of what we say is nonsense.

(6) But it is surely not plausible to think that most of what we say is nonsense. When I go into a restaurant and say, "A cup of coffee, please," and the waitress brings me a cup of coffee, could it be that I did *not* place an order which the waitress understood and acted on? Surely not! What would placing an order *be,* if not what I've just described. And yet if we adopt Moore's interpretation of this order (wherein a cup of coffee is a transcendent object), it becomes nonsense.

(7) So if we now retrace our steps through the foregoing reasoning, we arrive at the following results:

(a) When I go into a restaurant and say, "A cup of coffee, please," this is not nonsense.

(b) Since it is not nonsense, a cup of coffee is not (contrary to Moore) a transcendent entity, i.e., ordinary language does not here bear a Realist interpretation.

(c) But since the grammar of "cup" appears to support a Realist interpretation (for we say things like, "The cup slid off the table while no one was looking"), we are obliged to say (i) that our utterances about cups and tables and chairs contain misleading forms of words and (ii) that it is the *use* of language (in placing orders in restaurants and the like) that gives words their meaning.

(d) But if the use of language is what gives words their meaning, then since religious utterances have a *use*, i.e., play a role in human activities, then religious language, too, is meaningful.

(e) In the matter of religious utterances, then, it is the philosopher's job to describe their use and thereby show that they do not contain references to transcendent beings and that religious believers do not necessarily hold beliefs about the world over and above their secular beliefs.

I will refer to this henceforth as "the master argument."

I would not want to defend the opinion that Wittgenstein at some point in his life thought through the steps of the master argument in just the order in which I've presented it. But I feel sure that had he been asked whether this argument properly represented his views, he would have said that it did.[1] In any case, his various remarks about religion bear out such an interpretation.

We can most usefully survey those remarks by seeing how they fit into the master argument. Let us review, then, what we should expect to find Wittgenstein saying if the master argument represents his own thinking. We should expect to find him maintaining the following: (i) that religious utterances are really about something in the given world (about one's life, for example) and not about a transcendent world, i.e., that they do not mean what they may appear to mean, (ii) that religious utterances have a meaning because of their use, i.e., because of their role in religious practices, (iii) that what pass for religious *beliefs* are not really beliefs — at least not in the more usual sense of "belief", (iv) that people who take a Realist view of religious language are mistaken in this, (v) that 'believing' in God is like 'believing' in material things and 'other minds', i.e., 'believing' in God is not really *belief* but something more like an attitude.

These are the things we should expect Wittgenstein to say, and they are in fact the very things he does say.

(i) *Contrary to appearances, religious 'doctrines' are not really about a transcendent world.* Wittgenstein makes this point in several ways, one of which is the following:

Christianity is not a doctrine, not, I mean, a theory about what has happened and will happen to the human soul, but a description of something that actually takes place in human life. For 'consciousness of sin' is a real event and so are despair and salvation through faith. Those who speak of such things (Bunyan for instance) are simply describing what has happened to them, whatever gloss anyone may want to put on it (CV 28).

Predestination: It is only permissible to write like this [Wittgenstein seems to have been thinking here of Paul's epistles] out of the most dreadful suffering — and then it means something quite different. But for the same reason it is not permissible for someone to assert it as a truth, unless he himself says it in torment. — It simply isn't a theory. — Or to put it another way: If this is truth, it is not the truth that seems at first sight to be expressed by these words. It's less a theory than a sigh or a cry (CV 32).

Another of the ways this point shows up in Wittgenstein's writings is in the way he regards different religions. He writes:

Was Augustine mistaken, then, when he called on God on every page of the *Confession*?
Well — one might say — if he was not mistaken, then the Buddist holy-man, or some other, whose religion expresses quite different notions, surely was. But *none* of them was making a mistake except where he was putting forward a theory (RGB 28–29).

Wittgenstein means to say here that what is said in a properly religious spirit will contain no theoretical element and therefore different religions cannot clash. In particular, although Christians call upon God, while Buddists do not, this is not to be taken as showing that Christians believe that there is a supreme being, while Buddists do not. To think that Christianity and Buddism differ in this way is, according to Wittgenstein, a mistake that arises from the fact that "God" is a substantive: "Let us look at the grammar of ... such terms as 'God', 'soul', 'mind' ... One of the chief troubles is that we take a substance to correspond to a thing" (AWL p.31). This, according to Wittgenstein, is a typical philosophical mistake: "This kind of mistake recurs again and again in philosophy; e.g. when we are puzzled about the nature of time, when time seems to us a *queer thing*. We are most strongly tempted to think that here are things hidden. ... And yet nothing of the sort is the case. ... But it is the use of the substantive 'time' which mystifies us" (BB p.6). And so, too, with the substantive

'God'. "The way you use the word 'God' shews, not *whom* you mean, but what you mean" (RPP I §475). To think that 'God' is the name of a Supreme Being, then, is a mistake that we are drawn into by a misleading form of words.

(ii) *Religious utterances have a meaning because of their use, i.e., because of their role in religious practices.* Wittgenstein explicitly makes this point when he writes:

> When someone who believes in God looks around him and asks "Where did everything that I see come from?" "Where did everything come from?" he is *not* asking for a (causal) explanation; and the point of his question is that it is the expression of such a request. Thus, he is expressing an attitude toward all explanations. — But how is this shown in his life? It is the attitude that takes a particular matter seriously, but then at a particular point doesn't take it seriously after all, and declares that something else is even more serious.
>
> In this way a person can say it is very serious that so-and-so died before he could finish a certain work; and in another sense it doesn't matter at all. Here we use the words "in a profounder sense". What I actually want to say is that here too it is not a matter of the *words* one uses or of what one is thinking when using them, but rather of the difference they make at various points in life. How do I know that two people mean the same when both say they believe in God? And one can say just the same thing about the Trinity. Theology which insists on the use of *certain* words and phrases and bans others, makes nothing clearer (Karl Barth). It, so to speak, fumbles around with words, because it wants to say something and doesn't know how to express it. *Practices* give words their meaning (ROC III §317).

Perhaps the same point about use and meaning can be gathered from the following passage in the *Investigations*:

> Religion teaches that the soul can exist when the body has disintegrated. Now do I understand this teaching? — Of course I understand it — I can imagine plenty of things in connexion with it. And haven't pictures of these things been painted? And why should such a picture be only an imperfect rendering of the spoken doctrine? Why should

it not do the *same* service as the words? And it is the service which
is the point (PI p.178).

In these passages Wittgenstein is invoking his use theory of meaning in
order to defend religious utterances against the charge that they are nonsense.

(iii) *What pass for religious beliefs are not really beliefs — at least not
in the more usual sense of "belief."* Wittgenstein makes this point as
follows:

> It strikes me that a religious belief could only be something like
> a passionate commitment to a system of reference. Hence, although
> a *belief*, it's really a way of living, or a way of assessing life. It's
> passionately seizing hold of *this* interpretation (CV 64).
>
> Christianity is not based on a historical truth; rather, it offers us
> a (historical) narrative and says: Now believe! But not, believe this
> narrative with the belief appropriate to a historical narrative, rather:
> believe through thick and thin, which you can do only as the result
> of a life. *Here you have a narrative, don't take the same attitude to
> it as you take to other historical narratives!* Make a *quite different*
> place in your life for it. — There is nothing *paradoxical* about that!
> (CV 32).
>
> Queer as it sounds: The historical accounts in the Gospels might,
> historically speaking, be demonstrably false and yet belief would lose
> nothing by this: *not*, however, because it concerns 'universal truths
> of reason'! Rather, because historical proof (the historical proof-
> game) is irrelevant to belief. This message (the Gospels) is seized on
> by men believingly (i.e. lovingly). *That* is the certainty characterizing
> this particular acceptance-as-true, not something else (CV 32).

Wittgenstein was also making this point about religious belief when, in lectures, he said: "In religious discourse we use such expressions as: 'I believe
that so and so will happen [e.g., that there will be a Judgment Day],' and
use them differently to the way in which we use them in science" (LA 57).
And he further explained this by saying: "Here believing obviously plays
much more this role: suppose we said that a certain picture might play the
role of constantly admonishing me, or I always think of it. Here, an enormous difference would be between those people for whom the picture is
constantly in the foreground, and the others who just didn't use it at all"

(LC, p. 56). Wittgenstein is saying: The difference between these two sorts of people is not that the first sort act and think as they do because of something they *believe*, namely, that there will be a day of judgment; rather, what we call their "belief in a day of judgment" is nothing other than the fact that they use and are constantly admonished by a picture.

(iv) *People who take a Realist view of religious language are wrong about this.* Drury records Wittgenstein as having said:

People who call themselves modernists are the most deceived of all. I will tell you what modernism is like: in *The Brothers Karamazov* the old father says that the monks in the nearby monastery believe that the devils have hooks to pull people down into hell. 'Now,' says the old father, 'I can't believe in those hooks.' That is the same sort of mistake that modernists make when they misunderstand the nature of symbolism.[2]

Evidently, Wittgenstein thought that the Realist view of religion is a modern aberration, a recent misconception.

(v) *'Believing' in God is like 'believing' in material things and 'other minds', i.e., it is not really belief (as Moore thought) but something more like an attitude.* Wittgenstein makes these comparisons at several points. For example, he says: "If someone can believe in God with complete certainty, why not in Other Minds?" (CV p.73). This seems to echo Wittgenstein's remark in the *Investigations*: "My attitude towards him is an attitude towards a soul. I am not of the *opinion* that he has a soul" (PI p.178). As for the comparision with the 'language-games' we play with words such as "apple" and "chair" and "cup," Wittgenstein says: "Life can educate one to a belief in God. ... Experiences, thoughts, — life can force this concept on us. So perhaps it is similar to the concept of 'object'" (CV 86). I take this to mean: just as the way in which our sense-data behave (i.e., they aren't chaotic) leads us to employ nouns having the grammar of "apple" and "chair" and "cup," so the exegencies of a person's life, such as his feelings of guilt, can bring him to the point of using religious language, i.e., in neither case do we make inferences about transcendent objects but rather come by these forms of words spontaneously.

What are we to make of all this? I want to comment first on Wittgenstein's comparison of what religious people say with what all of us say about material things and about other people's pains and hopes and fears. Wittgenstein was surely wrong in lumping together the problem of religious belief with the problems of 'belief' in other minds and material things. In the latter two cases the problem arises only because of what philosophers themselves have invented: 'bodies' and 'sense-data.' In these cases we have come to see in recent years (thanks largely to the work of Frank Ebersole) that the philosophers' inventions are philosophical fictions. It is these fictions, and nothing else, that make it seem that material things and other people's thoughts and feeling are transcendent and thus make it seem plausible to say, with Moore, that we *believe* in other minds and material things. Accordingly, it is inappropriate to speak of our believing in 'other minds' or material objects, etc. — not only 'believing' in the way Moore thought of it but also 'believing' in the way Wittgenstein thought of it (as an attitude). By contrast, it is not just philosophers who say that God is transcendent and that people have religious *beliefs*, for everyone else says this, too. So *prima facie* this case is not like the other two, i.e., only a phenomenalist could say what Wittgenstein says here.

To see whether this *prima facie* difference holds up, let us turn to Wittgenstein's other remarks about religious language and belief. What we find in the passages quoted above is reductionism in its most patent form. All the signs of it are evident. Wittgenstein says: religious language does not mean what, at first sight, it appears to mean; appearances to the contrary, Christianity is a description of something that takes place in human life; although it is belief, in a special sense of the word, it is *really* a way of living, a way of assessing life. Gone from this account are all the things that have kept people in thrall for centuries: God and the devil, heaven and hell, the prospect of salvation or eternal damnation, forgiveness from a loving God. Wittgenstein, by dismissing all of this, has turned religion into something an empiricist can embrace, something intellectually comfortable, even if emotionally taxing.[3]

What is remarkable about Wittgenstein's reductionistic account of religion and religious belief is that he makes no attempt to support it with any sort of evidence that this is how things are in religion. This belies his claim that what he does is "to replace wild conjectures and explanations by quiet weighing of linguistic facts" (Z §447). Wittgenstein did not arrive at his account by weighing anything at all. He was simply driven to it by what I have called "the master argument."

Perhaps this can be more easily seen by reviewing a bit of the history of his account. At the time of the *Tractatus* he wrote in his notebook: "To pray is to think about the meaning of life" (NB 73) and "To believe in God means to see that life has a meaning" (NB 74). This was an early attempt to fit religious language ("prayer" and "God") into a world of sense-data. In 1930, before he had come to think of meaning as use, he tried a different strategy: he maintained that religious speech is not really *speech*.

> Is talking essential to religion? I can well imagine a religion in which there are no doctrinal propositions, in which there is thus no talking. Obviously the essence of religion cannot have anything to do with the fact that there is talking, or rather: when people talk, then this itself is part of a religious act and not a theory. Thus it also does not matter at all if the words used are true or false or nonsense.
>
> In religion talking is not *metaphorical* either; for otherwise it would have to be possible to say the same thing in prose (WWK 117).

Here Wittgenstein is saying that since praying, reciting creeds, and so on are religious *behavior*, like genuflecting, it would be a mistake to think that what is 'said' is true or false or nonsense.[4] Later, when he had come to think of meaning as use, he could retract this bizarre suggestion, for he could now allow that religious speech is indeed speech, i.e. that the words, like any words, have a meaning inasmuch as they have a use. But he now had to find a way to bring out the meaning of religious language in a way that did not clash with his empiricism, and accordingly he offered the reductionist account that we find in the passages quoted above.

Another possible source of his reductionist account may lie in the fact that he was greatly influenced by his reading, during the First World War, of Tolstoy, especially Tolstoy's *The Gospel in Brief*.[5] What Tolstoy did was select out of the four gospels mainly the human history and the moral teachings of Jesus. It is, as we would now say, a demythologized version of the gospels. Wittgenstein may have thought that Tolstoy had in this way captured the essence of Christianity.[6] But of course Tolstoy's version, which depicts Christianity as consisting chiefly of ethical teachings, is very far from orthodoxy, so that if one wants to know what orthodox Christians believe, the place to look is not in Tolstoy's book.

What, then, *do* orthodox Christians believe? And how does one find out? How else could one find out but in the way Evans-Pritchard found out what the Azande believe? One must ask them or listen to them reciting their creeds. But if one does this, one hears nothing like what Wittgenstein's account would suggest. Orthodox Christians say they believe in supernatural beings and miraculous events, and they say they believe in life after death.

Faced with this, some of Wittgensein's followers insist that we must *not* ask such people what they believe. Peter Winch, for example, explicitly affirms that in defending the Wittgensteinian account of religion he is prepared to disregard what religious believers themselves *say* they believe:

> Here I only want to remark that how a term refers has to be understood in the light of its *actual* application with its surrounding context in the lives of its users. I italicize '*actual*' by way of contrasting what I am talking about ... with what users of the term may be inclined to *say* about their application of it if asked.[7]

But Winch will have to discount not only what people say about their beliefs *when asked* (which he perhaps thinks will be naively philosophical), but also the way religious leaders have always presented religion. I have at hand a recent advertisement for one of Billy Graham's revival meetings which pictures an elderly couple walking arm-in-arm and is captioned: "You planned for life after retirement. What about life after death? The Bible has thrilling news. Our creator designed us as immortal creatures. Our bodies die, yes, but the *real* us, our immortal spirits, live on and on! With Christ in our lives, we live forever with Him in Heaven. Without Christ, we're doomed to separation from God. ... How are *you* going to spend forever? If you are not sure, you must hear Billy Graham tonight!" What we find here is not a piece of philosophical misunderstanding of religion, but rather an illustration of the way the vast majority of religious believers understand their faith.

Consider another example, this one from Catholicism. In 1986 Pope John Paul preached a sermon in which he insisted on the reality of the devil as a person and warned of demonic possession. Exorcism is still practiced by the church, and in 1989 Cardinal O'Connor of New York authorized two such rites, reporting afterward that he believed them to have been "successful."

We needn't look only at things such as this; we can look at the creeds orthodox Christians recited each Sunday. When people recite such creeds they are not philosophizing, they are reciting what they believe. Only an *a priori* theory like Wittgenstein's would lead one to think otherwise. Just as his *a priori* theory about the magical practices of primitive peoples can be seen to be wrong by looking at the facts[8], so his *a priori* theory of religion is found to be wrong when we notice what people actually say in pursuing a religious life.

Here we must deal with a matter that I have so far not mentioned: the matter of miracles. Wittgenstein maintained that an extraordinary event is not *in itself* miraculous, for whether we regard it as miraculous or not is a matter of whether we would hope to explain it.[9] But he does not mean that adopting a religious attitude amounts to believing (predicting) that science will find no (Humean) cause of some extraordinary event. If that were all it amounted to, then one's religious attitude would be always in jeopardy of being overturned if a scientist someday found a (Humean) cause of the event. So Wittgenstein presumably thought that adopting a religious attitude toward the event involves playing a different language-game, namely, the 'indeterministic' language-game. And that means that, in adopting a religious attitude, one will simply regard any explanation that science may offer as being no explanation at all. The religious attitude is one in which a person does not think that there must be 'hidden' causes of what is not yet explained.

But what about divine agency as the cause of miracles? If we judge by what religious people *say*, we can only think that they understand miracles to be events brought about by God, as events having a *transcendent* cause. The Red Sea is not thought to have parted *causelessly* (in Exodus 14:21 we read: "and the Lord caused the sea to go back by a strong east wind all that night, and made the sea dry land, and the waters were divided"), nor is it thought that Mary became pregnant with Jesus causelessly (in Matthew 1:20 we read: "that which is conceived in her is of the Holy Ghost"). And what about the ascension of Jesus into heaven? The biblical account, accepted by orthodox believers, is that "he was taken up; and a cloud received him out of their sight" (Acts 1:9). The passive voice here is surely meant to imply divine agency. But Wittgenstein would have a problem with the idea of divine agency just because the cause is transcendent, not given in experience. Indeed, the problem he would have seen here is the same as that which led him to reject the causal theory of perception, in which the causes of sense-data are said to be 'beyond' experience. He said of this theory: "All propositions about causation are learned from sense-data. Therefore no proposition can be about the cause of sense-data" (LWL p.81). Wittgenstein would surely have thought that this undercuts not only the idea that sense-data are caused by something not found in experience, but also the belief that extraordinary events — such as Mary's pregnancy and the ascension of Jesus — were caused by something not found in experience. He was faced, then, with only two options: either to declare that belief in miracles is nonsense or to declare that a religious person, in regarding some event as miraculous, would allow nothing (and certainly not divine agency) as the cause of it. But in choosing the latter alternative, he was misrepresenting both Judaism and Christianity. Had he remained true to his claim to be replacing wild conjectures with quiet weighing of linguistic facts, he would have opted, given the premises of the master argument, for the other alternative, that religious belief is nonsense.[10] But by that standard, he should have come to the same conclusion wherever he found a collision between empiricism and what we say. "One cannot," he said, "guess how a word functions. One has to *look at* its use and learn from that" (PI §340). But Wittgenstein very seldom looked; he guessed, and in the case of religious belief guessed wrong.[11]

Endnotes

1. Defenders of Wittgenstein's account of religion sometimes explicitly state that their aim is to show that, since a belief in something metaphysically transcendent would be nonsensical, religious people do *not* believe in anything metaphysically transcendent. Ilham Dilman, for instance, puts the matter as follows:

> When I said "this [namely, something metaphysically transcendent] cannot be what [religious people] mean " I was assuming they do mean something. A whole tradition of thought, one which has played a role in people's lives for centuries and enriched their life and literature cannot be inherently confused. To put it simply, if a form of words which people have uttered again and again is not an idle wheel, but has a use, then it cannot be logically defective ("Wisdom's Philosophy of Religion: Part II: Metaphysical and Religious Transcendence," *Canadian Journal of Philosophy*, Vol. V, No. 4 (December, 1975), p. 500).

Wittgenstein's 'use' theory of meaning is clearly in evidence here as the means by which religious belief is to be rescued from the charge that such beliefs are nonsense.

2. M. O'C. Drury, "Conversations with Wittgenstein," in *Recollections of Wittgenstein*, ed. Rush Rhees (Oxford University Press: Oxford, 1984), p. 107.

3. Wittgenstein was not alone in proposing such an interpretation of religion, for R. B. Braithwaite's "An Empiricist's View of the Nature of Religious Belief" (1955) took much the same line. The difference was that Braithwaite lacked Wittgenstein's 'use' theory of meaning and so lacked what, in Wittgenstein's case, looked like grounds for such an interpretation.

4. Wittgenstein, having been raised a Catholic, may have been encouraged in this idea by the fact that the mass was in Latin, including responses by the choir and altar boys. He may have thought that the fact that Latin was used in place of the languages people spoke showed that one was not meant to understand. Such a view would, of course, have to ignore the fact that the worshippers' missals contain a translation of the mass — and also the fact that the worshippers have been catechized.

5. "Certainly, Tolstoy was as much in his thoughts as Frege during this crucial period; his fellow soldiers nicknamed him 'the man with the Gospels,' because he never was seen without his copy of Tolstoy's *The Gospel in Brief*, which he mentions acquiring in a letter to Russell, and which he also referred to as the book which 'saved my life'" (Allan Janik and Stephen Toulmin, *Wittgenstein's Vienna* (Simon and Schuster: New York, 1973), pp. 200-201).

6. Wittgenstein's cousin, F. A. von Hayek, in his "Unpublished Sketch of a Biography of Ludwig Wittgenstein," relates the following events during Wittgenstein's stay in prison camp at the end of World War I:

Another topic for lively discussion was provided by Wittgenstein discovering in the camp a copy of the Bible and reading, apparently for the first time, the original version of the Gospels. He had been so impressed by Tolstoy's interpretation that he was greatly disturbed by much that he found in the original and was only with difficulty convinced of its genuineness.

Von Hayek cites no source for this account, so one cannot give it full credence. But Wittgenstein's refusal to believe that the genuine Bible was genuine would not have been out of character. Norman Malcolm, in his memoir, relates the following incident:

The weather was unusually hot that summer [in Ithaca] and Wittgenstein's room on the second floor was often very uncomfortable. He once pointed out to me that the wire mesh of the window screens restricted to some extent the movements of air through his windows, and wondered why they could not be removed. I replied that if this were done great numbers of insects would enter and prove even more disagreeable than the heat. Wittgenstein doubted that this was so. He remarked that in England and on the Continent windows were commonly left unscreened. I answered that there were more insects in America. Wittgenstein didn't believe this, and when he went out for a walk later that day he made a point of looking at a number of houses in order to see whether their windows were screened. He found that all of them were but, oddly enough, instead of inferring that there must be a good reason for it, he concluded with some irritation that Americans were the victims of widespread and unthinking prejudice as to the necessity of window screens (*Ludwig Wittgenstein: A Memoir*, Op. Cit., p. 94.)

I suspect that this trait carried over to his philosophizing, so that when he found something that conflicted with his views, including his views about religion, he simply dismissed it or sought a way to dispell the appearance of conflict.

7. "Meaning and Religious language," in *Reason and Religion*, ed. Stuart C. Brown (Cornell University Press: Ithaca, 1977), p. 200.

8. See my "Magic, Witchcraft and Science," *Philosophical Investigations* (January, 1983), pp. 2-36.

9. "Wittgenstein's Lecture on Ethics," *Philosophical Review* (January, 1965), pp. 10-11.

10. I am not recommending this verdict, for I do not accept the philosophical notion of 'nonsense.' Nor do I accept the current view that we should concern ourselves with 'religious language,' for I do not accept the idea of 'religious language.' (See my essay "Wittgenstein and Religious Belief," *Philosophy*, October, 1988, pp. 427-452). We should be concerned with what religious believers believe, and I think those beliefs can be cogently criticized.

11. He did sometimes look, but what he found did not suit him. Drury quotes him as saying: "It is a dogma of the Roman Church that the existence of God can be proved by natural reason. Now this dogma would make it impossible for me to be a Roman Catholic. If I thought of God as another being like myself, outside myself, only infinitely more powerful, then I would regard it as my duty to defy him" ("Conversations with Wittgenstein," Op. Cit., pp. 107-108). It was not just the idea of proofs that he found unacceptable, but also the conception of God as a being outside himself.

CHAPTER X

Knowing What One Was
Intending to Say

J.F.M. Hunter

§633. "You were interrupted a while ago; do you still know what you were going to say?" — If I do know now, and say it — does that mean that I had already thought it before, only not said it? No. Unless you take the certainty with which I continue the interrupted sentence as a criterion of the thought's already having been completed at that time. — But of course the situation and the thoughts I had contained all sorts of things to help the continuation of the sentence.

§634. When I continue the interrupted sentence and say this is how I had been going to continue it, this is like following out a line of thought from brief notes.

Then don't I *interpret* the notes? Was only one continuation possible in these circumstances? Of course not. But I did not *choose* between interpretations. I *remembered* that I was going to say this (see also §337).

Various hard questions of interpretation arise in these sections, and I will discuss these, and at a minimum declare what answers to them I will be assuming when I go on to treat of the interesting philosophical questions we encounter here. I will number the exegetical problems.

1. In §633 Wittgenstein quite flatly denies that if we know what we were going to say, and say it, that means that we had already thought it before, only not said it; but perhaps he is just denying that we *must* have thought it before. His view might be that although the case in which we have thought the whole sentence before the interruption is very common, and when it occurs, easily explains our knowing what we were intending to say, we do sometimes know how we would have completed a sentence, although before being interrupted we had not inwardly enunciated the

whole sentence. And Wittgenstein might be proposing to concentrate on this rarer and supposedly mysterious, but still possible, kind of case.

There is very little textual evidence to go on in answering these questions, but since it is not true that we usually plan out what to say beforehand, while it is usually true that we know how we would have continued an interrupted sentence; and also since it is arguable that even when we do spell out to ourselves beforehand what we will say, it is not by recalling that plan, that we are able either to continue the sentence or to say how we would have continued it — I like to think that Wittgenstein did not believe it normal and unproblematic to have a linguistic plan and proceed to carry it out. The prior formulation of what one may say, for example in answer to someone's question, when that occurs, and the actual giving of an answer to that person's question, are exercises of the same ability; and if one were interrupted in the *former* activity, for example if one had said to oneself 'I shall say ...' and then been interrupted, but still knew how one would have continued, that would surely not require us to suppose that the 'inner' sentence had already been completed, perhaps in the unconscious.

2. What does Wittgenstein mean by 'Unless you take the certainty with which I continue the interrupted sentence as a criterion of the thought's already having been completed at that time'?

Again there is a shortage of textual evidence, but I will take Wittgenstein to be saying 'Unless when you say he had completed the thought when the interruption occurred, you *just mean* that he continued the sentence with certainty'. We might derive this interpretation from the fact that it would be wrong to take someone's completing an interrupted sentence with certainty to prove without more ado that the thought had been complete before the interruption. It is an empirical question whether a person has thought out a sentence before embarking on saying it, but making the certainty with which he continues it the *criterion* of his having thought it out beforehand would make it, in a case in which he does continue with certainty, true that he had planned it, independently of what had happened. (cf. §625, in which someone says he knows he has raised his arm because he recognizes the feeling, and Wittgenstein says 'You are certain that you raised your arm; isn't that the criterion, the measure, of the recognition?' Here it is virtually certain that Wittgenstein thought it humbug that we know we raised an arm because we recognize the feeling. Therefore in calling the certainty that we raised it the criterion of our having recognized a feeling, he can't be saying the certainty is what shows we recognized the feeling: that would involve taking seriously the idea that we do recognize the feeling. So in §633 too he probably means 'unless saying that the thought was already completed at that time was *just saying* that the interrupted sentence was continued with certainty.')

3. There are problems in the final sentence of §633, about what sorts of things would help in the continuation of the sentence, and how they would help, but I will leave them until later, and just note that talking of 'all sorts of things' helping the continuation of the sentence strongly suggests it was Wittgenstein's view that we *put together* the continuation of the sentence, we do not have it complete and ready (or, if we should forget it for a time, have it return complete and ready).

4. When Wittgenstein says that continuing the sentence is like following out a line of thought from brief notes, it may sound as if he is raising the possibility that the part of the sentence spoken before the interruption counted as brief notes on how the sentence should be continued. But I am not *enlarging* on 'I would have chosen ...' if I continue '... the red one'.

More likely he had in mind the case in which a squiggle (not a logical symbol or a stenographer's shorthand) somehow reminds us where we were and we then can get right on with what we had been going to say. I think the fact that in the second paragraph of §634 he says, not that he remembered planning to say this, but that he remembered that he was going to say this — shows fairly clearly that he had in mind, not the case in which something shows us how we had been going to continue, but the case in which we can simply (that is without guidance) complete the interrupted sentence. The squiggle or the brief notes do not tell us what we would have said, but as it were put us in a position to carry on out of our own resources.

5. Although Wittgenstein seems generally to be mindful of the difference between an interpretation and a continuation, he seems to be mixing them up when he says (§634): "Then don't I *interpret* the notes? Was only one continuation possible in these circumstances? Of course not. But I did not *choose* between interpretations. I *remembered* that I was going to say this."

One might think he would have been better to say 'I didn't choose between *continuations*. I remembered that I was going to say this', because the *continuation* of a sentence from any given point is not an interpretation at all, and hence not an interpretation that he remembered, rather than chose. So I am inclined to think Wittgenstein wrote carelessly here; but still it is a valuable point that the speaker does not in the normal case *work out* what she would have said, at least not in any way like that in which we work out interpretations. We are not in the dark about what we would have said, and do not labor to produce hypotheses about this.

6. Wittgenstein says 'I *remembered* that I was going to say this'; but what should we suppose this remembering consisted in? We may be very apt to think that it is a matter of having a re-appearance to the mind of something previously thought. That is the kind of supposition that goes with the direct object grammatical construction. What we remember is planning to say this or resolving to say that. But Wittgenstein used an indirect form of speech. Instead of e.g. 'I (vividly?) remember *planning* to say such and such', he said 'I remembered *that* I was going to say ...', and he could so express himself if all that happened was that when the interruption passed, he went on with the sentence previously embarked upon.

(Here we do not need to go into the question whether direct object remembering must be conceived as a conscious mental process. When we remember something vividly, all that need be true is that we could on demand give a richly detailed description. When we know we could on demand say what flowers Martha had in her garden, and where they were and what were their colours, it may seem that we must have a mental picture from which all this is derivable, but we do not feel much inclined to say that if from memory we can reproduce word for word a paragraph that someone read to us, it will be from a mental reproduction of her voice that we are apprized what to say.)

That Wittgenstein would say that we need no props in order to complete an interrupted sentence is clear from §633, where as we saw he denies that knowing what one had been going to say requires that one should have thought it before, only not said it.

The point that he did not think remembering is calling something specific before the mind is also clear from §338. When Wittgenstein says in that section that 'we grasp at the image of dancing, speaking, etc.', as showing what it is we want, the fact that he is talking here about wanting, rather than remembering, makes no difference; and just as he no doubt regards it as a mistake to grasp at the image of dancing etc. as showing what it is we want, he would likewise assuredly say it is a mistake to grasp at the image of a completed sentence running through the mind as showing what we were intending to say.

With these preliminaries out of the way, we can take up some of the philosophical questions arising in this affair.

It is hard to be sure whether Wittgenstein thought of knowing how the sentence would have been completed as a matter of knowing of what words and in what order the complete sentence would have been composed, or only as a matter of knowing what the burden of the completed sentence would have been, whatever the words in which it might be expressed. Since the text provides no clear indications about this, I propose simply to consider both kinds of case. We may very well scarcely doubt that composing a sentence having the same burden as the interrupted one would be by far the more usual state of affairs; and initially one might well be doubtful whether, except perhaps in the case of having planned the complete sentence, it is possible to know in just what words the sentence would have been completed.

Yet cases in which we do know this are not far to seek, or fantastic. A lawyer is drafting a client's will. She wants no uncertainty about how the testator's assets are to be handled, and she knows various standard formulae, to be used depending on whether the client wishes this or that. She is clear about the client's wishes, and it follows, and she knows it follows, that the will should be written thus and so at a certain point; but she need not and will not normally *rehearse* the way it should be written, before dictating it to her secretary. She *knows* how to write a clause in a will if such and such is the client's wish, and she can deliver the right words on demand at any time. So again not only is it her legal expertise that enables her to continue if she is interrupted, that expertise will often require her to continue in a particular way.

Perhaps a more common case in which, without having rehearsed it, a person may know verbatim what he would have said, is that in which either there is only one way of saying something, or only one way that he would ever use. If Wilfred says he does not want to go just now because... , and then is interrupted, he may know that he would have continued '... it is raining too hard' — in those words and no others — even if he (like anyone else) had not earlier thought the complete sentence. There scarcely are other ways of saying the 'it is raining' part of what he would have said; and while 'too heavily' or 'too much' are alternatives to 'too hard' that *someone* might have used, perhaps Wilfred would never in fact express himself in either of those ways, and always says 'too hard' in such a case.

So even in what we may initially have regarded as the hardest case, it is not mind-boggling after all, that a person should know without having planned it out, in what sequence of what words she would have completed an interrupted sentence; and perhaps the other case, in which we know how we will complete a sentence, but not in what words, is after all the more remarkable.

An example: a person who is intending to go to town to shop for some shoes and has said 'I am going to town...,' and been interrupted, later would not necessarily say '... to shop for a pair of shoes', but in a particular case would have said either that or something having the same sense. This person would not, just before speaking, have resolved 'I will say either "to shop for a pair of shoes" or something having the same sense'; and one may, if one thinks that intending certainly consists of *something*, wonder what her intending could have consisted of in this kind of case, if no particular string of words was settled upon, — or equally what form her recollection of this intending might take.

Part of the difficulty here may be that we keep looking for something that *shows* us what we were intending to say. We suppose there is a point at which we do not know, and have to be informed some way. Then we grope for an explanation of how we get back on track, although no such explanation is necessary, because (normally) we were never off track.

In a normal conversation there is nothing going on over and above my saying this and your saying that, no relevant words, pictures, or messages in code, that the memory might store and later reproduce. We do not rehearse what we will say, but just get on with it. But even if we recognize that usually there will be nothing for the memory to keep a record of, it may appear the more mind-boggling how it is possible that one should remember that one was going to say such and such. It will of course sometimes be true that we do not know what we were intending to say — if an incident about which we were being interrogated was not recent or if the point we were making was quite subtle. But even in such a case what we need is not to be informed of it — we may get past such conversational mishaps by thinking further about the problem that was under discussion, and re-inventing the point we had nearly made earlier.

We do sometimes forget what we were going to say, but if we do, our ability to complete the sentence is restored, not when some of the words we would have used float through the mind, but for example when we remember some of the drift and direction a conversation had been taking. Then, as Wittgenstein said (§633) 'the situation and the thoughts [we] had [will contain] all sorts of things to help the continuation of the sentence'. Here it is not that something makes the rest of the interrupted sentence come to mind, but rather that, putting ourselves imaginatively in essentially the position we had been in, we will continue on from there as we would have done, had there been no interruption. (Cf.PI §343, §648.)

I was in the thick of answering Emily's question; it was on a complex topic, about which I knew a good deal, but I had had a bright idea about how to simplify it. Knowing a good deal about a topic and being a little inventive are perhaps the sorts of thing Wittgenstein thought would help; but there would be no point in my reviewing *such* things: their being the case would be enough.

I am suggesting that these affairs work along something like the following lines: completing an interrupted sentence is a matter of resuming the conversational activity that had been in progress, starting where we had been when the interruption occurred. Normally we will simply continue, almost as if a recording of the conversation had been turned off for a moment and then on again. But sometimes we bog down. Having this happen is not like forgetting the lines of a poem, and the remedy for it is not somehow making those lines come tumbling forth again in their characteristic way. Suppose I am explaining what is wrong with the ontological argument. I know something about this, and can explain it in various ways, and this time I set about it using a somewhat novel example. There is an interruption, and when it passes I say 'Now, where were we?' Someone reminds me that I was using the example of someone listing the excellences of a house she is thinking of buying. I say 'Oh yes, I remember', and continue my explanation. Here remembering is not as it were digging out a script from which one had been reading, and reading further. It is rather returning to the project of explaining a point, and using some acquired skills in doing so. In pursuing such a project I may get in a muddle into which I might not have got, had the interruption not occurred, but that does not mean I have deviated from the script. There was no script.

If a cook says 'I make meringues this way because...', and is interrupted, his experience in cookery will provide him with plenty of material with which to continue his explanation. In doing this he does not draw on what was running through his mind when he began the sentence, but on some of his observations over the years on what happened if he made meringues in other ways.

When we ask what someone had been intending to say, we may seem to be assuming that some intending was undoubtedly part of what had been going on just before the interruption, and that intenders are likely to remember and focus in on the intending they had been doing, and in that way inform themselves about what they would have said. Something like this is perhaps the misleading picture of the use of the word 'intend' that Wittgenstein said (§337) we construct. The following is a possible way of enlarging on this suggestion.

Intending to go on in a particular way is not something that occurs as one talks, or just before one begins. It does not *occur*. *Later on* people may ask how I had intended to complete the sentence, and it will sound as if they were referring back to something that happened before the interruption; but in these contexts 'intend' is used only 'later on', and is shown not to refer back to something that took place, by the interchangeability of sentences in which it appears with constructions like 'What would you have gone on to say?', 'How would you have continued the sentence?', and so on, none of which carries the suggestion that a specific process of shaping the future was occurring. If these equivalent locutions carry no suggestion of something occurring alongside of or just prior to someone's saying something (and they do not), then neither does 'How did you intend to complete that sentence?'

In the first person singular, the expression 'to intend to say ....' is not used concerning conversation that is currently under way. I may conjecture what you intend to say to the prime minister tomorrow, but not what I intend to say to him, (as distinct from trying to decide what *to* say to him), as if I already had an intention, and would like to know what it is. 'To intend to say ....' is in its element in retrospective discourse, in recognition of an interruption or when a breakdown occurs. This is not because, although intending will of course be going on while a person is speaking — as it were organizing what to say next — we do not take an interest in it until we are thwarted by a stoppage in the flow. The question here is not whether anything occurs as well as the speaking we actually do, but whether any of what also occurs *is called* intending. We need not deny that thoughts that are connected to the speech endeavour we are engaged in do occur alongside of the speaking we do. As we talk, we wonder whether the other person has understood, whether we might provide more examples, whether such and such an example would be helpful, and so on. But this working on what to say that sometimes takes place concurrently with speaking is not called intending. When we ask what a person was intending to say, we are not wondering whether she had thought 'Perhaps I'd better not say that', 'Perhaps this will amuse her', and so on, but at most wondering what was the upshot of any such deliberations as may have occurred. And when a person who has spoken ambiguously is asked 'Is that what you intended to say?' we know what she did say and want to know, not whether her saying this was preceded by an intention to say it, but which of two inerpretations she endorses.

We do not use the word 'intend' in thinking about what to say. We do not say to ourselves 'Should I intend to say *this*?' 'Yes, I think I'll intend to say *that*', and so on. I may ask myself 'What was I intending to say at this point?', but that is another breakdown use; and if we say 'What *do* I intend to say about the really tough question?', either this use of 'intend' is mystifying or the question is the same as 'What *shall* I say?'. When Wittgenstein goes on (in §337) to say 'An intention is embedded in its situation, in human customs and institutions', I have great difficulty understanding him. When he continues: 'If the technique of the game of chess did not exist, I could not intend to play a game of chess', that seems hardly more worth noting than the fact that if bricks didn't exist, I couldn't intend to build a brick outhouse. But I begin to see light at the end of the tunnel when he adds: "Insofar as I do intend the construction of a sentence in advance, that is made possible by the fact that I speak the language in question."

I suggest Wittgenstein is saying here that to explain our ability to complete interrupted sentences we need only recognize that people can talk: can ask and answer questions, describe scenes and moods, express enthusiasm, and so on. Here we have a bag of skills, and one of the ways we can put them to work is in explaining what we had been intending to say. Wittgenstein says something quite *like* this in §692:

> Is it correct for someone to say: "When I gave you this rule, I meant you to.....in this case"? Of course it is correct. For "to mean it" does not mean: to think of it. But now the problem is: how are we to judge whether someone meant such-and-such? — The fact that he has for example mastered a particular technique in arithmetic and algebra ... is such a criterion.

In a case like this I will have meant her to do *this* here, *that* there, and so on indefinitely. It can look as if a great deal of meaning this and meaning that must have gone on in the twinkling of an eye and without my even noticing it happening; but I just wanted her to do what I or any other trained practitioner would do in each case. In this way what I mean you to do at the eleventh place, that is, what I would do at that point, is a spinoff from the workings of the habit set I have acquired in my mathematical training.

What may be analogous to this in the case of knowing what one would have said is the fact that although as we begin a sentence, we have most often not chosen the words with which we will complete it, if we are interrupted and someone wants to know what we would have said, we can generate an answer to his question by going back to where we were when the interruption occurred, and proceeding from there, in the direction we had been heading. Our linguistic habits will work to complete the sentence, just as they would have done, had no interruption occurred. This does not mean that I was *destined* to use just those words — only that I would have said either this or something having the same sense. '*This* is what I was intending to say' will not mean that I had *thought* those words, any more than '*This* is what I meant you to do' (in §692) does. It means something more like 'This is what my way with the language would have yielded at that point in the activity in which I was engaged.'

I will conclude with a brief consideration of a sentence in §337 that I have found extremely difficult:

> But didn't I intend the whole construction of the sentence (for example) at its beginning? So surely it must have existed in my mind before I said it out loud! — If it was in my mind, still it would not normally be there in some different word order.

Here we see Wittgenstein seeming to treat the fact that if the continuation of an interrupted sentence appeared in the mind, it would not appear in a different word order, as obvious and important; but is it obvious? What reason is there to expect that if there were a sentence running through the mind that expressed what I intended to say, its words should occur in an order different from that of the words I may in due course use? These questions seem uncommonly tough, but I will suggest answers that once seen provide a simple and effective solution.

There is in fact no reason whatever to expect a different word order, and it is of no consequence whatever whether the order is the same; but silly people like those described in the preceding section of the *Investigations* may suppose that in the language of thought, words have a natural and proper order, and only a very few fortunate languages preserve this order. Hence (they suppose) the language in which someone has thought something will nearly always have a different word order from that in which the thought is explained. If there were a language of thought, and if an intended sentence would of course appear in that language, then for sure part of the job of translating the mental sentence and thus explaining what one had intended to say would be one of changing its word order into that of the language the person translating spoke.

Wittgenstein's point that the words expressing the intention to say such and such would not usually occur in a different word order would be a good one against anyone like the French politician in §336; but since such a person's beliefs in this matter are hardly to be taken seriously, we can only suppose that Wittgenstein intended what he said in §337 as a joke. The humour here, if it is such, is not high comedy, but perhaps we could indulgently let it pass as quiet philosophical fun.

J.F.M. Hunter
University of Toronto

CHAPTER XI

Consciousness:
The Cartesian Enigma and
Its Contemporary Resolution

Jeff Coulter

Introduction

One of the most enigmatic and enduring problems confronted by philosophers and behavioural scientists alike has been the nature of 'consciousness'. Many concur in the judgement of Quine that it is a mystery, "but not one to be dismissed. We know what it is like to be conscious, but not how to put it into satisfactory scientific terms",[1] or in the position of Johnson-Laird that: "No one really knows what consciousness is, what it does, or what function it serves".[2] Indeed Nagel has argued that its properties cannot in principle be known to science because *any* scientific inquiry is necessarily a 'third-person' endeavour, whereas only a 'first-person' perspective can logically aspire to depict its characteristics,[3] a position described by Dennett as 'auto-phenomenological'.[4] Notoriously, Watson's behaviourist legacy also incorporated the view that 'consciousness' was not a proper topic for scientific investigation, but from the position that "belief in the existence of consciousness goes back to the days of superstition and magic".[5] In the absence of any "objective evidence for their existence", science can and must dispense with the pseudo-phenomena of 'mind' and 'consciousness'.[6] This 'eliminationist' reaction to the enigma confronted by scientific psychology was parallelled by Broad's efforts to counter Huxley's 'emergentist' evolutionary theorizing about the mind in the philosophy of biology.[7]

Various kinds of eliminationism persist today in the range of reductionist 'psycho-neural' identity theories,[8] according to most of which 'consciousness' is nothing but a neural state or process. The general inadequacies of this perspective will, I hope, become apparent as we proceed. Nonetheless, 'mind' and 'consciousness' continue to appear to many as embarrassments to materialist, evolutionary theories of human capacities and attributes. Either they are relegated to a domain permanently beyond scientific scrutiny or penetration (Nagel), dismissed as fictional constructs (Watson, Skinner) or 'reduced' to physical entities or processes (Place, Smart, Armstrong).

I shall seek to argue in what follows that many of the perplexities encountered in efforts to reconcile a commitment to evolutionary biology with 'consciousness' are a function of the entrapment of the development of Darwinian thought within a Cartesian conceptual framework, a framework whose many features are tacitly but demonstrably shared by eliminationist, reductionist and 'auto-phenomenological' approaches alike. I shall chart a course through the relevant contributions of Mead, Husserl, Ryle and the later Wittgenstein in the service of showing that an emancipation from the major tenets of the Cartesian legacy is not only possible but essential for the development of the behavioural sciences after Darwin. I believe that the philosophical developments to be tracked in pursuit of this anti-Cartesian objective exhibit progressively greater clarity and sophistication; whether the conclusions to be drawn amount to the 'solution' I claim is left to the reader to decide.

Consciousness: The Cartesian Conception

Descartes' dualism divided the human being into two components, the corporeal (physical, biological) body, the *res extensa*, and the immaterial (metaphysical) *res cogitans* (thinking thing/substance). By 'thought', Descartes meant "everything which takes place in us so that we are conscious of it, in so far as it is the object of our consciousness".[9] As Kenny indicates: "What is common to all the operations of the mind [according to Descartes -JC] is consciousness. Consciousness carries with it indubitability and thus makes the *cogito* suitable as a first principle."[10] Ambiguities pervade Descartes' account, however.

Sometimes, consciousness appears to be something that accompanies thought, as when he says that thought is that *of which* we are conscious ... Sometimes consciousness appears to be something identical with thought, as when he says that it is our seeming to see that is strictly to be called sensation or thought... And in passages in which thought and consciousness are identified, it is often unclear whether particular mental acts are species of thought consciousness or are accompanied by thought consciousness.[11]

Nonetheless, for Descartes 'consciousness' is the quintessential property of the 'res cogitans' - the mind - which sharply demarcates it from the corporeal vessel of the body, and he bequeathed to us a way of conceptualising the body-mind relationship according to which consciousness transcends the material, physical, biological properties of human beings while still possessing the capacity to control (and be reciprocally influenced by) the brain. In his *Treatise of Man* (1664), he proposed that the pineal gland receives sensory input (e.g., from the eyes) by means of vibrations through the fluid in the chambers of the brain. The mind's will then dispatches signals from the brain to the muscles, causing them to respond. The pineal gland was assigned the responsibility of mediating the relationship between the conscious mind and the material brain.[12] Animals, according to his general conception, were 'thoughtless brutes', lacking consciousness, and therefore amenable to analysis in terms of concepts derived purely from mechanics. Human beings, however, possessed a 'vital' power fundamentally irreducible to mechanical processes. Such an account naturally augured badly for incorporation into evolutionary biological thought with its exclusively materialist emphasis upon explaining the attributes and capacities of Man in terms of purely physical and ecological processes of reproduction, organism-environment interaction, natural selection, genetic adaptation and so on. Indeed, much of the debate between 'vitalists' and 'mechanists' in the nineteenth century turned upon the vexed question of how the brain (or any of its parts) could 'generate' thought or consciousness. Clearly, any internally consistent scheme of explanation compatible with the tenets of evolutionary theory would have to find some way of 'naturalising' the putative 'phenomenon of consciousness'.

As noted earlier, one relatively simple, although vacuous, way of dealing with the enigma was that of Watson, consisting in the denial of the *explanandum*. However, later behaviouristic efforts to come to terms with consciousness admitted it into the ontological canon and sought less drastic ways of handling the problems it created. Among these attempts at pacification, perhaps the most ambitious and influential was that of G.H. Mead.[13]

Mead postulated what may be termed a 'sociobiological' conception[14] of human consciousness. Focussing upon the human capacity for 'reflective thought' (also referred to as 'reflective awareness'), which Descartes had identified (or more generally associated) with human consciousness, Mead argued that this capacity depends, phylogenetically and ontogenetically, upon the capacity for speech which in turn is facilitated by the evolution of the vocal chords and their corresponding neurophysiological structures. Originating from primitive inter-organismic gesturing,[15] *vocal* gesturing emerged with its greater expressive and communicative power. Adaptionally advantageous, this new behavioural faculty formed the basis for the development of social *symbolisation* within hominid society. Reflective thought is derived from (and made possible by) social, interactive communication which, in its advanced form, consisted in the vocal articulation/manipulation of symbols. Its derivation consists in the *individuation* (Mead speaks of the 'individual importation') of a process which is originally interactive.

> Consciousness [reflective awareness] is an emergent from such beha-
> viour; that so far from being a precondition of the social act, the
> social act is a precondition of it. The mechanism of the social act can
> be traced out without introducing into it the conception of conscious-
> ness as a separable element within the act; hence the social act, in
> its more elementary states or forms, is possible without, or apart
> from, some form of [reflective] consciousness.[16]

The human being does not first think and then acquire the capacity to speak (as classical wisdom from Augustine to Descartes and Locke had assumed); rather, reflective thought consists in the symbolically-mediated (albeit non-articulated) communication 'between' a single individual and himself in which process he treats himself as he would another individual. In this way, argued Mead, a link can be established between a biologically evolved capacity in humans (speech) and a putatively 'mental' phenomenon (thought) via the analysis of the social phenomenon of linguistic behavior and its obvious survival functions. Little was said, however, about the precise nature of the 'sub-vocal', 'non-articulated' aspect of this 'internalised' process of communication with oneself, and in many passages Mead invokes a clearly Cartesian conception of the mind as a domain *within which* this process occurs.[17] The enigma thus remained partially intact.

Despite its difficulties, Mead's account had several significant and attractive features. It sought strenuously to resist the mystery-creating 'entelechistic' conception of consciousness, and began to decompose it into analyzable elements or aspects (sensory awareness, reflective awareness, self-consciousness, etc.), seeking to relate each element to a biologically and anthropologically plausible developmental picture. Such a demystification, however restricted in scope, was a step in the right direction, a move toward the more comprehensive dereification of 'consciousness' which is a prerequisite for a non-metaphysical approach to the topic.

'Consciousness' as a Gloss

A more thorough 'decomposition' of 'consciousness' was advanced by Husserl in the articulation of his project of 'phenomenology'. Although pursuing intellectual objectives quite independent of Darwinian thought, Husserl's analyses paved the way for a later, more radical transformation of the Cartesian account. Husserl's best-known contribution consisted in building upon an argument presented by Franz Brentano.[18] Widely discussed under the heading: 'the thesis of the intentionality of consciousness', Brentano's argument was designed to show that whenever one makes reference to someone's 'consciousness', including one's own, there is a necessary, even if implicit, linkage to some object or topic. In other words consciousness is consciousness *of* something: the concept of consciousness is *essentially* relational or transitive.[19]

> Every mental phenomenon is characterized by ... what we might call, though not wholly unambiguously, reference to a content, direction towards an object (which is not to be understood here as meaning a thing), or immanent objectivity. Every mental phenomenon includes something as an object within itself, although they do not all do so in the same way. In presentation, something is presented, in judgement, something is affirmed of denied, in love loved, in hate hated, in desire desired and so on.[20]

Husserl seized upon this insight to undermine a central aspect of the Cartesian picture: the 'entification' or substantialized conception of consciousness. He wrote, echoing Brentano:

> We understood under Intentionality the unique peculiarity of experiences 'to be the consciousness *of* something.' It was in the explicit *cogito* that we first came across this wonderful property to which all metaphysical enigmas and riddles of the theoretical reason lead us

eventually back: perceiving is the perceiving of something, maybe a thing; judging, the judging of a certain matter; valuation, the valuing of a value; wish, the wish for the content wished, and so on. Acting concerns action, doing concerns the deed, loving the beloved, joy the object of joy.[21]

From here, Husserl proposed to analyse consciousness without residue into 'acts' and their 'objects' (*noeses* and *noemata*).[22] 'Consciousness' is *identified* with such sequences and acts (and their correlative objects).[23] Thus if say, 'imagining' is an 'act', whatever is imagined thereby is its 'object'. Thinking, remembering, wondering, pondering, reflecting, perceiving, hearing, recognising, imagining, and so on - the array of 'modalities' of consciousness - are tied to *some* topic or object. The connection is often through a (grammatical) object-complementizer such as 'about', 'of' or 'that' (etc.). There is no 'consciousness' over and above, or independent of, the 'acts/objects' identifiable by analytic reflection. There is no 'thought' or 'act of thinking' *simpliciter*. There is only a thought *of* or *about* something, or *that* something is the case (etc.). There can be *no* 'thinking' independently of what it is of or about. The radical implications of Husserl's linkage of a (post-Kantian) 'activist' conception of mind to Brentano's 'intentionality' thesis for the classical Cartesian account are clear: 'consciousness' is wrongly construed by Descartes and his followers as a kind of 'entity' or 'substance'. Logically, 'consciousness' is not a term for a unitary phenomenon at all, but rather a gloss for a vast variety of diverse activities, achievements and dispositions of human beings, each of which (excluding the few 'intransitive' cases) is necessarily linked to some topic or 'object'.

Husserl proposed a mode of inquiry into this domain of (mental) acts and their objects which he referred to as 'eidetic (essential) intuition'. By means of such analytical contemplation, involving the method of 'free fantasy variation' of the elements that appear to be constitutive of one or other mental act/object,[24] one might aspire to reveal the essential properties constitutive of, say 'remembering that *X*' or 'listening to *Y*'. Against this programmatics for an *a priori* 'science' of mind, Ryle was to remark that:

> ... the moment we are told by Husserl that there is a process of directly contemplating universals we feel a certain scruple. For we know quite well not only that there do not in fact occur any such contemplations but, more, that there is some absurdity in supposing

that there should. What is the source of this scruple? For the doctrine is widely regarded as at least respectable which holds that the using of concepts does presuppose the finding of special entities; yet explicit talk about this finding does cause a sense of intellectual embarrassment. Why is it not merely a tasteless metaphor but a flat impropriety to speak of 'peering at Remorse'. 'gazing at Induction', 'taking a long look at Choice' or 'happening to light on Conscience'?[25]

Expressing forcefully his own preferred strategy for studying such topics, Ryle continues:

> We elucidate their significations by fixing the rules of their uses and not by any operation of gazing at any wearers of labels... It is, therefore, nonsense (as we felt in our bones) to speak of 'intuiting essences'... Phenomenology, if it moves at all, moves only by the procedures by which all good philosophers have always advanced the elucidation of concepts, *including consciousness-concepts*.[26]

The 'conceptual' transformation of what had been approached as an 'ontological' problem enables one to avoid postulating logically inappropriate strategies of inquiry into 'consciousness', strategies which result in failure, but which encourage their proponents to locate the *source* of such failure not in the misguided mode of inquiry itself but in the 'mysterious' or profoundly enigmatic nature of the putative 'phenomenon' under investigation. Ryle's strictures against efforts to introspect, to 'peer at Remorse', can with full force be directed against efforts to 'fix our attention upon Consciousness' in order to discern its features. G.E. Moore, for example, was apparently a victim of this (Cartesian-inspired) 'phenomenological' strategy, and his frustration is clearly displaced onto the object of his search:

> Though philosophers have recognised that *something* distinct is meant by consciousness, they have never yet had a clear conception of *what* that something is. They have not been able to hold *it* and *blue* before their minds and to compare them, in the same way in which they can compare *blue* and *green*... the moment we try to fix our attention upon consciousness and to see what, distinctly, it is, it seems to vanish: it seems as if we had before us mere emptiness.[27]

The diaphanous or evanescent quality of consciousness is an illusion created by supposing it to be an object amenable to an experiential or perceptual investigation of some kind, rather than a concept with a range of uses none of which are discretely referential. 'Consciousness' is not a name for a realm to be explored but a concept whose grammar awaits elucidation. Just as Ryle proposed to explore the logical geography of consciousness-concepts rather than to employ a method of subjective intuition, Wittgenstein also had, independently, begun to use logico-grammatical techniques to decipher the Cartesian hieroglyphics of the mental. Wittgenstein is similarly dismissive of the idea that one can discover what is *meant* by 'consciousness' (or any other mental concept/predicate) by introspection:

— But what can it mean to speak of 'turning my attention to my own consciousness'? This is surely the queerest thing there could be! It was a particular act of gazing that I called doing this. I stared fixedly in front of me — but not at any particular point or object... My glance was vacant... [28]

We can only determine the meaning of 'consciousness' by explicating the rules for the use of the word and the expressions containing it: no one ever acquired such rules by a process even remotely resembling a non-directed gaze or an inwardly-directed act of ostension. For, let us suppose that a language learner did indeed 'find' something inner when instructed to introspect - how could such a learner determine that he had indeed 'found' (the essence of) 'consciousness'? He does not even have a criterion he could use, and no way of satisfying his teachers that he had correctly identified this (peculiar!) 'phenomenon' (as distinct from thinking that he had). Moreover, any such hypothesised 'inner grasp' or 'intuition' of the essence of 'consciousness' could not instruct him in the proper uses of the word, could not in itself ensure his conformity to the rules for its use. Wittgenstein demonstrated at length the insufficiency of *any* act of ostension - 'inner' *or outer* - for learning how to use a word properly, which capacity is entailed by, and thereby ensures, our 'understanding its meaning'. 'Consciousness' is *not* a technical term, nor is it a theoretical construction which acquires its meaning exclusively from a theoretically stipulated system: it is, *ab initio*, as ordinary as 'lamp', 'number' or 'picture'. Just as looking at something that is called a lamp is not in itself sufficient to inculcate a mastery of the many uses of the word 'lamp' involved in understanding what 'lamp' means, what a lamp *is*, so any putatively successful operation of mentally indicating 'consciousness' to oneself, were this an intelligible possibility, would still not suffice to yield its *meaning*, to make available its various rules of proper employment in utterances in situations of (attributive and other kinds of) communication.[29]

If one follows the implications of the kind of investigative strategy proposed by Ryle and Wittgenstein, one soon discovers that the Husserlian analysis or decomposition of 'consciousness' into a consecutive array of distinguishable acts or modalities (thinking, expecting, hearing, looking, recollecting, imagining, regretting, hoping, understanding, recognising, noticing, gazing, etc., etc.) leads to difficulties. The troubles are of three kinds. Firstly, one might encounter an objection like this: granted, 'consciousness' is not a substance nor an entity, but perhaps it is a common element or aspect of all these admittedly different 'mental' orientations. Secondly, we may simply have contributed to *ramifying* the problem: after all, it could be suggested, one is 'conscious' *in a different way* when one is, e.g., 'imagining' than when one is 'listening', and in different ways again when one is, e.g., 'looking at something' as contrasted to 'recollecting something or 'sensing someone's presence', etc. And, thirdly, we still need to come to terms with the class of 'intransitive' cases in which one can say of someone that 'he/she is conscious' *without* such a usage entailing any specific mental act/orientation *or* any specific 'object' of consciousness. The Husserlian 'multiple acts/orientations-plus-their-objects' decomposition of 'consciousness', while productively generating a systematic dereification of the concept, nonetheless itself requires a logico-grammatical corrective. We need to explore the rules governing 'conscious' and 'consciousness' as (parts of) predicates *independently* of the other mental-conduct concepts.[30]

On 'Being Conscious' and 'Having Consciousness'.

Commonsensically, we say that human beings but not earthworms "have consciousness". What are we signifying with such an expression? We may say of a person but not of an ant that he "is conscious". What can we mean when we say this? In reference to the first predicate, "has consciousness", Hunter argued that such an expression enables us to say, "in an economical way",[31] that:

> the pairs of predicates, 'hears' and 'is deaf', 'sees' and 'is blind' and so on (when 'hears', 'sees', etc. are used intransitively), are applied

to human beings in such a way that if a person does not hear, he is deaf, and if he does not see, he is blind - whereas although we can say of flowers and buses that they do not see or hear, in their case it does not follow that they are blind or deaf.[32]

With respect to the first of the considerations identified as possible troubles for an Husserlian decomposition of consciousness, viz., that 'consciousness' might be postulated as a common element or aspect suffusing each and every noetic act or orientation, thereby again raising the question of its 'nature', Hunter's elaboration of his point is highly pertinent. He argues:

> Having 'consciousness' is not having something, the having of which explains the fact that we see or hear. The use we assigned to the expression is *only* to mark the difference between beings which, if they do not see, are blind, and those which, although they do not see, are not blind.[33]

It is not that a single unifying thread links all of our experiential and mental orientations, whose nature is mysterious, nor that there are many diverse *kinds* of 'consciousness', differing as do the various modes of experience and mental orientation.[34] As Hunter observes, to say of a being that it "has consciousness" is *not* to predicate any element, aspect, state or entity to it, nor some *variety* of these, but rather it is to signal the relevant applicability to it of ranges of *paired* predicates (*inter alia*, 'sees/is blind', 'hears/is deaf', 'hopes/has given up hope', 'thinks that *X*/has no opinion about *X*', 'believes *X*/disbelieves *X*' and so forth).

Let us now consider the first person uses, "*I* have consciousness" and "*I* am conscious". Are such locutions governed by a rule which provides that they express knowledge of the presence of a *phenomenon*, whether or not 'its' properties are describable? Consciousness is not itself any kind of *experience*, nor is it an object of experience. Wittgenstein sought to demonstrate that "I am conscious" has *no* fact-reporting use: it is not, appearances notwithstanding, an experiential *proposition*,[35] although it is certainly a sentence. To understand what *kind* of sentence it could be, we have to consider in what kinds of situations it could be uttered. Wittgenstein comments:

Whom do I really inform, if I say 'I have consciousness'? What is the purpose of saying this to myself, and how can another person understand me? - Now, expressions like 'I see', 'I hear', 'I am conscious' really have their uses. I tell a doctor 'Now I am hearing with this ear again', or I tell someone who believes I am in a faint 'I am conscious again', and so on.[36]

Norman Malcolm remarks:

If I have been injured in an accident, someone bending over me might say 'He seems to be unconscious', and I might murmur in response 'I am conscious'... My utterance, 'I am conscious', would show the other person that I am conscious, just by being an utterance and not by virtue of the supposed 'propositional content' of the utterance.[37]

My utterance would entitle the hearer to assert of me that I had "regained consciousness". But any *other* utterance might similarly so entitle him! Elsewhere, my utterance of "I am conscious" *simpliciter* would not function as a 'truism'; it would be *unintelligible*. Uses of expressions involving "I am conscious *of..* ", by contrast, may indeed be intelligible and informative, but what they *say* will vary contextually. Any one such usage may be analyzable (as Husserl strove to demonstrate) into some particular activity, orientation or achievement-type. Consider: "I suddenly became conscious of his weapon hidden behind his jacket", in which 'becoming conscious of' amounts to 'noticing' or 'spotting'. Or consider: "Whenever I meet her these days, I am conscious of a change in her attitude towards me", in which 'I am conscious of' can be simply paraphrased, without distortion or residue, into 'I notice' or 'I detect/discern/am struck by' (etc.). The methodological technique being employed here is not to *substitute* 'semantics' for ontology, but to approach an ontological issue ('What is consciousness?') from a conceptual or 'logical' vantage-point (asking: What is the meaning of the term 'consciousness'? - which equals 'According to what rules can this term be intelligibly used?'). Wittgenstein, in considering 'mental images', made this point clearly (and one could replace 'image', 'imagine' and 'imagination' with 'conscious' and 'consciousness' throughout the following passage):

> One ought to ask, not what images are [what consciousness is -JC]
> or what happens when one imagines anything [is conscious of any-
> thing - JC] but how the word 'imagination' ['consciousness' - JC]
> is used. But that does not mean that I want to talk only about words.
> For the question as to the nature of the imagination is as much about
> the word 'imagination' as my question is. And I am only saying that
> this question is not to be decided - neither for the person who does
> the imagining, nor for anyone else - by pointing; nor yet by a
> description of any process.[38]

Nonetheless, we do speak of (parts of) our brains being the "seat of consciousness", and many neuroscientists have sought to describe the physiological and biochemical transformations relevant to understanding how "altered
states of consciousness" arise. Does this mean that the brain is to be
thought of as somehow 'generating' consciousness? Wittgenstein rejected
what he disparagingly called "the prejudice in favour of psycho-physical
parallelism", claiming that it is "a fruit of the primitive conception of
grammar".[39] What does this mean?

To postulate a 'parallelism' presupposes the separate identifiability of
two 'states', 'processes', or 'events' which could subsequently be understood as 'existing', 'operating', or 'running' simultaneously. Wittgenstein
argued, giving many brilliant examples, against the "primitive conception
of grammar" according to which the 'mental' predicates are all names for
discretely identifiable 'states', 'processes' or 'events'. Many favoured cases
within psychophysical theorising (such as thinking, understanding, remembering, forgetting, imagining, desiring) cannot be fully (and some not at
all) analyzed into 'state', 'process' or 'event' categories.[40] 'Consciousness', however, seems to constitute a 'state' - of 'mind' or of a person.
This impression is deceptive; while we may speak of someone's 'being
conscious' (in very special circumstances, discussed earlier), as we may
say of someone that he has 'regained consciousness', we do not speak of
his 'consciousness' as a 'state of mind' as we may so characterise his
'depression', 'grief', or 'anxiety'. We do *not* say of anyone that he is "in
a state of consciousness", but we *can* speak of his being "in an altered state
of consciousness", where what we mean is restricted to certain fairly determinate possibilities (being 'high', 'stoned', 'drunk', hypnotised', etc.).[41]

With respect to the brain or its parts being the 'seat' or 'basis' of our
'consciousness', we find that 'being awake' and 'being conscious' are

sometimes treated as interchangeable predicates in theorising. Hearnshaw, for example, writes:

A striking advance was the discovery of the role of the reticular activating system in the brain stem and basal diencephalon by Moruzzi and Magoun in 1949. Stimulation of this system marked changes in EEG rhythms and in behaviour, and was shown to be related to the induction and maintenance of the waking state. This has thrown light on the basis of sleep, and also on the physiological basis of alertness and consciousness generally.[42]

Although they may on occasion be interchangeable, the grammars of 'awake/wakefulness' and 'conscious/consciousness' exhibit some critical divergences. For example, one cannot (claim to) be 'awake *of*' anything as one can claim to be 'conscious of' it. Thus, one cannot adequately generalise the neurophysiological findings pertaining to the biological basis of 'wakefulness' to a 'theory of consciousness'.

A more thorough review and assessment of the biological data relevant to sleeping and waking has recently been provided by Churchland in the course of developing an argument for the relevance of such data to the question of the nature of consciousness.[43] She is willing to entertain the prospect of what she terms a "smooth" reduction of consciousness to neurobiological phenomena. I think that this view is a result of her generic treatment of 'consciousness' and 'being conscious' as *state* categories/descriptions.[44] The grammars of these expressions, as we have explored them above, are incompatible with such an analysis. Further, she appears willing to countenance the possibility of 'eliminating' the concept of consciousness altogether after the fashion of 'caloric fluid' or 'vital spirit'.[45] This is untenable because, unlike these latter cases, 'consciousness' is not a *theoretical* construction but an ordinary concept with many (diverse) communicative functions. Churchland does not discuss the contributions of Husserl or Wittgenstein to our understanding of consciousness at all. This is puzzling, but perhaps may be explained by her apparent allegiance to a 'scientific' view of philosophical analysis, according to which it is the business of philosophers to construct theories or meta-theories based upon scientific 'findings'. Although Husserl *did* characterize his inquiries as 'scientific', it is clear that they took the form of conceptual investigations, and Wittgenstein was quite antagonistic to any conflation of empirical science with philosophy. Many proponents of cognitivism, however, falsely contend that

Wittgenstein was opposed to scientific endeavours, or hostile to the 'scientific spirit'. I would prefer to say that it was his seriousness about science and about its proper place in the pantheon of knowledge which precluded Wittgenstein from offering misplaced quasi-scientific 'solutions' to complex logical, grammatical or conceptual problems. 'Consciousness' is a term in need of clarification *prior to* any meaningful *empirical* investigation.

Concluding Observations

The 'problem' for evolutionary biological theory and post-Darwinian behavioural sciences posed by the apparently "unbridgeable gulf between consciousness and brain processes",[46] and the equally strong attractiveness of the idea that 'consciousness' is an emergent property in evolution, must both be viewed as *artifacts* of a 'primitive' rendition of the grammar of the concept of consciousness. Notwithstanding some prominent neurobiological claims to the contrary,[47] it makes no sense to predicate 'consciousness' - *nor* lack of consciousness - to brains, any more than it makes sense to attribute consciousness of a lack thereof to a finger (for what, metaphor aside, could a 'conscious finger' - or an 'unconscious finger' - *mean*?). It is, therefore, a red herring to invoke here the fact that certain invasive operations on the cortex generate no sensations for the person whose cortex it is. Consciousness is attributable to whole organisms of a certain complexity *of behaviour* or to human beings, not to constituent parts of them, and then only for certain purposes in certain contexts. Brains are no more conscious than eyes can see: *we* are conscious, and *we* see *with* our eyes (but as Hacker reminds us, we are not conscious with our brains: thus, while we may speak of our eyes as organs of vision, we cannot speak of our brains as organs of consciousness![48]). While it is certainly true that a wide range of neurophysiological structures and processes subserve an even wider range of human faculties, powers, dispositions, and forms of behaviour, *none* of them constitutes a 'basis' for 'consciousness' (as distinct from, e.g., wakefulness). This is not an empirical finding nor a hypothetical assertion subject to confirmation or disconfirmation; it is a *grammatical* truth.

> We attribute consciousness to a creature on the grounds of its behaviour in the circumstances of its life, not on the grounds of its neural organisation and complexity... Consciousness does not 'emerge', like an ethereal halo or 'astral body', from inanimate matter. Rather, the

biological constitution of living creatures becomes more complex as one ascends the evolutionary scale, and more forms of response and reaction to the environment are made possible. When these are manifest in certain forms of behavior, the concepts of consciousness... get a grip; but these are not concepts of an inner realm.[49]

Wittgenstein's assertion, that only of a living human being and of what resembles (behaves sufficiently like) a living human being can one say that it is conscious or unconscious,[50] remains a potent insight in these days of reductionist theoretical impulses.

Endnotes

1. W.V. Quine, *Quiddities: An Intermittently Philosophical Dictionary* (Harvard University Press/Belknap Press, Cambridge, 1987), p.133.

2. P.N. Johnson-Laird, *Mental Models* (Harvard University Press, Cambridge, 1983), p.448.

3. Thomas Nagel, *The View from Nowhere* (Oxford University Press, Oxford, 1986).

4. D.C. Dennett, "How to Study Human Consciousness Empirically: or Nothing Comes to Mind", *Synthese*, Vol. 53, 1982, pp. 159-80. See also his *The Intentional Stance* (Bradford Books, M.I.T. Press, Cambridge, 1987), pp. 153-5. (Dennett attempts to dispute this restriction, although his efforts lead him in a very different direction from the one followed here).

5. J.B. Watson, *Behaviourism* (Kegan Paul, Trench, Trubner & Co., London, 1913), p. 2.

6. *Ibid.*, p. 18.

7. See T.H. Huxley, *Man's Place in Nature* (1863; University of Michigan Press, Ann Arbor, 1959) and C.D. Broad's *The Mind and Its Place in Nature* (1923; Humanities Press, N.Y., 1951).

8. For a selection of classical contributions to the development of this doctrine, see C.V. Borst (Ed.), *The Mind/Brain Identity Theory* (Macmillan, London, 1970).

9. R. Descartes, *Oeuvres de Descartes*, Eds. Adams and Tannery, Vol.8 (Cerf, Paris, 1913), p. 7. While Descartes' 'cogito ergo sum' proposition may have lost some of its fascination for us, his associated metaphysics of mind and consciousness continue to haunt us all.

10. Anthony Kenny, *Descartes: A Study of His Philosophy* (Random House, N.Y., 1968), pp. 70-1.

11. *Ibid.*, p. 74.

12. For a detailed discussion of Descartes' 'psychophysiological' theorizing, see Edward S. Reed, "Descartes, Corporeal Ideas Hypothesis and the Origin of Scientific Psychology", *Review of Metaphysics*, Vol. 35, June 1982, pp. 731-52.

13. Especially as articulated in the posthumously edited lectures published under the title of *Mind, Self and Society: From the Standpoint of a Social Behaviourist* (Ed. C.W. Morris; University of Chicago Press, Chicago, 1934).

14. Provided that this characterisation is not confused with the doctrine propagated by E.O. Wilson under the same name, but with which it has nothing in common.

15. Gestures were behavioural phenomena in which Darwin, and later Wundt (with whom Mead studied), had taken special interest.

16. Mead, *op. cit.*, p. 18. A similar point is made also in his *The Philosophy of the Act* (University of Chicago Press, Chicago, 1938), p. 411. For a fuller discussion of this aspect of Mead's thought, see Thomas Natsoulas, "George Herbert Mead's Conception of Consciousness", *Journal for the Theory of Social Behaviour*, Vol. 15, No. 1, March 1985, pp. 68-75.

17. For some commentary on the residual Cartesian assumptions in Mead's theorising and its later elaborations in the social sciences, see David Rubinstein, "The Concept of Action in the Social Sciences", *Journal for the Theory of Social Behaviour*, Vol. 7, 1977, pp. 209-36.

18. Franz Brentano, "The Distinction between Mental and Physical Phenomena" in Oskar Kraus and Linda McAlister (Eds.), *Psychology from an Empirical Standpoint* (1924; Routledge and Kegan Paul, London, 1973).

19. Norman Malcolm has remarked that there is also an 'intransitive' use: "If we think that a person who was knocked unconscious has regained consciousness, we can say, 'He is conscious', without needing to add an 'of' or a 'that'... It may be noted that when 'conscious' is used

intransitively it cannot be replaced by 'aware': to be aware is always to be aware *of* or *that.*" ("Consciousness and Causality" in D.M. Armstrong and Norman Malcolm, *Consciousness and Causality: A Debate on the Nature of Mind* (Basil Blackwell, Oxford, 1984), p. 3.)

20. Brentano, *op. cit.,* p.88

21. Edmund Husserl, *Ideas: General Introduction to Pure Phenomenology* (1913: Trans. W.R. Boyce Gibson; Collier Books, N.Y., 1972), p. 223.

22. Edmund Husserl, *ibid.,* Chapters 9-11. It should be pointed out that Husserl disagreed with certain aspects of Brentano's formulation of the 'intentionality' thesis, even though he maintained its essential point as a cornerstone of his thinking: see Aron Gurwitsch, "On the Intentionality of Consciousness" in Joseph J. Kockelmans (Ed.), *Phenomenology: The Philosophy of Edmund Husserl and Its Interpretation* (Doubleday-Anchor, N.Y., 1967) pp. 118-37.

23. Husserl was equivocal about this strict identity of consciousness with intentional acts, and Sartre was later to accuse him of contradicting his basic position where he introduces a pure 'Ego' *behind* the sequences of intentional acts. (Jean-Paul Sartre, *The Transcendence of the Ego: An Existentialist Theory of Consciousness* (Trans. & Annotated by F. Williams & R. Kirkpatrick: Noonday Press, Farrar, Straus & Giroux, 1957)). For some discussion of this issue, see my *The Social Construction of Mind* (Rowman & Littlefield, N.J., 1979), 118-21.

24. Husserl depicted his method as a ratiocinative procedure requiring the analyst to focus upon any phenomenon and to suspend its mundane typification(s); subsequently, the 'phenomenologically reduced' exemplar is to be 'freely varied' in imagination so as to reveal the limits to its conceivable variability while sustaining its identity. Thus, "in such a fully free variation, released from all restrictions to facts accepted beforehand, all the variants (examples) belonging to the openly infinite sphere - which includes the (initial) example itself, as optional and freed of all its factualness - stand in a relationship of synthetic interrelatedness and integral connectedness.... But...what necessarily persists throughout this free and always repeatable variation comes to the fore: the *invariant*, the indissolubly identical in different and ever-again different, the *essence* common

to all, the universal essence by which all 'imaginable' variants of the example, and all variants of any such variant, are restricted. This invariant is the ontic essential form (a priori form), the *eidos*, corresponding to the example, in place of which any variant of the example could have served equally well." (Edmund Husserl, *Formal and Transcendental Logic*, Martinus Nijhoff, The Hague, 1969, p. 248). For a further elaboration of Husserl's method, see Richard Zaner, "The Act of Free-Fantasy in Rigorous Phenomenological Science" in Fred Kersten & Richard Zaner (Eds.), *Phenomenology: Continuation and Criticism* (Martinus Nijhoff, The Hague, 1973). For a lively Wittgensteinian critique, informed by Wittgenstein's observation that: "*Essence* is expressed by grammar" (*Philosophical Investigations,* para. 371) and by the analysis of 'family resemblances' and 'common properties' which Wittgenstein proffers to counter competing, introspective essentialisms, see James L. Heap, "Free-Fantasy, Language and Sociology: A Criticism of the Methodist Theory of Essence", *Human Studies*, Vol. 4, No. 4, October-December, 1981, pp. 299-311. It is almost as if Wittgenstein's remarks on these methodologically relevant topics were directed against Husserl's point of view, although there is no evidence for any such direct connection.

25. Gilbert Ryle, "Review of Martin Farber, 'The Foundations of Phenomenology" in his *Collected Papers, Vol. 1: Critical Essays* (Hutchinson & Co., London, 1971), p. 220. (This essay was originally published in 1946.)

26. *Ibid*. p. 221. (Emphasis added).

27. G.E. Moore, *Philosophical Studies* (Harcourt, Brace & Co., N.Y., 1922), p. 25.

28. Ludwig Wittgenstein, *Philosophical Investigations* (Trans. G.E.M. Anscombe: Basil Blackwell, Oxford, 1968), para. 412.

29. For an excellent analysis of this issue, which is explored by Wittgenstein in his *Philosophical Investigations* (op. cit.), paras. 27-64, see G.P. Baker and P.M.S. Hacker, "Ostensive Definition and Analysis" in their *Wittgenstein: Understanding and Meaning* (University of Chicago Press, Chicago, 1980), Chapter Two. Wittgenstein remarked: "Whereas, of course, if the words 'language', 'experience', 'world', have a use it

must be as humble a one as that of the words 'table', 'lamp', 'door'."
(*Philosophical Investigations*, para. 97).

30. In particular, we need to be wary of confusing *pleonastic* uses of
'conscious' with genuinely informative uses. A failure to distinguish
between these engenders the confusion which posits a mysterious state or
property over and above the phenomenon being so qualified. For example,
if I say that "I was conscious of having thought such-and-such", this is
simply a way of saying that I can recall having thought such-and-such or
simply that I did indeed think such-and-such. To treat the expression otherwise can generate a misconception according to which there are apparently
two states of affairs being depicted, the 'having been conscious' and the
'having thought such-and-such', where one is at a loss to specify any content to the former.

31. J.F.M. Hunter, "Consciousness and the Chief" in his *Understanding
Wittgenstein: Studies of 'Philosophical Investigations'* (Edinburgh
University Press, Edinburgh, 1985), p. 142.

32. *Ibid.*

33. *Ibid.*, p. 143.

34. Note, however, that we may speak intelligibly of 'altered states of
consciousness' in very particular contexts. We shall touch on this in more
detail later. The point being made here is simply that we should refrain
from misconceiving of 'consciousness' as differentiated according to
whatever mental or experiential predicate is being applied. Thus 'looking'
is not a different 'state of consciousness' from 'listening' in the sense in
which e.g., 'being high' is (or involves?) a different state of consciousness
from 'being drunk'. I may have to be *awake* in order to look or to listen,
but being awake and being conscious are not synonyms. Again, more on
this later.

35. Ludwig Wittgenstein, *Zettel* (Eds., G.E.M. Anscombe & G.H. von
Wright; Trans., G.E.M Anscombe: Basil Blackwell, Oxford, 1967), para.
401.

36. Ludwig Wittgenstein, *Philosophical Investigations*, op.cit., para. 416.

37. Norman Malcolm, *op. cit.*, p. 37.

38. Ludwig Wittgenstein, *Philosophical Investigations*, op. cit., sec. 370.

39. Ludwig Wittgenstein, *Remarks on the Philosophy of Psychology, Vol. 2* (Eds. G.E.M. Anscombe & G.H. von Wright; Trans. G.E.M. Anscombe: University of Chicago Press, Chicago 1980), para. 906.

40. This is a topic explored at length in both the *Philosophical Investigations* and *Zettel*. I discuss its significance in "Theoretical Problems of Cognitive Science", *Inquiry*, Vol. 25, No. 1, 1982, and further in *Rethinking Cognitive Theory* (Macmillan, London, 1983), Chapters 1, 4 & 8, and in "Two Concepts of the Mental" in K.J. Gergen & K. Davis (Eds.) *The Social Construction of the Person* (Springer International, N.Y., 1985).

41. Descriptive, experiential psychopharmacology is becoming a growth industry; see, e.g., Benjamin Wallace & Leslie E. Fisher, "Consciousness-Altering Drugs" in their *Consciousness and Behavior* (Allyn & Bacon, Boston, 1983).

42. L.S. Hearnshaw, *The Shaping of Modern Psychology* (Routledge and Kegan Paul, London, 1987), p. 255.

43. Patricia Smith Churchland, "Reduction and the Neurobiological Basis of Consciousness" in A.J. Marcel & E. Bisiach (Eds.) *Consciousness in Contemporary Science* (Clarendon Press, Oxford, 1988).

44. *Ibid.*, p. 285.

45. *Ibid.*, p. 301.

46. Ludwig Wittgenstein, *Philosophical Investigations*, op. cit., para. 412.

47. See, for example, Steven Rose, *The Conscious Brain* (London, 1972).

48. P.M.S. Hacker, "The World of Consciousness" in his *Wittgenstein: Meaning and Mind* (Basil Blackwell, Oxford, 1990), p. 523.

49. *Ibid.*, p. 525.

50. Ludwig Wittgenstein, *Philosophical Investigations*, op. cit., para. 281.

CHAPTER XII

Wittgenstein versus James and Russell on the Nature of Willing[1]

Stuart G. Shanker

§1. Wittgenstein's Response to Descartes' Dilemma: The Will is Neither Mover Nor Moved

The Descartes who emerges from Wittgenstein's (covert) reading of the history of philosophy is like a founding father who has created a constitution that commits his nation to a never-ending cycle of Labour and Conservative governments. Wittgenstein, on the other hand, stands out as the radical reformer who hopes to install a new party committed to proportional representation; should he be elected it will mean the inevitable downfall of the old order, and with it perhaps, the type of political chaos which Russell feared in his famous letter to Trinity College on behalf of Wittgenstein's 1930 application for a research grant.

The point of this analogy is that mechanism must be seen, not just as an alternative to dualism, but as its foil: both are the product of Cartesianism, both serve to define the other's legislative programme. Just as a rigid two-party system depends for its survival on a 'first-past-the-post' electoral process, so too the mechanist/mentalist debate hinges on Descartes' thesis that all bodily movements are caused by 'agitations in the brain': i.e. by the parts activated when animal spirits are released. Descartes gives two explanations as to how this might occur: either the soul deflects the pineal gland, or external objects and/or internal physiological processes impinge on the senses. His 'animal automaton hypothesis' turns on the claim that involuntary movements occur without any intervention of the will, while "the movements which we call 'voluntary'" are those which "the soul determines" (Descartes 1649: 315). To the eye of the observer, voluntary and involuntary movements *look* exactly the same; it is only because we are able to see and report on our own volitions that we are able to make this fundamental distinction (and because animals lack a similar capacity that they are ruled automata).

However much mechanists and mentalists may have differed in their attitudes towards 'privileged access' they were agreed on one thing: the attack on the continuum picture of vegetable-animal-human intelligence which Descartes mounted with this argument must somehow be repulsed. For two and a half centuries mechanists had sought to restore what Russell called the 'continuity hypothesis' by establishing that conscious voluntary movements are brought about by the same mental causes (viz, sensations and images) as unconscious involuntary ones, and thus, that the distinction between adaptation, tropisms, habituation, accommodation, animal and human learning (with all of the levels which the latter involve) is one of degree, not of kind.

James and Russell saw Ideo-Motor theory as the consummation of this empiricist tradition, but from a cognitivist perspective their argument is an obsolete reminder of the limitations of pre-computational mechanism (of the failure to appreciate how the complex workings of the mind can only be explained if the brain is seen to process representations of goals and strategies for obtaining them). Whereas from Wittgenstein's point of view, Ideo-Motor theory constitutes a profound illustration of the manner in which Cartesianism forces one to construe the conceptual distinction between voluntary and involuntary movements on the wrong paradigm.

Unfortunately, one aspect of the method whereby he develops this theme has been a source of much anxiety amongst cognitivists. The problem which they have with his scrutiny of the actual ways in which the words 'voluntary' and 'involuntary' are used is that this appears to bear out Russell's dire prediction that such an approach would render philosophy an exercise in lexicography; dismissing this as 'ordinary language philosophy' effectively removes any need to consider the *point* of these investigations. But Wittgenstein's intention was certainly not to thwart the process of conceptual evolution which drives science (cf. his remarks on Faraday's *The Burning of a Candle* in the Bouwsma notes). The target here is rather epistemological asymmetry, and all of the theoretical confusions which this entails.

When the mechanist denies the Cartesian picture of acquaintance with mental causes, he restricts himself to one of two alternatives: embrace eliminative materialism, or some form of reductionism which will reformulate the epistemological status of first-person psychological utterances by revealing their 'real' logical form. There is an allusion to the former strategy at RFM II §62 (where Wittgenstein asserts: "Finitism and behaviourism are quite similar trends. Both say, but surely, all we have here is.

... Both deny the existence of something, both with a view to escaping from a confusion"). In the discussion of Russell it is the latter thesis which captures his attention.

In *The Analysis of Mind* Russell construes first-person psychological utterances of desire or belief as inferences about the causes of one's behaviour (see Shanker 1992). To say that experience (or an external observer) can always overturn an agent's belief that he desired (intended, chose to do) x amounts to saying that statements of desire (intention, choice) are not *avowals*: are not the foundation of the language-games of wanting, intending, choosing, believing. Although it is not obvious, Wittgenstein is thinking of this argument when he asks: "What is the natural expression of an intention? — Look at a cat when it stalks a bird; or a beast when it wants to escape. ((Connexion with propositions about sensations.))" (PI §647) The connection he has in mind here is with the argument at §244 that sensation-words are "connected with the primitive, the natural, expressions of the sensation and used in their place." The conclusion drawn in §244 is that "the verbal expression of pain replaces crying and does not describe it." Similarly, phrases like 'I want (will, intend to do) x' are rooted in primitive behaviour. The exclamation 'I want x' (as uttered e.g. by a small child, or by Henderson's inner voice in *Henderson the Rain King*) is akin to a cat stalking a bird, not to the description of a fact: the verbal expression of desire or intention replaces crying or stamping one's foot and does not describe it.

This theme that first-person psychological statements are avowals and not descriptions (of mental states or processes) is developed over the next fifty passages and culminates in the argument presented at §290 that when I say 'I am in pain' "What I do is not, of course, to identify my sensation by criteria: but to repeat an expression. But this is not the *end* of the language-game; it is the beginning." In case we have missed the bearing which this conclusion has on the argument initiated at §243, Wittgenstein spells out in the second part of §290 that the sense in which we (legitimately) speak of describing a mental state is categorially different from describing one's room (cf. LW §§43,50). If the same use of 'description' were operating in both then first-person expressions of desire (intention, belief, choice), like reports of pain, must begin — as Russell postulated — with sensations or images which we perceive and identify. (Cf. Nisbett and Wilson's thesis in 'Telling More than we Can Know' that we perceive 'mental contents', but the processes which determine these are said to 'transcend our introspective powers'.) The difference between expressions of pain and intention must either be accounted for phenomenologically (*pace* Russell, i.e. in terms of the sensations) or inductively (*pace* cognitive attribution theory, i.e. in terms of mental models which the Mind maps on-to behaviour).

The reason why Wittgenstein argues that the language game of sensat-ions or desires (intentions etc.) begins with the *utterance* is to block both of these moves: to clarify that the epistemological considerations relevant to physical descriptions do not apply to first-person psychological state-ments. An expression of desire or intention is not based on observation; we do not justify such expressions as we might a belief or knowledge-claim. Hence the kind of agent-observer 'conflicts' recorded by Nisbett and Wilson must equally be (re)interpreted in terms of the shift from episte-mological to logico-grammatical asymmetry. But before this latter problem can be addressed we must first clarify the 'nature' of psychological causali-ty; otherwise we shall indeed be led to conclude, from the fact that the so-cial psychologist's judgments about the causes of an agent's behaviour often undermine the agent's own explanation, that all first-person statements giv-ing the reasons for one's actions are *hypotheses* based on "implicit, *a priori* theories, or judgments about the extent to which a particular stimulus is a plausible cause of a given response" (Nisbett & Wilson 1977: 231).

Wittgenstein's carefully mounted campaign to reveal the misconception of psychological causality lying at the heart of the mechanist/mentalist debate comes to a head in the passages on 'willing' at PI §§611-30 (which shades imperceptibly into the remarks on intentions at §631). It is no coin-cidence that this discussion should come near the end of the *Investigations*, just as it does in both the *Principles of Psychology* and *The Analysis of Mind*; for our understanding of the 'nature of psychological causality' turns on the resolution of the continuum hypothesis.

In §571 occurs the famous warning of the "Misleading parallel: psychol-ogy treats of processes in the psychical sphere, as does physics in the phys-ical": i.e. which treats willing (seeing, hearing, thinking, feeling) as "the subject of psychology *in the same sense* as that in which the movements of bodies, the phenomena of electricity etc., are the subject of physics." But Wittgenstein says no more about this problem here, other than to con-clude that "the psychologist observes the *external reactions* (the behaviour) of the subject." That this is not intended as a behaviourist thesis is borne out in the next passage, in which Wittgenstein considers the criteria which establish that someone is in a state of expectation (i.e. that the person, not his body or mind, is in that state). The passages that follow (on expecting,

believing, feelings of tendency, familiarity, recognition) are all closely tied
to prominent themes in James and Russell. But it is not until §§611ff that
we are presented with the sustained clarification of the point hinted at in
§571. This is not just a further element in what might begin to take on the
appearance of a personal vendetta (cf. his remark in MS 124 p.129 that
"James is a goldmine for the psychology of the philosopher"); rather, these
passages mark the culmination of Wittgenstein's reading of James and Russell: of the confusions which result when psychology is approached on the
paradigm of physics.

The structure of the discussion of voluntary behaviour is almost as significant as its content. We begin with an attack on the idea that willing is an
experience, followed by an attack on the idea that willing is an action, and
then a series of remarks that can apply to either theme. In essence this
amounts to a criticism of mechanism, followed by one of vitalism, and then
a generalizing of the issue in order to clarify how it is the framework
which is the source of both misconceptions. Looked at more closely, the
argument begins with a clear reference in §611 to Ideo-Motor theory ("the
'will' too only 'idea'"), shifts to the commonsense response in §612 that
"this is the region in which we say significantly that a thing doesn't simply
happen to us, but that we *do* it," and then broadens the scope in §613 so
as to focus on the underlying problem involved in Cartesianism: viz,
"wanting to think of willing as an immediate non-causal bringing-about".
As important as the argument is that philosophy should "study the use of
a word, point to mistakes in the description of this use" (RPPI §548), here-
in lies an even more significant aspect of Wittgenstein's methodology: what
begins as a 'local' criticism is only retained because there is some larger
implication to be drawn from it. This is really what we should understand
by 'Wittgenstein's method': isolate a philosophical problem and show why
it is confused; relate this to its contrary thesis and show why that is equally
confused; limn the picture underpinning both views and show how this in-
duces one to misconstrue the concept(s) in question on the wrong paradigm; tie this in with related issues where the problems involved can be
seen to arise from the same picture; continue with this process until you
arrive at the *fons et origo* of the theories involved. Hence the status assigned to Augustine: i.e. Augustine serves as a metaphor for Wittgenstein's
search for the *Urbilder* which 'keep seducing us into asking the same questions' and pursuing the same 'solutions'.

§2. *PI* §§611-30

Given the heavy demands placed upon it, it is hardly surprising that the discussion of willing should, like all of the major 'chapters' in the *Investigations*, be such a challenging text to decipher. These remarks are especially difficult to relate to cognitive science: in part because they are the highly condensed residue of extensive earlier writings on the topic, partly because the argument becomes ever more abstract in the process of being reworked, and partly because the very issue seems so distant from contemporary psychological concerns.

The preliminary argument developed in §§611-13, which sets the stage for the next twenty sections (if not for the remainder of the first part of the book), assumes a considerable amount of background knowledge. The first problem that it poses is: who exactly is it that would want to say: "'Willing too is merely an experience,' It comes when it comes"? The *Nachlass* makes it clear that James and Russell are the intended target here (see Candlish 1991, Ter Hark 1990); i.e. the Jamesian idea that once attention fixes on an idea or kinæsthetic image this "produces immediately its appropriate motor effects" (PP II 524).[2] This is more problematic than might at first appear. For one thing, there are the important differences between James and Russell's attitudes towards Ideo-Motor theory outlined in Shanker 1992; as we shall see, it is not always clear which of the two versions Wittgenstein is thinking of: a complication that does have some bearing on the point he is making. Furthermore, Wittgenstein's criticisms sometimes appear to distort the theory in question, which raises the difficult problem of deciding whether this was deliberate or unintentional on his part, and more importantly, significant or inconsequential.

In §611 Wittgenstein reduces Ideo-Motor theory to the premise that willing is a passive experience. His main objection here is that neither James nor Russell can explain the notion of 'bringing about' an action. This would seem a more pertinent criticism of James than of Russell; for James' 'fiats' are an attempt to reconcile free will with Ideo-Motor theory by salvaging the internal relation between the concepts of willing and effort (e.g. "*The question of ... free-will ...* relates solely to the amount of effort of attention or consent which we can at any time put forth" (PP II 571)). But §611 only works as a criticism of James if it assumes that this strategy is a failure (that it only succeeds in shifting the problem of what 'constitutes' willing to a lower level): an argument which is present in the *Nachlass* but not in the *Investigations*.

As far as Russell is concerned, this objection would seem to be completely beside the point; for Russell never suggests that we cannot bring about the experience of willing or the image before our mind. His argument is that such an image or kinæsthetic sensation triggers a causal mechanism, the nature of which entirely dispenses with any need to retain 'will' or 'effort'. (This appears to be the misreading Wittgenstein is committing at BB 154, where Ideo-Motor theory is presented as the thesis that we try to bring about kinæsthetic sensations before the mind's eye.) Hence §611 conceals a substantial leap in Wittgenstein's reasoning if it is to be read as a criticism of Russell. The 'it' in the first sentence of the second paragraph is what is most troubling here, since it is precisely this pronoun which Russell would claim to have removed with his logical analysis of volitional statements. Yet Wittgenstein can also be read as making the point that you can only talk of analysing or reducing 'willing' if you talk (*pace* James) of trying to bring about the movement associated with an image or kinæsthetic sensation. In other words, the alternatives here are reductionism and materialism, and you cannot have it — as Russell seeks — both ways.

In any event, Russell is committed to the minimal thesis that what we call willing is an experience that we cannot bring about, which elicits from Wittgenstein the concluding remark that the statement 'You cannot bring about this experience' is not an empirical proposition; for then it would be possible to conceive what it would be like to bring about such an experience. It is rather a grammatical proposition whose meaning is completely distorted when not construed as such. §612 then starts to probe the deeper philosophical significance resulting from Ideo-Motor theory's transgression of this point.

This is the first of several remarks contrasting voluntary and involuntary movements. The passage begins with an echo of the argument at BB 151. In the latter, Wittgenstein describes an example where we would speak of something happening to us (of *finding* our arm rising). But the same cannot be said of willing (cf. the remark at PG 144 that "'The will can't be a phenomenon, for whatever phenomenon you take is something that *simply happens*, something we undergo, not something we *do*. The will isn't *something* I see happen, it's more like my being involved in my actions, my *being* my actions'."). This sets the stage for a long discussion (largely missing in the *Investigations* but hinted at in a couple of places: most clearly at §659) about how the sense in which we speak of observing our own movements is when they are involuntary, and conversely, that "it is the peculiar impossibility of taking an observant attitude towards a certain action which characterizes it as a voluntary one" (BB 153; cf. Z §§591—2). This early argument is potentially misleading, however, for it sounds as if Wittgenstein is trying to explain subjectively the "many striking differences between the case of observing my arm rising in this experiment or watching someone else getting out of bed and the case of finding myself getting up" (e.g. in terms of the "perfect absence of what one might call surprise" in voluntary movements): a mistake which he implicitly warns against at §§624 and 628.

The *Investigations* version of the argument proceeds much more cautiously. §612 is confined to clarifying that whereas the concept of involuntary movement is internally related to that of passive experience, the logical grammar of *voluntary movement* is tied to the dynamic (cf. Z §588). Z §589 and BB 152-3 render it clear that Wittgenstein is thinking of James here. In the former Wittgenstein merely makes the point that the introduction of 'effort' cancels the possibility of treating an agent's action as a passive experience. The *Brown Book* discussion takes this a step further. Here Wittgenstein alerts us to the danger of over-emphasizing the internal relation between voluntary movement and effort; for this will quickly reinstate the confusion sustaining Ideo-Motor theory. James' argument is based on an analogy between the strain involved in lifting a heavy weight and that of making a difficult decision. But there are all sorts of cases where it makes no sense to speak of the effort involved in a voluntary movement (e.g. writing, pointing, looking). James' theory has the effect of severing the internal relation between free will and voluntary behaviour; but the fact that "When I raise my arm I do not usually *try* to raise it" or that we only speak of *trying* to get to that house when there is some difficulty about this (PI §§622-3) hardly entails that such behaviour was not voluntary. Furthermore, Ideo-Motor theory ignores the grammatical fact that the concept of voluntary movement is also internally related to the family of intentional concepts: i.e. that it only makes sense to speak of doing something voluntarily when one speaks of choosing, deciding, trying, wanting, intending (PI §615; RPP1 §805). Typically, when we speak of an absence of effort in these contexts this does not mean that e.g. a decision was made involuntarily but rather, signifies that the agent was lazy or irresponsible.

The question which remains is: to what extent do these damning criticisms of James apply to Russell. The most important thing to notice here is that Wittgenstein's argument does not trade on the (deceptive) surface grammar of 'voluntary' and 'involuntary movement'. On the contrary, Wittgenstein makes much the same point as Russell when he explains how

"The forms of expression of our ordinary language fit most obviously certain very special applications of the words 'willing', 'thinking', 'meaning', 'reading', etc., etc. ... We speak of an 'act of volition' as different from the action which is willed" (BB 151). He goes on in §613 of the *Investigations* — in terms which Russell could not but approve — to remove this principal misconception created by the ordinary use of 'willing': i.e. that willing an action is itself a form of action. This anticipates what has come to be known as Ryle's 'regress argument' (or rather, one part of it) that an act of willing cannot be brought about by a further act of willing. (If the willing is involuntary then it is a passive experience; if voluntary, then it must have been brought about by a further act of willing, *ad infinitum*.) Significantly, Wittgenstein makes exactly the same criticism of this 'volitionist' idea as of the thesis that willing is an experience: viz. "it makes no sense to speak of willing willing". This point is elaborated in §618: it makes sense to speak of willing to do something yet being unable to do it, but not, of willing one's will. The sense in which one cannot fail or try to will, just like the statement that the will cannot be a phenomenon, is the grammatical.

The parallel between this criticism and that of Ideo-Motor theory makes it clear that this is only one side of a two-pronged attack. In the *Brown Book* Wittgenstein underscores that Ideo-Motor theory is no less at fault than its mentalist complement: that in the former "One takes one's idea, and one's language, about volition from this kind of example [lifting a heavy weight] and thinks that they must apply — if not in such an obvious way — to all cases which one can properly call cases of willing" (BB 150). It is not just this particular analogy that Wittgenstein is concerned with, however: it is any case of misconstruing *voluntary movement* on the wrong paradigm. Thus, the real conflict between Russell and Wittgenstein on the explanation of voluntary behaviour is not between logical analysis and 'ordinary language philosophy': it is over the interpretation of what Russell would call the 'depth' and Wittgenstein the 'logical' grammar of *voluntary movement*.

This strategy is most evident in the second half of §613, where Wittgenstein hints that both sides of this mentalist/reductionist debate stem from one and the same picture. The section begins unpromisingly enough with an obscure answer to the question posed at the end of §611: viz. the sense in which we can speak of bringing about an experience is the same in which we speak of bringing about an action. The concept we are meant to be scrutinizing here is that of *bringing about* an action. Wittgenstein is deliberately playing on the causal overtones of *herbeiführen* (see Candlish 1991). The mentalist sees the problem as that of explaining how I (my mind) cause(s) this action to occur; the reductionist, how an experience x caused me to ϕ (while the cognitivist lurks in the background with an explanation of how the latter can satisfy the demands of the former). The remainder of the discussion of willing — indeed of the rest of the first part of the *Investigations* — is devoted to weaning us from this causal misconception of 'herbeiführen' *vis-à-vis* mental concepts.

In the *Brown Book* Wittgenstein asks: "does our volition, as it were, play on a keyboard of muscles, choosing which one it was going to use next?" (BB 153) The same point is picked up in §613, where the mentalist is accused of wanting to treat volition as "an immediate non-causal bringing-about" (i.e. a non-causal cause). Only now, the argument is expanded so as to apply to mentalist and reductionist alike; for it is the same "misleading analogy" which lies at the root of both ideas: viz, "the causal nexus seems to be established by a mechanism connecting two parts of a machine." For the mentalist, the connection is somehow forged between noumenal and phenomenal mechanical parts; for the Ideo-Motor theorist, it remains within the compass of the body. Thus Wittgenstein speaks at §618 of "a motor which has no inertia in itself to overcome." That is, he reformulates the debate between mentalist and reductionist so as to be seen as turning on the question of whether or not there is any physical inertia to be overcome in bodily and mental actions: whether the will is mover or moved.

James equivocates on this point in the *Principles*; but what Wittgenstein found most interesting about his argument is how James was drawn into treating free will as quite literally the force needed to overcome the resistance of conflicting mental causes. (Wittgenstein makes exactly the same point about 'feelings of innervation' at GWL 202.) Russell is much more consistent on this score: the picture of mental resistance is still there, but it is now an issue whose outcome is decided solely by experience. Hence Russell espouses (e.g. in *Religion and Science*, chapter VI) and James occasionally inclines towards indeterminism (see 'The Dilemma of Determinism'); for whatever 'freedom' accrues to man must be the same as that exhibited by any other causal phenomenon in the natural order.

The preliminary argument sketched in §§611-13 has landed us in the following dilemma: either there is no such thing as 'bringing about' an image or idea, or willing is ineffable. (The eliminative materialist might regard this as proof that volitional terms are otiose. Wittgenstein pays no attention to this attempt to 'escape the confusion by denying the problem' in the *Investigations*, but he does touch on it in his lecture on free will (see §4).)

The impetus for Ideo-Motor theory stems from the obvious need to remove the taint of metaphysics from the fledgling science of psychology. In the following eight sections Wittgenstein builds carefully on this tension, bringing us ultimately to what sounds like a remark straight out of the *Tractatus* (e.g. it might be TLP 5.65): "*Doing* itself seems not to have any volume of experience. It seems like an extensionless point, the point of a needle. This point seems to be the real agent" (PI §620). This alarming conclusion seems to be supported in §621: since nothing is left over in experience, the will must be an extensionless point 'doing the doing'. The parenthetical remark at the end of §621 apparently directs us to consider whether Ideo-Motor theory has an answer to this question.[3] Had this been written thirty years later the question would no doubt have read: 'Are readiness potentials my willing?'; for in neither case is the 'subtraction' regarded as metaphorical. 'Willing' is assumed by both mentalist and reductionist to be an event that occurs prior to an action/bodily movement. (This could be taken as the defining feature of 'connationism'; see Candlish 1986.) The conflict has thus become one of determining whether the 'subtraction' takes us out of or remains within the bounds of experience: whether the 'doing' or 'trying' is, as Wittgenstein puts it in *Philosophical Grammar*, 'redundant' (PG 145).

The attack which follows on the Ideo-Motor theorist's affirmative response leads us back to the same problem as was encountered in the private language arguments (cf. §625 with §§258, 260, 265, 270, 378). In keeping with the point made above about the connection between §647 and §244, perhaps the most pertinent comparison here is once again with §290. For my certainty that I have raised my arm (as in the §624 experiment) cannot be justified; but this 'cannot' is grammatical. I do not *observe* or *identify* my kinæsthetic sensations or *recognize* that they are the same as I have experienced on other occasions when my arm has risen. To be sure, there are cases where I describe my sensations (e.g. on the phone to my doctor's nurse when begging for a house call), but my expression of certainty in the type of experiments outlined in §§617, 624 is an avowal which serves as a criterion for describing me as trying to raise my arm. Thus Wittgenstein remarks: "But how do I know that this movement was voluntary? — I don't know this, I manifest it" (Z §600). When I represent my behaviour in voluntary or intentional terms my "words are a signal; and they have a *function*" (Z §601; see Shanker 1991).

The upshot of §625 is that it makes no sense to speak of being certain or uncertain of whether I have recognized my kinæsthetic sensations correctly: not because my judgment cannot be justified, but simply because my statement is an avowal as opposed to a judgment. As in §289, the answer to the question, 'On what is our certainty that we have raised our arm based?' is: on nothing — but not on something either; for avowals *exclude* justification. Moreover, just as it makes no sense to ask whether I am (or could be) aware of making the inference, 'Since this is the same sensation as I experience at t_1 when my arm was rising, I must be raising my arm', so too it makes no sense to ask whether I make this inference *pre-consciously* (and no sense to suppose that the §617 and §624 experiments are examples of 'volitional illusions' from which one can discover the hypothesis-generating procedures used to categorize one's own behaviour as voluntary or involuntary).

One can well appreciate how a positivist might come to the conclusion after working through this argument that Wittgenstein had succumbed to his notorious 'yellow streak'. But the last thing Wittgenstein was trying to do here was force us into accepting the metaphysics of §§620-1. The discussion of willing is rather a *reductio* where the premise to be rejected is Cartesianism. Perhaps the single most telling remark that Wittgenstein makes about this issue is at Z §590, where he explains how

> The connexion of our main problem with the epistemological problem of willing has occurred to me before. When such an obstinate problem makes its appearance in psychology, it is never a question about facts of experience (such a problem is always much more tractable), but a logical, and hence properly a grammatical question.

Once we see how the logical grammar of first-person expressions of voluntary behaviour excludes the possibility of doubt, we shall see that it makes no more sense to suppose that my 'certainty' that an action was voluntary was based on privileged access than that my 'judgment' is actually a hypothesis based on an implicit theory about human behaviour. This emphasis on the point that this is a *psychological*, not a philosophical problem, is a reminder that far more is at stake here than e.g. searching for ways to escape from Ryle's regress; for Cartesianism is not just an abstract enquiry into what kind of 'event' it is which brings about a certain species of behaviour. The essence of Cartesianism lies in the contest between science and philosophy to account for the difference between voluntary and involuntary movements.

It is easy enough to overlook this overriding concern in the *Investigations*, where what is in fact the crux of the issue is reduced to four passages (§§627-30). These represent the corollary to the preceding *reductio*: viz, that, as in the discussion of solipsism, "*this* is what disputes between Idealists, Solipsists and Realists look like. The one party attack the normal form of expression as if they were attacking a statement; the others defend it, as if they were stating facts recognized by every reasonable human being" (PI §402). In concrete terms what this means is that mechanism has been placed on the same level as mentalism: both are the metaphysical result of misconstruing the logical grammar of first-person expressions and third-person descriptions of voluntary — and involuntary! — behaviour. This must seem paradoxical, given that mechanism has always presented itself as the champion of the scientific cause; but if Wittgenstein is right, mechanism does not *proceed from* but rather, *imposes* an *a priori* schema on the hard data yielded by experimental psychology: a set of presuppositions which stem from mechanism's constitutional goal of overturning Descartes' 'animal automaton hypothesis'.

It is highly significant that Wittgenstein introduces his remarks on voluntary and involuntary movements in his 1946-7 lectures on the philosophy of psychology with a reminder of the importance of the shift from epistemological to grammatical asymmetry. (We want to say that "If the third person is verified by observation of behaviour, and the first not, then this might be due to a fact that first person verbs express states of affairs *of which only I can be aware*; others know it directly. We have already spoken of this: (i) There is no question of knowing indirectly if there is no chance of knowing directly; (ii) There is difficulty about "observations'.... (iii) the 'can't' is a logical 'can't'" (GWL 276).) As the lecture progresses it becomes increasingly clear that Wittgenstein sees the problem of distinguishing between voluntary and involuntary movements as not just a further element in the Cartesian framework, but as a fundamental, perhaps *the* fundamental problem. After all, when Descartes argues for epistemological asymmetry in the second Meditation it is on the grounds that, while he knows that his own actions are mentally caused, he can only infer that the movements of the passersby whom he observes crossing the square are those of purposive beings and not automatons (Descartes 1641: 21). That is, the difference between voluntary and involuntary movements consists in some form of internal causal antecedent which only philosophy (Descartes) or science (mechanism) can disclose. Given that the attack on Cartesianism (virtually from §§242-626) has successfully exposed this fatal misconception, the next step in the argument must be to go back to this originating confusion and reconsider what exactly is involved in seeing behaviour as voluntary or involuntary.

§§577-94 in *Zettel* are variations on the theme that what makes a movement voluntary or involuntary is its 'character and context' (Z §587). What, for example, "is the difference between a gesture of the hand without a particular intention and the same gesture which is intended as a sign?" (RPPII §182) An appropriate answer to this question will be one in terms of the *surrounding* of the movement — e.g. whether it occurs against the background of an agent's intending, learning, or trying to do something — not some mysterious neural or mental event (Z §577). There is "a particular interplay of movements, words, expressions of face, as of manifestations of reluctance or readiness, which are characteristic of the voluntary movements of a normal human being" (Z §594). What makes it so difficult to distinguish categorically between voluntary and involuntary behaviour is that there is not one single criterion operating here but rather, a cluster of different (occasionally overlapping) language-games. First (and perhaps most important), there is the passive versus active distinction: viz. behaviour as phenomenon versus actions. Here the relevant grammatical truths are that it makes sense to speak of *x* happening to one and of trying to ϕ, of observing or experiencing surprise at one's involuntary but not one's voluntary behaviour; and to perceive the same effort or reactions in somebody else. To this must be added the rules of grammar that only of a voluntary action does it make sense to speak of deciding or choosing — of being able to explain, justify, or rationalize one's decision or choice — and conversely, of the exclusion of such responses for involuntary movements. Hence "One draws quite different conclusions from an involuntary movement and from a voluntary: this *characterizes* voluntary movement" (Z §599).

This internal relation between voluntary behaviour and the ability to give one's reasons for ϕing steers us in the direction of the array of considerations which most concern moral philosophers: e.g. doing something willingly or unwillingly; between obligation and choice; between verbs which do or do not take imperative forms (Z §51). One of the primary reasons why these cases are so intimately connected with the problems of free will and responsibility is that all of these distinctions hinge on the grammatical proposition that, unlike third-person contexts, it makes no sense to speak in the first person of the *criteria* for judging whether one has ϕ'd voluntarily or involuntarily. It should, moreover, be noted that the use of 'judge' as opposed to 'see' in third-person contexts is only warranted because of some distinctive criterial aspect of the agent's behaviour and/or its surrounding (which may leave us in doubt as to whether the agent intended to ϕ, or perhaps surprised that such an agent would have chosen to ϕ, or that any agent would have wanted to ϕ in such a situation). In other words, the use of 'judge' is the exception, not the rule: normally we *see* that an agent's behaviour is voluntary or involuntary. That is not to say that all uses of 'see' are indefeasible (although if most were it would be peculiar to continue employing 'see'[4]); only, that when such uses are defeated it is because of some further criterion present in the situation: not an inference about some hidden mental or physical event.

This emphasis on the themes that I do not judge on the basis of criteria whether I ϕ'd voluntarily or involuntarily, that the criteria for ϕing voluntarily are as varied as the actions that we do voluntarily,[5] that differing criteria can lead us to describe the same physical movement as voluntary in one context and involuntary in another (e.g. winking and blinking), and that the concept of voluntary behaviour is internally related to intending (wanting, trying, deciding) has profound implications for the 'continuity hypothesis'. When we speak of the criteria for voluntary movements we are referring to rules of grammar that apply to persons; if the movement of my arm is voluntary this means that *I* am raising or waving my arm. Involuntary movements are slightly more complicated as there are both person and bodily concepts involved. To describe a bodily movement as involuntary (e.g. the phenomenon of one's arms rising after pressing them against a door jamb) means that the agent was not trying to lift his arms: that no *psychological significance* can be attached to the movement in question. That involuntary movements (or the lack thereof) can have great physiological significance is all too often discovered at an annual check-up.

It is not quite so straightforward, however, when we are dealing with involuntary actions: with those concepts that apply to persons and not their bodies. In some cases the significance of these actions remains primarily physiological (e.g. Wittgenstein mentions the examples of somnambulism and of someone in a narcotic state at RPPI §902); but in other instances the description of an action as involuntary may have considerable psychological import: not just in the obvious circumstances of coercion or compulsion, but also in the more subtle cases where we regard involuntary actions as manifesting unconscious thoughts or intentions.

The crucial question in all this as far as mechanism is concerned is: where do reflexes enter into this picture? The answer is: on the level of bodily movements. Except in extraordinary cases, it makes no sense to speak of trying (intending, wanting) to dilate one's pupils in the dark. With reflexes, the relation between movement and judgment is inductive, not criterial; a pupil that fails to constrict when light is shone in it does not *mean* but is rather *evidence* for the fact that the patient is suffering from some neurophysiological disorder or is on some form of drugs. Thus, if we go back to §613 we can see how Wittgenstein's target there is the very foundations of mechanism; for the 'misleading analogy' which he attacks constitutes the starting-point for mechanism.

Where reflexes are concerned, it is entirely appropriate to speak of the "causal nexus established by a mechanism connecting two parts of a machine." The philosophical problems contained in Ideo-Motor theory — which is very much a descendant of Hartley's 'secondarily automatic motions' — only result when reflexes are taken as the paradigm for a continuum of involuntary/voluntary experience. There is rather a logico-grammatical continuum ranging from reflex movements (where intentional concepts are excluded) through involuntary movements (where intentional concepts may or may not apply depending on the circumstances) to voluntary movements (where they must apply — i.e. logically 'must'). Perhaps the greatest irony in all this is that Wittgenstein's shift from epistemological to grammatical asymmetry has the effect of resurrecting Descartes' attack on the continuum, but for reasons totally foreign to Descartes' outlook. For Wittgenstein does indeed leave us with a break between mechanical and intentional behaviour, but this is a *categorial*, not an *epistemological* consequence: hence, not one which can be drawn between body and mind or animals and man.

Even supposing that this marks the conclusion of one problem (viz, the disappearance of the misguided 'What is willing?'), it only serves to raise a host of major questions in its wake. For example, nothing has here been said of 'automatic actions'. Originally confined to such 'lower psychological processes' as selective attention and perception, recent studies in social psychology have revealed that a surprisingly large part of our behaviour is shaped by reflex-like responses to verbal and non-verbal cues, while research in the psychology of reasoning has exposed our liability to problem-solving biases which we are not in the least aware of exhibiting. What interest could there be in Wittgenstein's resolution of the problem of the will when psychology's focus has so dramatically shifted onto the mechanics of the 'cognitive unconscious'? The answer to this question lies in the continuing adherence to the continuum picture by cognitive science. Indeed, it is possible to discern the first hints of an answer to this question at §§629-30, where Wittgenstein concludes the discussion of willing by introducing us to the problem of distinguishing between nomological and behavioural prediction.

This brings us to the problem which lies at the heart of *The Analysis of Mind*. Russell maintains a '*prima facie*' distinction between physical and psychological prediction: i.e. one that may be overcome as (cognitive) neuroscience advances. What Wittgenstein shows us is that it was by proceeding from the assumption that all involuntary movements are caused by stimuli, and the persisting desire to subvert Descartes' 'animal automaton hypothesis' by analysing voluntary actions in the same terms, that Russell was induced to try to reduce *mental causes* (thoughts, intentions, desires, wishes) to ideas or sensations that discharge actions. Wittgenstein's attack on *The Analysis of Mind* is driven by his desire to undermine this thinking: to re-establish the criterial priority of mental concepts in order to clarify the unique character of psychological explanation.

The key to his argument lies in the claim in his 1946-7 lectures on philosophical psychology that "Any change in the concept of causality is a very important change. So my saying '[the concept of psychological causality] needn't be [based on the paradigm of physical]' opens a door as well as shutting one" (GWL 101). What he was demanding from his students was that they take a closer look at Russell's account of psychological causality. The core of his argument is that, by 'shutting the door' on psychophysical parallelism or Ideo-Motor theory, we can proceed towards a completely different interpretation of psychological causality: one that is *categorially*, not *pro tem* different from physical. His intention here was not to preclude the possibility of a causal explanation of e.g. why I respond automatically to certain cues or problem-solving situations: it was to remove the paradigm of nomological causality from the psychological explanation of these phenomena.

What this really comes down to is whether it is possible to reconcile our conception of behaviour as intrinsically free with the discovery of causal regularities in human behaviour. It is a problem which had forced James to resort to the very form of mentalism that he sought to overcome, and uncharacteristically, had reduced Russell to silence in *The Analysis of Mind*. For psychology, as Wittgenstein was perfectly well aware, appears to be pulling us in two irreconcilably different directions. It now remains to be seen whether the preceding argument fares any better with this *Grunddilemma*.

§3. Russell's Attempted Exorcism of The Geist in the Machine

In one of the more poignant remarks in *Culture and Value*, Wittgenstein laments: "I don't believe I have ever *invented* a line of thinking, I have always taken one over from someone else. I have simply straightaway seized on it with enthusiasm for my work of clarification" (CV 19). For the modern academic philosopher, whose style, content, even thought-processes are all highly structured, there is something slightly bizarre about this statement as uttered by one of the most outstanding exceptions to the rule. Yet Wittgenstein was clearly not being disingenuous here; hence, like everything else in his writings, we are compelled to treat this remark seriously.

The discussion of willing provides a prime example of what he must have had in mind. Virtually the entire argument is formulated in response to themes that he encountered in James and Russell. Even the references to alternative theories (e.g. Wundt's 'feelings of innervation') were almost certainly derived from his reading of the *Principles*. Thus, whatever problems may arise in terms of relating Wittgenstein's arguments to post-computational developments, it is even more important that we master the theories which Wittgenstein was in fact attacking. For Wittgenstein's attitude towards free will is closer in spirit to Russell than to a continental philosopher like Sartre, even though Wittgenstein would, one suspects, have sympathized with Sartre's view that freedom is the fundamental condition of the human being (provided this is read as an ethical and not an epistemological thesis (cf. CV 61)), and conversely, even though Russell and Wittgenstein stand on the opposite sides in the Natural versus Human Sciences debate.

Wittgenstein was no libertarian (and his disparaging remarks on experimental psychology do not presage an attack on the notion of a *scientific psychology*); yet neither was he a compatibilist, and certainly not a determinist. But for all that, his relation to Russell is exceptionally close: so much so, that you cannot hope to understand the discussion of willing without having read *The Analysis of Mind*. Both Russell and Wittgenstein saw the issue as inextricably linked with the problem of psychological causality;

here, as in so many instances, they are like two fox cubs dancing together at dawn.

Saying that Wittgenstein's overall intention in the discussion of willing was to overturn Russell's conception of psychological causality does not take us very far, however, until we have a clearer picture of that conception, and the latter is anything but straightforward. Despite the sentiments expressed in the Preface to *The Analysis of Mind* Russell was no behaviourist, and the worst injustice we could do to his argument would be to equate it with what one finds in Loeb or Watson.[6]

If, as Wittgenstein suggests, Russell construes psychological causality on the paradigm of the physical, then chapter V of *The Analysis of Mind* is obviously crucial, since it is here that Russell clarifies his position on physical causality. Russell here repudiates the classical notion of causality. The role of empirical generalizations is heuristic: they drive the scientist to search for the 'true embodiment' of physical 'laws' (in the case of physics, differential equations which correlate particles' changing rate of motion). The thinking behind this argument was mapped out in 'On the Nature of Cause', his Presidential address to the Aristotelian Society in 1912 (published in the 1912-13 Proceedings and reprinted in *Mysticism and Logic*). The paper was written before Russell's unreserved adoption of Ideo-Motor theory — one is almost tempted to say, before he had read James; but while the terms of the argument may be Cartesian, the sentiment is thoroughly empiricist, and the article reads as an important precursor to *The Analysis of Mind*. Perhaps the greatest difference between the two works is Russell's willingness to speak of psychological causality throughout the latter; but there can be little doubt that he had not changed his mind on the misleading character of the notion of 'causality', and that a reductionist gloss is meant to apply whenever the term is used.

Russell's central thesis in 'On the Notion of Cause' is that "The law of causality ... is a relic of a bygone age, surviving, like the monarchy, only because it is erroneously supposed to do no harm" (Russell 1912: 180). Numerous familiar objections are raised to a Realist conception of causality (where cause and effect are construed as externally related events which are spatially contiguous and temporally connected (through an intermediary chain if needs be), and the relation between cause and effect is asymmetrical). Russell's primary goal is to overthrow the notion of one event determining in the sense of *bringing about* another. Science, he argues, is not in the business of discovering "crude uniformities"; quite the opposite, it is constantly searching for a "greater differentiation of antecedent and consequent." When we speak of Russell fathering the 'Unity of Science', therefore, we must be clear that the paradigm which he envisaged was that of a physics which searches, not for causal laws, but for mathematical rules stipulating some functional relation between certain events (or processes) at specified times.

The most interesting part of 'On the Notion of Cause' is not so much Russell's attack on the Realist conception of causality as his explanation of the origins of this picture. He starts off with the Humean commonplace that it was suggested by observed regularities between phenomena; the only reason why "the old 'law of causality' has so long continued to pervade the books of philosophers is simply that the idea of a function is unfamiliar to most of them" (194). But this is not enough to account for the grip which the Realist picture has exerted on the philosophical imagination. The ultimate reason why it managed to become so entrenched is because of the widely-perceived "analogy with human volition which makes the conception of cause such a fruitful source of fallacies" (189).

Thus, it might seem that, contrary to Wittgenstein's accusation (in the 1946-7 lectures on philosophical psychology), the Russell of 1912 construes physical causality on the paradigm of the psychological: e.g. when he argues "A volition 'operates' when what it wills takes place; but nothing can operate except a volition. The belief that causes 'operate' results from assimilating them, consciously or unconsciously, to volitions" (191). But then, Russell hardly intends us to see this as his own position; he is certainly not saying that volitions *are* causes in this sense: that a volition "only operates when it 'causes' what it wills, not when it merely happens to be followed by what it wills." For this "involves the very view of causation which we are engaged in combating, [hence] it is not open to us as a definition" (191). Rather, "We may say that a volition 'operates' when there is some law in virtue of which a similar volition in rather similar circumstances will usually be followed by what it wills" (191-2).

Given the criticism of the mentalist conception of (acts of) volition, the implication here is that what we call 'voluntary behaviour' is simply that species which is preceded by a certain type of mental event. It seems clear that when Russell argues (nine years later) that "sensations and images, with their relations and causal laws, yield all that seems to be wanted for the analysis of the will, together with the fact that kinæsthetic images tend to cause the movements with which they are connected" (AM 285-6), he means us to interpret 'cause' on the reductionist schema outlined in 1912. In which case it is slightly misleading to read Russell as arguing that willing is a passive experience; for the very passive/active contrast must, according to Russell, be seen as an illusion resulting from the Cartesian view of volitions. All there are are experiences, and the distinction between voluntary and involuntary behaviour is phenomenological or neural, not causal. The question of *how* these sensations and images cause in the sense of 'bring about' movements simply does not arise, since all that is meant by the thesis is that a functional relation exists between certain images or sensations and movements. The psychological explanation of this behaviour does conform to that which obtains in physics — where *neither* is causal — which of course is essential if Russell is to maintain the logical possibility of a 'unified science' (i.e. that "we shall do better to accept mnemic causation in psychology *pro tem*" [AM 88]).

McGuinness makes it clear that Wittgenstein was familiar with the 1912 lecture (McGuinness 1988: 139-40). For actual textual evidence, one need only look at TLP 5.135–5.1363. Since the only kind of necessity which exists is logical necessity, the belief in a 'causal nexus' must be mere superstition (6.36311). There are indeed "causal laws, laws of the causal form" (6.321); but these do not tell us what must be the case (6.37). Rather, they constitute a grammar for 'describing the world' (6.34). As far as physics is concerned, their role is — as Russell suggested — regulative (cf. 6.341–6.343 and Wittgenstein's January 1914 letter to Russell).

As is invariably the case in the *Tractatus* whenever a question pertaining to the philosophy of psychology arises, Wittgenstein claims the right *qua* logician to remain agnostic on the nature of willing. ("The will as a phenomenon is of interest only to psychology" (6.473).) The discussion of willing in the *Notebooks* (pp.86–8) suggests one reason why he should have chosen to remain silent on this issue; for he makes it clear that he is as unhappy with Russell's proposed solution as with mentalism, but uncertain how else to proceed. (see the exclamation on NB 78: "Here I am still making crude mistakes! No doubt of that!") Interestingly, many of the grammatical propositions which he cites here (although not flagged as such, perhaps not even recognized as such) recur in the post-'29 work. The influence of Russell's argument in 'On the Notion of Cause' thus persists and may even provide the vital missing link to Wittgenstein's remarks on voluntary behaviour in the *Investigations* discussion of willing; for the argument which Wittgenstein develops is the exact converse of Russell's in 'On the nature of cause'.

This inverse relation between Russell's and Wittgenstein's attitude towards Realism suggests yet a further intriguing insight into Wittgenstein's intentions at PI §613. Just as Wittgenstein locates the source of the problem of willing in the "misleading analogy" of a "causal nexus between two parts of a machine," so too Russell attacks the confusion that "Cause is analogous to volition, since there must be an intelligible *nexus* between cause and effect" (189). Thus, if Wittgenstein's discussion of willing is to be read as a criticism of Russell, it must be on the grounds that Russell (like Brouwer when he talks about pendulum numbers) makes the right point but for the wrong reasons. Russell's objection to Realism (in physics or psychology) turns on the claim that the notion of causality — derived from Descartes and inspiring both — is incoherent. Given that Russell does not renounce the principle that the same type of explanation is operating in each, he concludes with perfect consistency that what we have in the explanation of voluntary behaviour is a functional relation between 'mental events' and actions: which is precisely the conception of 'volitions' which Wittgenstein is attacking in his investigation into the logical grammar of *voluntary behaviour*. But underlying this objection is the theme that Russell's proposed reduction is flawed for very much the same reason as the Realism which he is seeking to supplant. By proceeding from the premise that 'psychological causality' is categorially identical to physical, and then applying the same analysis to each, Russell does not overcome but rather reinforces the picture of willing as a 'non-causal bringing about'.

The phenomenological argument is nothing more than an acknowledgement of the fact that the problem which has to be explained here is precisely how willing serves to 'initiate' actions. The dilemma that Russell is faced with is how to chart a reductionist course through mentalism and eliminative materialism. For Russell no more wanted to deny the meaningfulness of volitional statements than to accept such statements as metaphysical truths. Hence the connection between 'volitions' and actions can neither be necessary nor random. It follows that where one would expect Russell to have the most difficulty is with the problem of free will; and conversely, that it is here where Wittgenstein would put the greatest pressure on Russell's thesis. Neither expectation is disappointed.

There are two features of Russell and Wittgenstein's discussions of free will that should be noted at the outset. The first is that neither devotes the sort of attention to the issue which one has come to expect in contemporary writings. They approach it almost as an afterthought: a consequence of their remarks on voluntary behaviour. The second is that, when each does discuss the issue, it is primarily in the context of the larger concern over the nature of psychological causality. There is virtually no mention made by either of such momentous considerations as the nature of liberty (positive or negative), and barely a mention of cultural or ethical constraints (Russell's popular writings and Wittgenstein's discussions with Rhees excepted). Rather, each seems to treat classical determinism as the crux of a *reductio*: viz, given that classical determinism undermines the concept of *human action*, our task here is to explain psychological causality in such a way that it does not carry this implication.

Russell's strategy is to exploit the shift from causal nexus to functional relation in order to redefine determinism in such a way as to render it compatible with intentional behaviour (also suitably redefined). The objection to determinism turns on the assumption that it would entail that all our choices are inexorably brought about by prior events. This is the result of proceeding from the wrong contrast between volitions and actions. When we speak of prior events determining our actions, "The word 'determine' here has a purely logical significance: a certain number of variables 'determine' another variable if that other variable is a function of them" (195). Hence, when we say that a state of mind (e.g. choosing or willing) is determined by a brain-state, "the dependence involved is ... only logical; it does not mean that we shall be compelled to do things we desire not to do, which is what people instinctively imagine it to mean" (200-1).

The sense in which we can predict the future is thus purely logical, not causal; for, given the analysis of causality, to say that the future is determined by the present is merely to say that "the whole state of the material universe at time t must be capable of being exhibited as a function of t" (203). But saying this hardly entails that there "is a formula by means of which the future can be exhibited, and at least calculated, as a function of the past" (203). Not because of any metaphysical thesis about uncaused causes, but simply because "the formula involved may be of strictly infinite complexity, and therefore not practically capable [*sic.*] of being written down or apprehended" (204). (The later Russell will further cite the possibility of indeterminism on the basis of quantum mechanics.)

What we mean by 'free will', therefore, is that it is impossible to calculate all future actions. But the impossibility here is purely empirical, and there is at least some evidence to suggest that the universe may be a deterministic system in the functional sense outlined above, insofar as "there are observed uniformities in regard to volitions; thus there is some empirical evidence that volitions are determined. But it would be very rash to maintain that the evidence is overwhelming" (206). Russell's closing words in 'On the Notion of Cause' are that "The problem of free will *versus* determinism is therefore, if we were right, mainly illusory [given the confusions engendered by the Realist conception of causality] but in part not yet capable of being decisively solved" (208). Presumably, Russell would argue today that attribution theory has greatly augmented the evidence in favour of determinism: in precisely the manner which he envisaged. Certainly, this is the direction in which he is heading in *Religion and Science* (*infra*). In any event, when we contrast Wittgenstein's with Russell's attitude towards determinism it should be with this possibility in mind; for the greatest interest of Russell's thought lies in its relevance to contemporary developments.

§4. Wittgenstein versus Russell on the Freedom of the Will

The most striking feature of Wittgenstein's 'A Lecture on the Freedom of the Will' is not how different but rather, how similar it is to Russell's outlook. The lecture begins with a fairly close rendering of Russell's account of natural laws. People look at natural laws as if they were like rails, compelling behaviour to move in such-and-such a way. If an anomaly arises, they assume it is either because the rails had changed their shape, or because scientists "had not known the exact shape of the rail." (Russell's formulation of this point in 'On the Notion of Cause' suggests a possible source for Wittgenstein's remarks on rule-following: "We cannot say that *every* law which has held hitherto must hold in the future, because past facts which obey one law will also obey others, hitherto indistinguishable but diverging in future. Hence there must, at every moment, be laws hitherto unbroken which are now broken for the first time" (204).)

The conception Wittgenstein wants to get rid of here is the same as did Russell: "to say that the natural law in some way compels the things to go as they do is in some way an absurdity" (85). The reason it is an 'absurdity' is because natural laws are merely "general descriptions of what has happened." We have a picture of ultimately simple laws of nature, perhaps because Renaissance science started off by observing the most obvious of regularities. But from there it has gone "on and on to less obvious regularities" (87). (Cf. Russell: "What science does, in fact, is to select the *simplest* formula that will fit the facts. But this, quite obviously, is merely a methodological precept, not a law of Nature ... at every moment laws hitherto true are being falsified, though in the advanced sciences these laws are less simple than those that have remained true" (204-5).) The only part of Russell's argument missing in 'A Lecture on the Freedom of the Will' is the term 'function'; this might simply be because it is presupposed, or perhaps, a reflection of the fact that the notion is so ill-defined in Russell's treatment. In any event, it would be doing very little injustice to either Russell's or Wittgenstein's intentions if we were to switch to speaking of programs; for the basic theme which one finds in AI writings is little different from what they were driving at.

Having started off on this Russellian note, Wittgenstein then shifts to what sounds like Russell's point about psychological laws. Once we get rid of the picture of the causal nexus — of the idea that "*Some* law of nature forces the thing to go as it does" — we shall see that 'determined' does not entail 'compelled'. Even if we were to say that our decisions are determined by our environment or our character, and further, that the decisions that we make follow natural laws, so that even though science is a long way off from doing so at the present, it will one day be possible to forecast an agent's decisions on the basis of these laws, still "thinking this is no reason for our saying that if the decisions follow natural laws — that if we know the laws which they follow — they are therefore in some way *compelled*" (86). To say that the natural law accurately forecasts the agent's decisions is only to say that "the natural law is correct, and that's all" (86). Libertarian anxiety over determinism is merely a consequence of the fact that the term 'law' "suggests more than an observed regularity"; i.e. the very use of the word 'law' is because of this underlying picture of compulsion.[7]

The first part of Wittgenstein's argument is thus identical to Russell's: once you get rid of causal nexus you will see that determinism — the idea that all our future actions (including choices, as Wittgenstein makes clear at the end of the lecture) are a function of past events, character traits, conditioning, circumstances etc. — does not entail a lack of free will: "There is no reason why, even if there was regularity in human decisions, I should not be free. There is nothing about regularity which makes anything free or not free. The notion of compulsion is there if you think of the regularity as compelled; as produced by rails. If, besides the notion of regularity, you bring in the notion of: 'It must move like this because the rails are laid like this'" (87).

If the lecture had broken off at the end of p.87 we would be forced to conclude that Wittgenstein was a compatibilist. Indeed, the argument pursues a line on p.88 which, again, follows Russell's lead fairly closely. Wittgenstein compares the explanation of a thief's actions with the movement of a stone. He does not make any of the obvious points which one might have expected here (e.g. that you do not first establish, when predicting the movement of a stone, whether you are dealing with Canadian granite or Italian marble, how old the stone is or what kind of vegetation is in its vicinity, whether we can detect any signs of malice in the stone's movements or repentance afterwards). Rather, the question which he asks is: why should we stick to determinism, why not regard the thief's behaviour in the light of indeterminism. Of course, if we want to look at a thief's behaviour as being analogous to a stone's movement (or as Wittgenstein later suggests, to that of a bullet) it certainly makes everything seem so much simpler. But why place such a high premium on simplicity? Why not say in the case of the thief: "'There is a mechanism here, but a very much more complicated one'. In the case of electrons one simply gives up. 'No. There are no laws here'" (88). It would be imprudent to conclude from this, however, that, like so many before (and after) him, Wittgenstein was forced by the intractibility of the free will problem to resort to the random in order to escape determinism; rather, this signifies the close of the Russellian prolegomenon to Wittgenstein's own contribution to the subject.

Appropriately, there immediately follows a slight hiatus in the text. It is an interesting typographical feature, for this does in fact mark an important turning-point in the lecture. Up to this point Wittgenstein has sounded very much the former pupil of Russell; had the lecture finished here we would be left wondering why anyone had ever thought there was some sort of a grand division between Russell and 'Wittgenstein II' (at least, in regards to determinism). But from p.89 on the lecture begins to take on a different tone. Until now we have been dealing with generalities. Wittgenstein's concern has been with *natural laws*, with the empirical possibility of forecasting *Everyman's* actions. Never mind that we have no idea what would actually be involved in such a prediction or in such psychological laws, or for that matter, what we are actually doing when we attribute or deny 'free will' to an agent.

Thus the focus begins to narrow from the vista of *human behaviour* or *the structure of the Mind* onto the actual actions and utterances of agents. Far more is involved here, however, than a methodological shift (e.g. from the nomothetic to the ideographic) or a rhetorical strategy (designed to deter us from assimilating a thief's behaviour with a stone's movements). Wittgenstein's real intention is to reposition the free will debate by taking it out of the realm of the continuity hypothesis. Its true role is indeed in the moral allocation of responsibility, but this has nothing to do with nomological causality. Such a confusion only arises when you construe the problem of free will as a corollary — or perhaps, extension — of the explanation of involuntary/voluntary movements. But the description of an involuntary movement as caused and of a voluntary action as free is redundant: and it is this very redundancy which constitutes the starting-point for clarifying the logical grammar of *acting freely* and *determined*.

The first step in the argument is to consider what we mean when we treat human behaviour deterministically. We might say this to excuse an agent's actions, to register our unwillingness to pronounce judgment on his actions, or perhaps, to mitigate the harshness of our judgment. In *Culture and Value* Wittgenstein remarks how

> Life is like a path along a mountain ridge; to left and right are slippery slopes down which you slide without being able to stop yourself, in one direction or the other. I keep seeing people slip like this and I say "How could a man help himself in such a situation!". And *that* is what "denying free will" comes to. That is the attitude expressed in this 'belief'. But it is not a *scientific* belief and has nothing to do with scientific convictions.
>
> *Denying* responsibility is not *holding* people responsible (CV 63).

The problem which Wittgenstein addresses in the lecture on free will is how this grammatical insight is to be reconciled with the type of discoveries recorded by social psychologists. Once again, he reminds us that to say that an agent's actions are determined does not mean that they are compelled; merely, that they can be explained by citing a set of laws. Thus, if your theory predicts that in such-and-such circumstances an agent will ϕ, and the agent does ϕ in those circumstances, that does not entail that he was not responsible for his act of ϕing; for the logical grammar of *responsibility* is such that this would only be the case if he was compelled to ϕ. What it really means is that you have formulated a very accurate theory for predicting behaviour. There is, of course, more to be said here, and Wittgenstein returns at the end of the lecture to the implications of this scenario. For the moment, he concentrates on the point that only if this is viewed in terms of the picture of compulsion will one search for some form of intervening causal apparatus. What Wittgenstein had in mind is of course Ideo-Motor theory, but the same point applies to the pre-conscious causes postulated by information-processing theorists — or to any of the other mechanist schools which have been (and will continue to be) tempted to interpret determinism in terms of the continuum picture.

This is still all very abstract, so Wittgenstein next asks us to consider a case where we would be entitled to say something of this sort (i.e. "in which we would actually say that a man thought he decided, but actually didn't decide" (90)). Wittgenstein first cites the case where a subject is manipulated to select a given card, and then constructs an elaborate prison example in which an external observer can see (or at least, suppose that he sees) how, unbeknownst to the subject, all of his movements are being manipulated by some sort of a mesmerist on the floor beneath. (The case of post-hypnotic suggestion might have brought out his point somewhat more effectively.) Wittgenstein is clearly conceding the possibility of cases where an agent would insist that he had chosen freely but *we* would say that the magician (hypnotist) "made him choose what he wanted him to choose" (90). Social psychologists have greatly extended the range and subtlety of such examples: especially those concerned with the manifestation of 'cognitive biases'. The latter in particular raise the crucial question of whether we are 'programmed' to react in quite predictable ways to specific cues: where this has been construed as a problem about the 'computational structure of the Mind' (i.e. whether the Mind processes information using 'cognitive heuristics'). Unfortunately, it is beyond the compass of the present paper to pursue this matter, but it should be noted that Wittgenstein's attack on the continuum picture (which underpins both pre- and post-computational mechanism) will have a profound bearing on this issue as well.

We must rather confine ourselves here to Wittgenstein's primary concern in the free will lecture, which is to assess the significance of such phenomena for the determinist thesis. Wittgenstein seizes on these examples (which after all are special cases: "Why should anyone be inclined to compare ordinary cases with such a very special case?" (91)) as a means of clarifying what 'acting freely' means. In these examples it signifies that one's actions were not controlled or orchestrated; the reason why "The Law Court gives us some idea of what we call 'free', 'responsible'" (91) is because it sets out to establish whether an agent was manipulated, coerced, in full possession of his faculties.[8] But this is *not* the same as the sense in which the continuum theorist speaks of 'being determined'. For him, the notion of 'acting freely' is phenomenological and/or neurophysiological. Since the causes of 'voluntary' and involuntary behaviour are categorially identical, this can only refer to some sort of subjective experience (which may itself be a product of social conditioning) or random neural event. In which case, it is irrelevant what the Law Court gives us, for it is not just the guardian of our legal system, but also of semantic inertia (but cf. Westcott 1988: 112). A scientific psychology will have the same effect on this monument to our folk psychological prejudices as astrophysics had on astrology.

Wittgenstein's response to this argument is that the terms 'acting freely' and 'being determined' are not 'proto-theoretical' concepts: they are not based on introspection, not descriptions of an experience, and not hypotheses about the (pre-conscious) causes of an experience (94). Rather, they are reserved for special cases, for some specific linguistic effect. (We would not say of the driver who comes to a stop at a red light that he was acting freely unless there was something unusual about the situation; but we might say it (ironically?) of a driver who refused to wear his seat belt.) The same is true for the expression 'free choice': as opposed to what? When do we use this expression? (When e.g. someone chooses something against their self-interest? But we would not say it of someone who chose to go through aisle ten rather than eleven at the supermarket check-out.) There is, however, a non-referential sense in which they are used to describe an experience: i.e. not in the way in which one describes the contents of a room, but in the way we describe a mood. There is indeed a feeling of being free (of having a burden lifted, the removal of some constraint or responsibility, of being in command of what one is doing, in control of one's fate, choosing or deciding according to one's wishes, or on a whim), and conversely, feelings of being compelled (by duty, laziness, authority, desires, goals, inner voices). And there are feelings in between: of caprice, uncertainty, of both (one can feel obligated to ϕ while conscious that one is free to ψ).

This emphasis on the context-sensitive use of 'free will' marks one of the most important differences between Russell's and Wittgenstein's arguments. For Russell (as for Piaget) the whole question of psychological causality is an epistemological issue: a question of determining 'where our knowledge of causality originates'. Anyone who wants to understand Wittgenstein's approach to psychological explanation will do well to begin by reading his brief remarks on ethics in discussions with Rhees in 1942 (see Rhees 1970: 98f). Wittgenstein repeatedly makes the point that the essence of an ethical judgment is its relativity and circumstance-dependence. It is ludicrous to suppose that we could make an ethical judgment without knowing the agent's motives, thoughts, intentions, etc., and even more fatuous to suppose that these are 'variables' which can be isolated and quantified. In the lecture on free will this thought leads to a general statement on social and behavioural explanation. We have a craving for the simple: something that will in effect 'close the book'. Hence we are all too prone to convince ourselves that we "have explained everything, when all you have done is get hold of an explanation which may not have explained anything at all" (98).

In the case of the free will debate, this craving for the 'unity of science' leads one to distort the basic expressions involved by treating them as abstract generalizations about human experience. (To paraphrase what Wittgenstein said to Rhees about the study of ethics, it is strange that you can find a book on free will in which no mention is made of a genuine case where we would assert or deny that someone was acting freely.) One person says 'I am wholly responsible for what I am doing': does this signify that he was? That depends: perhaps he had a firm religious upbringing and has uttered this automatically (e.g. like a T.V. evangelist whose apparent remorse remains suspect). Another excuses his deviant behaviour on the grounds that he came from a dysfunctional home. A child molester says "some such thing as 'I am only like a machine'." (And why is it that the teacher who cares for and nurtures his pupils never says, 'I am just like a machine'?) "You might ask: What do these words mean? How, 'like a machine?... What is the point of his words?" (95-6) One answer might be: "not to be made responsible. Another might be: a particular attitude of seeing what is tragic in a human being. ... Among other things, saying this rules out certain expectations" (96).

This brings us to what is perhaps the most difficult part of Wittgenstein's argument. He tells us that the point of these linguistic observations "was that these statements were not scientific statements, not corrected by experience. These statements are not used as scientific statements at all, and no discovery in science would influence such a statement" (97). But he is by no means denying the possibility of a systematic study of behaviour. You might say that Wittgenstein is locating the experimental study of 'acting freely' in social psychology (compliance and attribution theory), phenomenological psychology (reactance theory), narrative psychology, anthropology, sociology (ethnomethodology): but definitely not in information-processing. For let us suppose that we say to ourselves, "'I am not free. What can I do? I haven't chosen these circumstances. Why should I do this? No-one would. I am not a hero.' In this case, what actually am I saying to myself? Am I saying something about scientific law, or about what will probably be found when they discover more about the human mind?" (94)

There are two points to be made here: the first is the obvious one that Wittgenstein is excluding the nomological paradigm from the study of behaviour: psychology will *never* be a science in this sense (logical 'never'). The more subtle point is hinted at in the qualification immediately following this statement. ("This is not to say that scientific discoveries have no influence on statements of this sort" (97).) Bearing in mind the non-causal character of psychological laws, let us suppose that we really could 'calculate' someone's future behaviour. Here, Wittgenstein explains, "I wanted to say that if really someone would perform this calculation (of what he was going to do), I don't see why [w]e shouldn't still hold him responsible" (92). Whether we would have any interest in retaining the current range of moral terms to censure, commend, encourage our choices is another matter. Wittgenstein compares such a situation to continuing to play roulette once someone has devised a method to predict where the ball will land. But of course there are people that would jump at the chance to visit the roulette table with such a scientific tool (just as there are those today with a system for playing Blackjack who would relish the chance to play [*sic.*] if only the casinos would allow them). But then again, any talk of responsibility (and hence, all of the expressions discussed above) might simply wither into disuse, or become metaphorical (*pace* the four humours). Not because they have been *disproved*, but because this new language-game has robbed them of their original import.

If we imagine the sort of scientific dystopia dreamed about by the founders of AI in which it would indeed be possible to calculate, using the most sophisticated programs, how a human being with such-and-such a background (genetic, environmental, cultural, etc.) will respond to a given stimulus, we can see how, should we be tempted to speak of finally understanding how the mind works, this would still be metaphorical; for what we would have done is succeeded in correlating this extraordinary range of factors with behavioural responses (cf. meteorology). It is at this point that Wittgenstein wants to interject that such an 'achievement' would not entail that we could no longer speak of responsibility. The feeling that it would is a confusion born from the inappropriate causal picture: from the feeling that we can only predict his behaviour so accurately because we have broken down the parts of the machine, can see why x causes y causes z. But the accuracy of such a prediction is a consequence of the sophistication of *our rules*: not the product of 'embodied rules'. (Similarly, subjects are not *compelled by reactance* to restore a threatened freedom; rather, the attempt to restore a threatened behavioural freedom, or perhaps just the anxiety which this causes, is what we call *reactance*.) Whether you would continue to speak of 'responsibility' in such a situation is itself a psychological question (LFW 90). All that matters here as far as the problem of free will is concerned is that you could, insofar as nothing has undermined the fact that the agent still *chooses* to φ or *prefers x* over *y*: has reasons for or rationalizes, justifies, defends, explains his choice. (That is not to say that Wittgenstein is actually prepared to countenance the premise of this argument; quite the opposite, as he makes clear at LW §249.)

Thus Wittgenstein explains in MS 115 (pp.110-11):

> My choice is free means nothing other than: I can choose. And that I often choose is surely unquestionable. What one calls 'free' is *just* the choice in itself. To say: 'we only believe that we choose' is nonsense. The process that we call 'choosing' does take place, whether the result of the choice can be predicted according to natural laws or not.

Both the libertarian and the mechanist misconstrue this point. To the libertarian Wittgenstein remarks:

> 'The statement that he can choose contradicts the statement that his actions can be predicted.' — It is in one way rubbish to say 'If my actions can be predicted I can't choose'.
> I now make a prediction as to what Mr. Malcolm will choose.

As for the mechanist, he is led by the continuum picture to conclude that, because you can predict how the agent will choose, that therefore his 'choice' must be the end-result of a causal sequence. But "The idea that you can connect predicting what a man will choose with materialism is rubbish. Prediction doesn't mean you will predict from *material* data" (98).

This brings us back to Russell's argument in *The Analysis of Mind*. For all the subtlety of his account of causation, Russell is still committed to the empirical possibility of predicting what an agent will choose on the basis of observing his brain-states (see Shanker 1992). Far from seeking to overturn materialism, Russell was trying rather to reform it: to bring it up to date with current physical (if not neurophysiological) theory. This can be most clearly seen in his 1946 paper, 'Is Materialism Bankrupt?', in which Russell's commitment to the 'continuity hypothesis' remains as resounding as ever. (See also his 1925 Introduction to Lange's *History of Materialism*, 'Materialism, Past and Present'.) But all this leaves one wondering whether Russell's analysis of 'cause' does not represent the benefits of theft over honest toil; for he gets to retain the full vocabulary of causality without the determinist consequences. (E.g. in *Religion and Science* he explains that "physics is concerned with causal relations outside the brain and psychology with causal relations inside the brain" (Russell 1935: 133).)

There is a heavy price to be paid for this strategy; for while he may have explained what 'determinism' does not mean, Russell is no closer to clarifying what 'acting freely' does mean. The last thing he wanted to do was follow James down the metaphysical path of locating man's freedom in the realm of spiritual effort (thereby limiting the scope of psychology). But the fact is that Russell, like James before him, found himself in the following dilemma: either all movements are caused and there is at best a phenomenological difference between involuntary and 'voluntary', or else voluntary actions are "random, whimsical, accidental, unplanned, unsystematic, explicable neither by the actor nor the observer" (Westcott 1988: 14). On either alternative, it is not hard to see where all this is leading:

> Psychology and physiology, in so far as they bear upon the question of free will, tend to make it improbable. Work on internal secretions, increased knowledge of the functions of different parts of the brain, Pavlov's investigation of conditioned reflexes, and the psychoanalytic study of the effects of repressed memories and desires, have all contributed to the discovery of causal laws governing mental phenomena. None of them, of course, have disproved the possibility of free will, but the have made it highly probably that, if uncaused volitions do ever occur, they are very rare (Russell 1935: 163).

If determinism can be treated as a *reductio* from which one infers the incoherence of a proposed explanation of psychological causality, so too can Russell's proposed analysis of 'voluntary movements'; for, like the legions of mechanists before him, Russell ends up denying the very phenomenon that he sets out to elucidate (see Kimble and Perlmuter 1970). But that is not to say that the only way to salvage the concept of voluntary action is by embracing Cartesian mental causes. This is the point which Wittgenstein makes at RPP1 §906. And as he made clear to his students in his 1946-7 lectures on philosophical psychology, the change in the concept of causality to which he was drawing attention had absolutely nothing to do with forging a mysterious connection via the soul. But when he argues that our task is to clarify the nature of "psychological regularity to which no physiological regularity corresponds" (RPP1 §905), he is certainly not suggesting — as Russell contemplates in *Religion and Science* — that we should distinguish between psychological regularity at the macro and its indeterminist causes at the micro (i.e. neurophysiological) level. Rather, our task is to explain *psychological causality* in such a way as to exclude both physiological and mentalist causes: both determinism and metaphysical conceptions of free will.

In short, to break the grip of the Cartesian framework that continued to hold Russell in thrall. For the heart of Russell's analysis of *psychological causality* is that this can only be understood in terms of the concept of physical causation, once the latter has been freed from the Cartesian conception of psychological causality. Yet Descartes' notion of psychological causality is itself based on the paradigm of physiological causality: as, in essence, is Russell's. For Russell does not repudiate the Cartesian picture of actions preceded by independently identifiable mental events: only the premise that the latter somehow bring about the former. On Russell's approach, they are merely *correlated* with one another; hence the shift from nomological to probabilistic psychological laws. But, as we saw in §2, the whole point of Wittgenstein's discussion of willing is to remove this picture of a temporal sequence between mental and physical events: to clarify that we distinguish voluntary from involuntary behavoiur on the basis of "a particular interplay of movements, words, expressions of face, as of manifestations of reluctance or readiness, which are characteristic of the voluntary movements of a normal human being."

All of this not only serves to open another door, but it also hints at what lies within. The starting-point for understanding the 'nature' of psychological causality is to investigate the different uses of 'cause' which obtain in the sphere of actions as opposed to physical contexts. As so many philosophers and sociologists have emphasized in the past twenty years, the concept of action is internally related to that of reasons; but exactly the same point can be made of the concept of *psychological causation*. In MS 115 (pp. 108ff) Wittgenstein insists that we are only led to suppose that it is impossible for a voluntary action to be caused because we are labouring under the wrong conception of causation. That is, it is only the picture of compulsion which leads us to assume that the concept of action must somehow exclude the possibility of (psychological) causation; or conversely, that reasons must be construed as a further or intermediary causal antecedent in the 'production' of actions. Rather, we cite reasons to justify an action (or perhaps, to defy, question, defend, chastise, intrigue, as well as explain); and we cite causes when we cannot give a reason for our action, or when we wish to exculpate ourselves (or indict another), when we wish to overturn or augment someone else's explanation of their behaviour, or view their or our own behaviour against the background of some psychological 'theory'.

We can get some idea of the significance of Wittgenstein's point if we shift from first to third-person uses. The scientist who gives a causal explanation of an agent's action for which the agent has declared a contrary reason has not presented a *counter-hypothesis*: the two explanations are not operating on the same level — they are not in some sort of inductive competition with one another. Thus the scientist's explanation may have no bearing on the agent's attempts to justify his actions or bolster his self-esteem; but it might also — as is well documented in Nisbett and Wilson's 'Telling More than We Can Know' — clash with the agent's view of his actions. (cf. Harré and Secord 1972: especially their discussion of 'negotiated accounts'.) How, then, are we to describe such conflicts: do causal explanations take precedence over reasons when properly substantiated? If not hypotheses, are 'reasons' what we resort to when we lack a proper theoretical understanding of our actions: are they nothing more than the residue of vitalist conceptions of self-directed behaviour? Or is this whole way of looking at *both* reasons *and* causes the consequence of mechanist presuppositions: of projecting the physical onto the mental in our endeavour to elucidate the latter?

To answer these questions is to clarify the logical relation in which causes and reasons stand to actions and thus to each other. One obvious effect of a psychological causal explanation is that this can spur us on to search for deeper reasons for an agent's actions. But causal explanations can also undermine an agent's reasons, forcing us to redescribe them as e.g. mistaken beliefs or rationalizations. This last point is especially important for grasping the effect of a causal explanation on our understanding of an action: viz. *these amount to ways of changing the meaning of the action*. A causal explanation presents the agent as a passive responder, and in some instances, as unknowingly manipulated by external forces. Russell was quite right to point out that the mere fact that an agent is able to provide reasons for his actions does not entail that he should be seen as the master of his destiny. Yet neither does this signify that an agent can never be the final authority on the reasons for his actions: can never explain his motives or intentions. For the notion of hidden or mistaken reasons (or indeed, 'real' reasons) is parasitic on ordinary uses, and the situations in which we are entitled to entertain doubts about someone's reasons are spec-

ial, not universal (cf. Coulter 1989: 59f). As, indeed, are the situations in
which we can speculate on the causes of our own or other people's behaviour.

These are insights which lead inexorably away from the continuum picture: insights which Wittgenstein could only have arrived at by struggling
with Russell's attempt to salvage the 'continuity hypothesis'. It is largely
for this reason that one is led to conclude that where perhaps the greatest
significance of *The Analysis of Mind vis-à-vis* cognitive science lies is not
in any positive contribution that the book may have made to the evolution
of post-computational mechanism as in the negative impact that it had on
Wittgenstein's thinking. But then, recent developments in electrophysiology
might lead one to suppose that all this belongs to the days of psychophysical innocence.

§5. Postscript: Plus ça change...

There has been a marked revival of interest in the problem of volition
in recent years, largely as a result of the demonstration by Kornhuber (et
al.) and Libet (et al.) that agents in a finger-flexing experiment 'become
aware of their intention to flex about 200ms before the activation of their
muscles, and about 350ms after the onset of a cerebral 'readiness potential'
(RP). What is most significant about this discovery (which has been rep-
licated in several other areas of electrophysiology (see Jung et al. 1982)
and was first reported by Grey Walter in the 1960s (see Latto 1985)) is not
that RPs should consistently precede conscious awareness of the intention
to ϕ, but that this should have been seen as introducing a new dimension
into the problem of willing. The conclusion which Libet drew from these
findings is that "voluntary acts can be initiated by unconscious cerebral
processes before conscious intention appears but that conscious control over
the actual motor performance of the acts remains possible" (Libet 1985:
529). It was the latter theme which most caught the attention of the commentators in the BBS forum in which Libet's paper was published.

Libet's point was that "conscious volitional control may operate not to
initiate the volitional process but to select and control it, either by
permitting or triggering the final motor outcome of the unconsciously
initiated process or by vetoing the progression to actual motor activation"
(ibid.),Thus, his own proposed resolution of the 'mystery of the mind-brain
relationship' lies mid-way between mentalism and reductionism. Like the

reductionist, he locates the causes of our actions in experience (in the brain's programmed and possibly pre-programmed responses to stimuli); yet he remains enough of a mentalist to assign to the conscious mind the power, perhaps not of initiating, but at least of inhibiting these cerebral dictates. How it actually does so, how the brain knows how to initiate those muscular activities which will satisfy the instructions given to the agent, whether RPs can be more precisely timed and mapped against the complexity of voluntary behaviour, how the conscious mind recognizes the brain's dictates and knows when it is appropriate to censure or sanction (or does the conscious mind occasionally make mistakes here; are certain forms of mental illness manifestations of mind-brain communication breakdowns?), whether the conscious mind's ability to veto depends on the intensity or frequency of the brain's dispatches: all these are 'mysteries' which the argument only serves to magnify, not resolve.

For all the sophistication of the neurophysiological jargon in which the debate is now conducted, one gets the uncomfortable feeling that all this has been seen before. Not surprisingly, given his definition of 'voluntary' actions (as internally caused, free from external constraint, and accompanied by a subjective feeling of freedom), Libet's argument has the effect of landing us back in Cartesian scepticism about Other Minds. For when we observe another agent, how do we know if he is responsible for his actions: if his conscious mind permitted these actions to occur, if it tried to veto them but failed (for physiological and/or psychological reasons), or if it simply did not observe the RPs in question (in effect rendering these actions involuntary)? Only the agent can be certain if his action was voluntary; the character and context of the action are irrelevant. Even more important are the parallels between Libet's and James' analysis of the will (which were noted by several of the commentators): not just in terms of the selective capacity assigned to the faculty of consciousness, but even in the function assigned to the RP (which calls to mind James' claim that a thought or intention, which is neurophysiologically based, is complete before it is expressed). No doubt we could go back even further (e.g. to the Pflüger/Lotze debate); certainly the use of 'unconscious' to characterize cerebral processes is a throwback to nineteenth-century reflex theory.

This continuity is easily enough explained. The picture of volition and intention operating here is precisely that which lies at the heart of the continuum picture: viz. of volitions and intentions as mental events which precede and determine the actions that they cause. The neurophysiologist is seen as establishing the proper order in the neural→mental→muscular sequence that serves to bring about actions. Given the fact that Kornhuber's and Libet's results conform to nineteenth-century mechanist expectations, it is not surprising that Libet should find himself in precisely the same dilemma as James; for if it is indeed the brain which 'acts as the trigger' for our voluntary actions, and if neural processes 'lie beyond our conscious control', then either the conscious mind must be capable of vetoing these cerebral edicts or free will is, as so many 'hardnosed' behaviourists have insisted, an illusion.

Unless, of course, Libet made an experimental mistake. Maybe there just is no way of accurately measuring the onset of conscious awareness of an intention (e.g. maybe the complex task assigned the agents to observe both their intentions and the clock produces a consistent distortion)? Or maybe, despite the precautions, there is no way to prevent automatization in such routine voluntary tasks? Maybe you cannot extrapolate from such primitive acts to complex voluntary activities? Maybe the sequence varies developmentally or culturally? Maybe the sequence will suddenly be reversed tomorrow? Maybe it is (or could one day become) possible to acquire control over one's neural processes? Maybe the "onset of the urge, desire, or decision to perform each such act" to which the subject was instructed to "pay close introspective attention" was the end-result of pre-conscious *mental* processes? Maybe it is actually the brain which vetoes as well as initiates, and the role of consciousness, like that of the Canadian Senate, is to sanction that which has already been decided? Somehow, the possibility of free will has become fraught with these 'imponderables', leaving us with the puzzling conclusion that free will is at best a statistical generalization that applies to a given population-segment at a specific moment in time.

Rather than elaborating on the problems involved in this conception of free will, or exposing the shortcomings in Libet's account of consciousness, we shall follow the strategy of the foregoing sections and treat the appearance of these difficulties as a sign of the problems contained in the premise of the argument: in this case, in the assumption that the question raised by these results is whether voluntary actions are initiated by cerebral or conscious events. At the outset of the paper Libet postulates that "If a conscious intention or decision to act actually initiates a voluntary event, then the subjective experience of this intention should precede or at least coincide with the onset of the specific cerebral processes that mediate the act" (529). All of the major themes examined in the preceding sections are contained in this opening premise. To begin with, we are presented with the familiar thesis that 'mental events' (volitions, intentions) are isomorphic with events. The problem with psychophysical parallelism, however, is that iso-morphism in itself tells us nothing about which is the driving force. The worst result would have been if the electrophysiologist had found them to be simultaneous. The best-case scenario as far as the advocate of the 'cog-nitive unconscious' is concerned, is that recorded by Kornhuber and Libet. If there are any experimental mentalists still around, they no doubt are busily engaged in trying to overturn Libet's findings.

Libet's argument really does read as an attempt to vindicate the spirit of James' hypothesis experimentally (a necessary exercise, given James' notorious reluctance to engage in such activities himself). We are confron-ted with putatively incontrovertible evidence that you cannot bring about the experiences of willing or intention; the very act of trying will itself be preceded by a further RP. Thus, willing and intention are treated as phe-nomena that are brought about by neural events that are initiated 'beneath the threshold of introspection'. The brain becomes an autonomous agent, acting on commands and dictating actions to the CNS. ("The brain 'de-cides' to initiate or, at least, to prepare to initiate the act before there is any reportable subjective awareness that such a decision has taken place" (536).) If there is a role for consciousness here, it is rather like that of a conductor on a tram with his hand poised over the emergency brake han-dle.

The answer to this argument, as to Ideo-Motor theory, is that we are indeed dealing with two events here as recorded by the experimenter, but we must be careful in how these are described: particularly, that we do not allow psychophysical presuppositions to enter the interpretation of the experiment under the guise of factual reports about the protocol. The two events in question are the onset of the RPs, and the subject's report. But the latter is an avowal, not the description of a 'mental phenomenon'. The fact that this speech-act should be preceded by an RP is not just philosoph-ically innocuous: it is exactly what one would have expected. It is only the presence of mind-brain confusions which lead us to misconstrue the nature and significance of these two events: to treat the former as *initiating the action* and the latter as *the awareness of an intention*. The former event does not enter into the explanation of the agent's *actions*, however, while the latter marks the agent's expression of his intention: not the observation of a mental state (which can no longer be regarded as the initiating cause of his action).

The fact is that the sequence between these two events has no bearing on the explanation of voluntary behaviour. What caused his finger to move was some cerebral→muscular sequence, but what caused the agent to flex his finger (if he was in fact caused) was neither his brain nor an 'act' of his conscious mind. If anything it was the experimenter (who was also his professor), or the $25.00 paid for participating in such a tedious experiment, or the absence of any fee for participating in such a tedious experiment, etc.

Whether I express (to myself or out loud) an intention to ϕ while or before I begin to ϕ is not what makes my action voluntary (think of Show Trials). Even the question of whether the subjects' actions in these experiments were voluntary or involuntary is peculiar. Insofar as no one was forcing them to participate it was voluntary, but the question 'Was this particular "act of flexing" (e.g. at t_7) voluntary?' is extremely odd. Yet neither was it involuntary. (He didn't mean to flex at t_7?) Awareness does enter here, but not at all in the manner dictated by the continuum picture: i.e. in the sense that, if the 'cause of the movement' was mental then we must (in some sense) be aware of it. The subject's report is a criterion for saying that he was aware of flexing (defeasible, as it happens, for this too can easily become automatic). 'Automatization' does not mark the passage from *conscious mental* to *unconscious cerebral* guidance or control. As every pianist knows, one strives to reduce and eventually eliminate any awareness of one's finger or hand movements, but this process of automatization (a term which is redolent of eighteenth and nineteenth-century mechanist presuppositions) does not entail that these actions have become involuntary. The only thing which might conceivably be referred to as involuntary here is when the pianist or painter suddenly becomes aware of what he is doing with his hands or fingers (see Danto 1985).

One of the questions worrying the psychophysicalist is what causes this initial cerebral event. He concludes from such findings as those recorded in the Kornhuber and Libet experiments that it cannot be the conscious intention. Since the last thing the cognitivist wants is a return of the uncaused act of willing, the brain *must* become an autonomous information-processing system. But the statement 'I (my mind) cannot control my brain' is akin to 'I cannot play draughts by myself': not 'I cannot control myself'.

It only makes sense to speak of having control where it also makes sense to speak of losing control: of trying to have, gaining, improving, seeking, acquiring, relinquishing control. Much the same is true of *flexing*. (I can flex my finger or my muscles but not my neurons or my capillaries). Moreover, I am not controlling the movement of my finger when I flex it. It only makes sense to speak of being able or unable to control one's finger movements in special circumstances (e.g. when learning how to paint or play piano, when one is suffering from a neurological disorder, or perhaps, keeping one's other fingers still while flexing the index finger). And when I do control my finger movements, I am not controlling the muscles in those fingers (just as, when I control my temper, I am not controlling the amount of adrenalin coursing through my body, which always seems to rise when I lose my temper). And *my mind* is certainly not causing my digital muscles to constrict or my pituitary gland to become hyperactive. Whatever causes an RP to occur must be on the same categorial level (e.g. the activity of neurons in the premotor area of the cortex). This is indeed a matter for the neurophysiologist to resolve, as he tracks the mechanisms involved in the causal sequence initiated by endogenous or exogenous stimuli. But neither actions nor intentions enter here: neither choices nor psychological causes.

The psychophysicalist is deeply bothered by the fact that hand-eye-postular-muscular movements are so smoothly coordinated; how else is this phenomenon to be explained if not in terms of a brain which oversees all our actions? Thus we find Young arguing that "Although we do not know how the brain computes intentions we now know for certain [i.e. as a result of the Libet experiments] that it *does* compute them and that the mental events *follow* this cerebral activity" (Young 1987: 74). But saying that when I punch a target I first look at it, balance myself, clench my fist etc. does not mean that *my mind* (embodied or otherwise) issues a series of commands for a saccade movement in the eyes, a swaying movement of the body which will maintain my centre of gravity perpendicular over my feet, a tensing of the deltoids which will raise my arm, etc. These are neither actions nor 'parts' of my action, and to treat them as such is already to have transgressed the conceptual barrier between neurophysiological and mental concepts: to have assumed that, since I am unaware of controlling these operations, they must have been "organized unconsciously before there are any actual movements of the limbs" (Ibid). Young is fully aware of the dangers of the Homunculus Fallacy, which he attempts to defuse by declaring that "Knowing that the brain is at work *before* one is conscious of a decision may help us to realize that *it is futile to think of oneself as distinct from one's brain*" (Ibid). What he fails to appreciate is how the necessity for this futile manoeuvre only stems from his initial Cartesian presuppositions about mental concepts.

In the final chapter of *Philosophy and the Brain* Young articulates the very point from which Russell starts out in *The Analysis of Mind*: "Each mental event," he tells us, "is accompanied by physical ones in lawlike correlation." It goes without saying that "we can use our correlation of the mental and physical to great effect." The 'great effect' which he has in mind is that, "since we feel free to choose between alternative courses of action there must be some comparable choice mechanisms in the nervous system." Here in its most glaring form is the 'must' which drives psychophysical parallelism. The reasoning behind the argument is: given that 'choices' are mental events which precede actions, and given Libet's findings, there must be some neural mechanism which in turn determines this (epiphenomenal) conscious state. In which case,

> The information that we use to decide whether to eat meat or fish, or which colour to paint the walls, is [*must be*!] recorded in the coded memory systems of our brains. In the act of choosing, the various relevant representations are brought into play and balanced with the information coming from parts of the brain that indicate the needs of the moment. The outcome of this balancing operation depends entirely upon the characteristics of that individual, as built up over the centuries in the DNA of his ancestors and in the brain over his own years of growth (209).

That is, it is the brain which selects from a wide range of (neurally encoded) possible actions which one to perform, and then organizes all of the various bodily functions involved, sometimes (but not invariably) conveying its decision to the faculty of conscious awareness.

Given that the argument proceeds from the continuum picture, it is hardly surprising that it should lead to exactly the same conclusion as *The Analysis of Mind*. On Young's version, it is the 'neurophysiological mechanisms of *choice*' which are said to be hierarchically configured. "Even bacteria can adapt to a new medium. In this sense they make a 'choice' between a small set of possibilities. ... The characteristics of the 'higher' organisms include an increasing variety of possible alternative actions, culminating in man." As Russell speculated in the chapter on the 'Influence of Past History on Present Occurrences in Living Organisms', 'we ought to be able actually to see differences between the brain of a man who chooses to ϕ and that of a man who chooses to ψ.' For the time being, the champion of free will can take solace in the fact that, as Russell explained in his remarks on mnemic causation, since "the behaviour of an organism is influenced by its past history," it is "not easy to define the sense in which historical factors can be said to 'determine' the behaviour of any system" (210). Thus, "In simpler organisms we can analyse [the organism's encoded memories] and make reasonably accurate forecasts," but "In higher animals the complexity of choice and of motivational factors makes forecasting increasingly difficult" (211). Man is no more free than a storm system, therefore; or perhaps we should say, our judgment of which is more free will depend on which advances more quickly: psychology or meteorology.

Short of reiterating all of the arguments of the preceding sections, of showing why *choosing* is not a mental event which precedes — or accompanies! — an action, or of formulating such obvious grammatical truths as that bacteria are not capable of making and acting on decisions and that the appearance of such a consequence serves notice of a drastic need to clarify the logical grammar of *acting* and *deciding*, we can treat Young's argument as illustrating two important points. First, it manifests the continuity of mechanist thought: the fact that both the framework and the consequences of psychophysical presuppositions have remained remarkably constant over the past two centuries. And second, it epitomises what Wittgenstein was thinking of when he warned that

> The prejudice in favour of psycho-physical parallelism is also a fruit of the primitive conception of grammar. For when one admits a causality between psychological phenomena, which is not mediated physiologically, one fancies that in doing so one is making an admission of the existence of a soul *alongside* the body, a ghostly mental nature (RPP1 §906).

But, of course, the purpose of this paper, following on Wittgenstein's lead, has been nothing of the sort; rather, it has been to articulate the need to clarify the concept of *psychological causality* before we begin to investigate the causes of our behaviour: to escape from the physiological/mentalist straightjacket imposed on the social sciences by Cartesianism. In short, it has been to learn from *The Analysis of Mind* in order to escape the Santayanan consequences in which cognitive science now finds itself.

Stuart G. Shanker
York University

Endnotes

1. I have benefitted immeasurably in the writing of this paper by Stewart Candlish's 'Das Wollen Ist Auch Nur Eine Erfahrung' and Michel Ter Hark's *Beyond the Inner and the Outer*.

2. In the *Brown Book* Wittgenstein responds to James' 'getting out of a warm bed' example (which is supposed to "contain in miniature form the data for an entire psychology of volition" (PP II 525)):

> Now on the other hand it has been said that when a man, say, gets out of bed in the morning, all that happens may be this, he deliberates, "Is it time to get up?," he tries to make up his mind, and then suddenly *he finds himself getting up*. Describing it this way emphasizes the absence of an act of volition. ... Now there is something in the above description which tempts us to contradict it; we say: "We don't just 'find', observe, ourselves getting up, as though we were observing someone else! It isn't like, say, watching certain reflex actions" (BB 151).

3. One says 'apparently' since Ideo-Motor stipulates that it is the images of kinæsthetic sensations, not the sensations themselves, that constitute willing (see AM 285). But, like everything else in Wittgenstein, this remark should not be hastily written off as an oversight. After all, what exactly is an 'image of a kinæsthetic sensation': is it a kinæsthetic sensation itself? Is there a phenomenological difference between images of kinæsthetic sensations and of objects?

4. Contrast this with lying, where 'see' is the primary and 'judge' the secondary use for children, but the opposite becomes the case with age.

5. Just compare 'trying to open a jar', 'trying to make up one's mind', 'trying to leave', 'trying to quit smoking', 'trying to imagine what it would be like to walk on the moon', 'trying to keep a straight face', 'trying to keep still', 'trying to brush away an annoying fly' (see RPPI §§848-9).

6. Cf. Loeb's proposed resolution of the free will problem: viz, "We eat, drink, and reproduce not because mankind has reached an agreement that this is desirable, but because, machine-like, we are compelled to do so" (Loeb 1890: 33).

7. It is surprising that Wittgenstein even continues to speak of psychological 'laws' (cf. Gergen 1982).

8. Consider the recent case in Ontario where a man who had driven some distance and murdered his mother-in-law was acquitted of homicide on the grounds that he suffered from somnambulism.

References

Candlish, Stewart (1984) 'Absque Labore Nihil', *Australasian Journal of Philosophy*, vol.64.

— (1992) 'Das Wollen ist auch nur eine Erfahrung', *Philosophical Investigations*, Robert L. Arrington and Hans-Joachim Glock (eds), London: Routledge.

Coulter, Jeff (1989) *Mind in Action*, Oxford: Polity Press.

Danto, Arthur C. (1985) 'Consciousness and motor control', *The Behavioral and Brain Sciences*, vol.8.

Descartes, René (1641) *Meditations on First Philosophy*, in *The Philosophical Writings of Descartes*, John Cottingham, Robert Stoothoff, and Dugald Murdoch (trans), vol.I, Cambridge: Cambridge University Press, 1985.

— (1649) *The Passions of the Soul*, in *The Philosophical Writings of Descartes*, John Cottingham, Robert Stoothoff, and Dugald Murdoch (trans), vol.I, Cambridge: Cambridge University Press, 1985.

Gergen, K. (1982) *Toward Transformation in Social Knowledge*, New York: Springer-Verlag.

Harré, R. and P.F. Secord (1972) *The Explanation of Social Behaviour*, Oxford: Basil Blackwell.

James, William (1890) *The Principles of Psychology*, New York: Henry Holt & Co.

— (1905) 'The Dilemma of Determinism', in *The Will to Believe and Other Essays in Popular Philosophy*, New York: Longmans, Green.

Jung, R., Hufschmidt, A. and W. Moschallski (1982), 'Langsame Hirpotentiale beim Schrieben: Die Wechselwirkung von Schreibhand und Sprachdominanz bei Rechshändern', *Archiv für Psychiatrie und Nervenkrankheiten*, vol. 232.

Kimble, G. and L.Perlmuter (1970) 'The problem of volition', *Psychological Review*, vol.77.

Kornhuber, H.H. and L. Deecke (1965), 'Hirnpotentialänderungen bei Willkürbewegungen und passiven Bewegungen des Menschen: Bereitschaftspotential und reafferente Potentiale', *Pflügers Archiv für Gesamte Physiologie*, vol.284.

Latto, Richard (1985) 'Consciousness as an experimental variable: Problems of definition, practice, and interpretation', *The Behavioral and Brain Sciences*, vol.8.

Libet, Benjamin (1985) 'Unconscious cerebral initiative and the role of conscious will in voluntary action', *The Behavioral and Brain Sciences*, vol.8.

Loeb, Jacques (1899) 'Some fundamental facts and conceptions concerning the comparative physiolgy of the central nervous system', in *The Mechanistic Conception of Life*, Donald Fleming (ed), Cambridge, Mass.: The Belknap Press of Harvard University Press, 1964.

McGuiness, Brian (1988) *Wittgenstein: A Life*, London: Duckworth.

Nisbett, Richard E. & Wilson, Timothy D.W. (1977) 'Telling more than we can know: verbal reports on mental processes', *Psychological Review*, vol.84.

Rhees, Rush (1970) *Discussions of Wittgenstein*, London: Routledge and Kegan Paul.

Russell, Bertrand (1912) 'On the Notion of Cause', in *Mysticism and Logic*, London: Longmans, Green and Co. 1918.

— (1921) *The Analysis of Mind*, London: George Allen & Unwin Ltd.

— (1925) 'Materialism, Past and Present', in Friedrich Lange, *History of Materialism*, New York: Humanities Press, 1950.

— (1946) 'Is Materialism Bankrupt?', Girard, Kansas: Haldeman-Julius Publications.

— (1935) *Religion and Science*, New York: Oxford University Press, 1961.

Shanker, S.G. (1991) 'The Enduring Relevance of Wittgenstein's Remarks on Intentions', in John Hyman (ed), *Investigating Psychology*, London: Routledge.

— (forthcoming) 'Wittgenstein versus Russell on the Analysis of Mind', in Andrew Irvine and Gary Wedekind (eds), *Bertrand Russell and the Rise of Analytic Philosophy*, Toronto: University of Toronto Press.

Ter Hark, Michel (1990) *Beyond the Inner and the Outer*, Dordrecht: Kluwer Academic Publishers.

Westcott, Malcolm R. (1988) *The Psychology of Human Freedom*, New York: Springer-Verlag.

Wittgenstein, Ludwig (1960), *The Blue and Brown Books*, Oxford: Basil Blackwell.

— (1921) *Tractatus Logico-Philosophicus*, D.F. Pears & B.F. McGuinness (trans.), London: Routledge & Kegan Paul, 1961.

— (1946) 'A Lecture on Freedom of the Will', *Philosophical Investigations*, vol.12 (1989).

— (1946–7) *Wittgenstein's Lectures on Philosophical Psychology 1946–47* P.T. Geach (ed), Chicago: University of Chicago, 1989.

— (1953) *Philosophical Investigations*, G.E.M. Anscombe (trans), 3rd edition, Oxford: Basil Blackwell, 1973.

— (1958) *Remarks on the Foundations of Mathematics*, G.H. von Wright, R. Rhees, and G.E.M. Anscombe (eds), G.E.M. Anscombe (trans), 3rd edn, Oxford: Basil Blackwell, 1978.

— (1967) *Zettl*, G.E.M. Anscombe and G.H. von Wright (eds), G.E.M. Anscombe (trans), Oxford: Basil Blackwell.

— (1974) *Philosophical Grammar*, Rush Rhees (ed), Anthony Kenny (trans), Oxford: Basil Blackwell.

— (1975) *Philosophical Remarks*, Rush Rhees (ed), R. Hargreaves and R. White (trans), Oxford: Basil Blackwell.

— (1980) *Culture and Value*, G.H. von Wright (ed), Peter Winch (trans), Oxford: Basil Blackwell.

— (1980) *Remarks on the Philosophy of Psychology*, vol. I, G.E.M. Anscombe and G.H. von Wright (eds), G.E.M. Anscombe (trans), Oxford: Basil Blackwell.

— (1980) *Remarks on the Philosophy of Psychology*, vol. II, G.H. von Wright and Heikki Nyman (eds), C.G. Luckhardt and M.A.E. Aue (trans), Oxford: Basil Blackwell.

— (1982) *Last Writings*, G.H. von Wright and Heikki Nyman (eds), C.G. Luckhardt and Maximilian A.E. Aue (trans), Oxford: Basil Blackwell.

Young, J.Z. (1987) *Philosophy and the Brain*, Oxford: Oxford University Press.